MW00564131

Endorsements For
Breaking Free from Broke

"Thank you, George, for putting Breaking Free from Broke *on paper! Easy-to-read, sound fundamentals that seem to be lost in our crazy world. Not only did I enjoy it, I have copies for all my kids!"*

Willie Robertson
Duck Dynasty

"You've been pre-approved. *Without wasting a word, George helps you see that you're approved to get out of debt, walk away from the manipulations of the financial industrial-complex, and finally live. Our communities need your passion, your contributions, and your energy. The first step is to think hard about what really matters and to do something about it."*

Seth Godin
Author of *The Song of Significance*

"If you've ever felt like your finances are a constant struggle, you're not alone. In Breaking Free from Broke, *George Kamel offers a practical guide that will help you break the cycle of financial stress and embrace a life of freedom and peace. If you're ready for real change, this is the book for you."*

Craig Groeschel
Pastor of Life.Church and *New York Times* bestselling author

"Who knew personal finance could be both enlightening and entertaining? Breaking Free from Broke *is like having a conversation about money with your smart and snarky friend."*

Les Parrott, PhD
#1 *New York Times* bestselling author of
Saving Your Marriage Before It Starts

"In a world where financial advice can be boring and unattainable, Breaking Free from Broke *is a fresh dose of wit and reality. George doesn't just decode financial jargon; he breaks it down in a practical way with analogies, research, and humor."*

Jeffrey T. Dobyns, CFP®, CLU, ChFC
President, SageSpring

"One of George's superpowers is his ability to take what he does seriously without taking himself too seriously. With that, he has given us all one of the most gracious gifts imaginable in this book: a clear path to financial freedom where the journey is as fun and gratifying as the destination."

Will Guidara
James Beard Award-winning restaurateur

"George's passion for guiding folks through the wonderful world of finance shines in Breaking Free from Broke. *He makes personal finance entertaining and enlightening with his unique blend of smarts, snark, and common sense!"*

Brian Preston, CPA, CFP®, PFS
Host of *The Money Guy Show*

"George masterfully combines the timeless wisdom of Dave Ramsey's financial principles with a good dose of humor. Imagine learning about budgets and saving while simultaneously chuckling to yourself. That's a win."

Marie Forleo
#1 *New York Times* bestselling author of
Everything is Figureoutable

"In Breaking Free from Broke, *George provides a roadmap to financial freedom. After reading this book, you'll be telling your money where to go instead of wondering where it went."*

John Maxwell

"As a psychologist, I can attest to how much of people's anxiety is related to financial stress, worry, guilt, and fear. Much of that is tied up in one word: control. *They feel out of control with money and feel like finances have control of them—a recipe for anxiety and stress. George shows you very specifically how to regain control and put an end to ongoing, debilitating financial stress. It is simple yet profound."*

Dr. Henry Cloud
***New York Times* bestselling author**

"This is one of those books that is so compelling and simple that I can't imagine why everyone shouldn't read it. And it's really well-written, even funny!"

Patrick Lencioni
Author of *The Five Dysfunctions of a Team* and
The Six Types of Working Genius

BREAKING FREE FROM BROKE

The fruit of the Spirit is love, joy, peace, patience, kindness, goodness, faithfulness, gentleness, self-control; against such things there is no law.

Galatians 5:22–23

BREAKING FREE FROM BROKE

The Ultimate Guide to More Money and Less Stress

GEORGE KAMEL

FOREWORD BY DAVE RAMSEY

Published by Ramsey Press, The Lampo Group, LLC
Franklin, Tennessee 37064

This publication is designed to provide accurate and authoritative information with regard to the subject matter covered. It is sold with the understanding that the publisher is not engaged in rendering financial, accounting, or other professional advice. If financial advice or other expert assistance is required, the services of a competent professional should be sought.

Editor: Kris Bearss
Cover Design: Chris Carrico and Weylon Smith
Photography: Seth Farmer and Riley Clark
Interior Design: PerfecType, Nashville, TN
ISBN: 978-1-942121-78-7

Printed in the United States of America
24 25 26 27 28 WRZ 5 4 3 2 1

For Whitney
My radiant beacon on foggy days,
My co-captain keeping our ship afloat,
My heart's compass, pointing me toward love and truth.

For Mia
This book made me an author, but you made me a father.
And that's the only title that will ever matter.
You will teach me more than any book ever could.

For Olive and Blue
The furry duo that kept me company with snorts,
farts, snores, and barks.
Thank you for reminding me that the best life is simple,
and that dog ownership is really expensive.

CONTENTS

FOREWORD

BY DAVE RAMSEY

In 1992, I self-published a little blue book called *Financial Peace* and sold it out of the trunk of my car. It was common sense. God's and Grandma's ways of handling money. That book went on to become my first *New York Times* bestseller, and it's now sold over 3 million copies. Its big brother, *The Total Money Makeover*, has sold over 10 million copies since 2003, teaching people the same common-sense, exact Baby Steps process for taking control of your money, getting out of debt, and building wealth. About the time those books were published, George Kamel was just a kid—barely in high school. I won't claim to be thinking about him or the millennial generation when I wrote those books. I was just trying to show the folks who were already in a financial mess that they could dig their way out and have hope again. But I did know the principles I was teaching had no expiration date. They'd worked for generations, and they would keep working for future generations as long as there were people disciplined enough to follow through on them.

When George joined Ramsey Solutions over a decade ago as marketing intern, he was a typical 20-something. Broke. In debt.

Living paycheck to paycheck and trapped under the weight of his student loans and credit card debt. He'd bought into the lies his generation had been sold about money: You can't be a student without a student loan. You'll always have a car payment. Get a credit card so the great and mighty FICO will smile down on you. He knew he had a mess on his hands. But he didn't know how to clean up that mess. Like we do with all our team members, we showed George the principles from the *Total Money Makeover* and *Financial Peace.* We also enrolled him in *Financial Peace University*, where he learned the truth about debt and how to handle money. He also got good and mad about the toxic money culture that was designed to keep him broke. And he was determined to break free.

George immediately began living the principles he'd learned. He got out of debt. He saved money. But his turnaround didn't stop there. His career flourished. His personal life flourished. Not just because of us, but because that's who George is. He met his wife, Whitney, here at Ramsey. They began their marriage debt-free with a goal to buy a home of their own and pay it off fast. And that's what they did. By the time he was 32 years old, George was a Baby Steps millionaire. If you don't know what that is, it's what we call millionaires who got that way by following the Baby Steps. They don't have a million-dollar income. They have an actual net worth of $1 million or more by being debt-free with assets like a paid-for home and growing retirement accounts. Bottom line: George has proven for the millennials and the Gen Zers that the same common-sense principles work for every age group. And they still work.

When we hired George, he had no idea—and certainly we had no idea—that he would end up becoming one of our most popular Ramsey personalities. Most days, he's behind the mic as a cohost with me on *The Ramsey Show*. He's a YouTube sensation with several successful podcasts under his belt. His humor, his knowledge base in the money space, and his sarcastic, wonderful wit make him the man of the hour with audiences today. If you're one of the folks who say Ramsey's material is out-of-date because it comes from a boomer, spend a few minutes with this book. George disproves all that and makes learning and talking about money fun again. Reading his book feels like you're watching his YouTube show. It's deeply researched and extremely accurate. And every page is filled with humor. You're going to enjoy a completely new take on some old ideas. It's a lot like *Financial Peace* in that way, because that was a new take on old ideas back in 1992. In fact, *Breaking Free from Broke* is *Financial Peace* for a new generation. So, enjoy this ride with George. You'll have fun, and you'll come away informed and inspired to completely transform your life.

INTRODUCTION

Average Sucks

When the whole world is running toward a cliff, he who is running in the opposite direction appears to have lost his mind.
–C. S. LEWIS

It's December 15, 2021, and I'm standing in my front yard staring at some dead grass. (Which I often do, as if the longer I stare, the more likely I am to bring it back from the dead.) But something is different about this day. This day, it is *my* dead grass. I own every blade of it, free and clear, because my wife and I have just paid off our mortgage.

Whitney and I were thirty-one and thirty-two years old respectively, and I *never* thought we'd be here. I thought paid-for houses were mythical unicorns reserved for retirees, rich people, and trust-fund kids with inheritances. Not for the little guys like me who didn't learn about money growing up, and made money mistakes with several zeroes on the end.

In the third grade, Mrs. Plunkett asked us what we wanted to be when we grew up. I, of course, wanted to be an astronaut. I had recently picked up a copy of *The Adventures of Mary-Kate & Ashley: The Case of the U.S. Space Camp Mission* from the Scholastic Book Fair and was totally sold on the idea of exploring this great frontier. (In hindsight, I think eight-year-old George was just excited about the idea of floating in zero gravity. Still, a noble goal.)

In the fourth grade, my plans changed dramatically. I got my first electric guitar and decided I was destined to be a rock star. Back in those days, you could supposedly be whatever you wanted to be. As a millennial, I grew up in a generation where everyone was special and we all got a participation trophy (even if our soccer team never won a single game. Season. After. Season).

I had different goals back then. I had different fears back then. I went through a phase where I was genuinely concerned about the Bermuda Triangle. And quicksand. Both turned out to be much less of a problem than anticipated. Nobody warned me about the *real* problems, like money problems, that would drag me down (quicksand pun most intended) in adulthood.

THE (NOT SO) AVERAGE GEORGE

Like none of you, I grew up as an Arabic Baptist, pop-punk-loving skateboarder in a mostly Irish/Italian Catholic suburb of Boston, Massachusetts. I was fascinated by money at a young age, *especially* once I figured out how to get some of it. My dad would give me a dollar to go up to random people at church and say something in Arabic. I had no idea what these phrases meant, but they always got a laugh. And the bonus: I was a buck richer every time.

My dad and mom emigrated from Egypt and Syria (respectively) to the US back in the early 1980s. My brother and I were born stateside, and my parents worked hard to get good jobs and give us a good life. They adapted to American culture very quickly. Including its money culture, where everyone was encouraged to use *other* people's money to buy stuff with shiny plastic cards offering virtually unlimited dollars.

I learned that a high credit score meant you were crushing it with money. I learned that the secret to getting a cool car wasn't having the cash to pay for it but being able to negotiate the financing to get a good "deal" and manage the monthly payment.

What did I do with all this *learning*? I financed my way through college using Sallie Mae's monopoly money. All I had to do was sign the dotted line and the money was mine.

I had no idea what the interest was or what the payments would be. I just figured that at the end of the obligatory college-degree rainbow was a pot of gold that included a dream job and a big ol' salary. And it wasn't just me thinking that. This treacherous trail of hyped half-truths was sold to my entire generation. And it's still sold today by college marketers, student loan companies, and well-meaning guidance counselors and parents all over America.

What I can tell you is: Ignorance was bliss. Until it was *broke*.

There I was—a newly minted college grad who was banking on a job that would pay the bills. And that included the impending student loan payments that were about to kick in. Sadly, I didn't even know how much total debt I had until I experienced identity theft and pulled my credit report. Once I tallied up all my student loans, I discovered my total: 36 grand. (Narrator: "And there was nothing *grand* about that.")

Turns out it was not monopoly money after all. Like the schoolyard bullies of my youth, Sallie Mae shook me down for all I was worth—which wasn't much, considering I had a negative net worth thanks to, you know, all those loans she lent me.

I found myself at the crossroads of bright-eyed, bushy-tailed, and flat-broke. To cover the gap between my life and my bills, I turned to my Discover and American Express Delta cards to save the day. But $4,000 in credit card debt later, I had a decision to make. Was I going to pay on my student loans for the next 20 years? Was I going to continue racking up credit card debt while justifying it with 2 percent cash back and freakin' SkyMiles? Nah, it was time for a change. Getting *into* debt was remarkably easy, but even as a 23-year-old knucklehead, I knew getting *out* would be remarkably hard.

I also knew my debt was holding me back, because it was stealing from the little income I had. I remember depositing that first paycheck from my first job after college and realizing it was barely enough to cover my rent, utilities, and debt payments. That lump-in-the-throat, pit-of-the-stomach feeling was starkly different from the warm, fuzzy feeling I was given on the college campus tour. With no breathing room in my money or my life, I was riddled with anxiety and cynical toward adulthood. But I didn't know how to reverse course and get out of debt. I had fallen for the traps of a screwed-up financial system, and my new reality had left me in a dark place.

Thankfully, my first salaried job out of college happened to be at a company run by a guy named Dave Ramsey. As part of the onboarding process, I went through a course called *Financial Peace University*. Once a week for nine weeks straight, I'd meet up with a bunch of strangers at a local church to watch a video lesson about money, followed by some candid group conversation. Although these strangers came from all walks of life, we all had one major thing in common: We wanted to be better with money, and we realized our plan thus far wasn't cutting it. (The first step is to admit you have a problem, right?)

Through the videos, I learned about the toxic money culture in America today and how it thrives on keeping people broke. Even more importantly, I discovered the many ways I'd bought in to it and was being affected by it. I began deprogramming all the lies and myths I had come to believe about money for the first few decades of my life.

By the second week of *Financial Peace University*, we had a "plastectomy" where we took scissors to our credit cards and physically cut up those bad boys. It was weirdly emotional and even a little frightening. Those cards had been my security blanket and companion into adulthood, much like Woody was to Andy in *Toy Story*. And just like Woody, there were strings attached. The metal blades slicing through the plastic felt like cutting the strings from a toxic relationship—a one-sided relationship that cost me far more than the 2 percent "effort" it gave in the form of cash back. Feeling a newfound sense of liberation, I created my first budget ever, started tracking my expenses, and set big money goals. For the first time in my life, I felt like *I* was happening to my money instead of it just happening to me.

After 18 grueling months of budgeting, living on less than I made, side hustling, Uber-ing, Lyft-ing, selling stuff, and eating "rice and beans" (or in my case, Lean Cuisines), I paid off all $40,000 of my consumer debt! I was *debt-free*, baby! Less than six months later, I had saved up a fully funded emergency fund. Right after that, I started investing in my work's 401(k) plan, harnessing the magical power of compound interest.

That was a long time ago, but I still remember the feeling of living paycheck to paycheck. Every payday felt less like a celebration and more like a quick gasp for air before diving back into a sea of bills and expenses. Turns out, I wasn't alone. With almost 8 out of 10 American workers (78 percent) living paycheck to paycheck, I was *normal.*[1] And let me tell you, if broke is normal, then normal sucks!

ESCAPING AVERAGE

A few years into my career at Ramsey Solutions, I met my now-wife, Whitney. She was (and is) way better looking than me, way smarter, and way better at money management. Naturally, I didn't think I had a shot. But it turns out she's got a soft spot for pale Middle Eastern guys under 5'8"—and she gave me a chance. I turned the wit and charm up to 11 and somehow won her over. We started off our marriage with no consumer debt back in 2018 and decided to do something extra weird: save up a big down payment on a house, and then pay it off as fast as possible. Why?

Well, we asked ourselves some simple yet revolutionary questions:

How cool would it be to not have a mortgage payment in our early thirties?
What kind of freedom could we have?
What new and incredible options would that open up for us?
What kind of life could we live?

And with that unity and vision, we were off to the races.

From side hustles to no-spend months to selling anything collecting dust to strangers on Facebook Marketplace, we weren't

[1] "Living Paycheck to Paycheck is a Way of Life for Majority of U.S. Workers," CareerBuilder, August 24, 2017, http://press.careerbuilder.com/2017-08-24-Living-Paycheck-to-Paycheck-is-a-Way-of-Life-for-Majority-of-U-S-Workers-According-to-New-CareerBuilder-Survey.

fooling around. Twenty-six months later, way ahead of schedule, Whitney and I paid off the dang house!

To be honest, the payoff itself was hilariously anticlimactic. First off, the mortgage website didn't have a magic *Payoff* button with digital confetti. Instead, we had to request a *physical* payoff statement via snail mail. Ugh. Once we received that, we *still* couldn't pay it off online. We had to go to the bank in person to do a final wire transfer. The bank was sad and sterile, much like the DMV, but with less wait time and more lollipops.

The banker sat us down and began the process of the wire transfer. This was a life-changing moment for me and my wife—but seemingly just another financial transaction for this lady. Here's how it went down.

Us *(excited)*: "Hello! We'd like to do a wire transfer!"
Banker: "Is this for a home closing?"
Us *(still excited)*: "No, we're actually paying off our mortgage!"
Banker *(with as little emotion as possible)*: "Congratulations. That's the dream."

Seven minutes later, still typing and clicking.

Banker: "Alright, the wire transfer will happen at some point today. Is there anything else I can do for you?"
Us *(deflated)*: "Nope. Thanks."

While the bar is low, I hope your mortgage payoff experience is way more exciting than ours was. In any case, I tell you these stories from my journey, not to brag about how awesome I am with money, but to encourage you that if any normal, broke, average George like me can take control of their money and build wealth, *you can too*.

The financial transformation I experienced by following this proven plan was insane. Over 10 years, I went from a negative net worth to a $1 million net worth. I went from broke to millionaire. In a decade. I also saw huge personal transformation. And while it was hard, it was also incredibly simple.

There's a great quote that beautifully sums up my financial journey: "Most people *overestimate* what they can accomplish in a year and *underestimate* what they can accomplish in a decade." That was me for sure. For too long, I thought someone like me couldn't get ahead with money. Thank God for the ability to change our minds, our beliefs, and our actions.

It *was* possible for me. And the good news is, it's possible for you too. It won't be a cakewalk. Or a walk in the park. Or a piece of cake. Come to think of it, there's not much walking or cake involved here at all. But by the time you're done with this book, you'll be confident in your ability to buck the system, ditch debt, and build wealth. And the financial peace you'll feel as a result is the icing on the cake.

WELCOME TO THE GAP

Quick spoiler alert before we go any further—because I'd hate to mislead you. This isn't *really* a book about money. It's a book about turning money from a stressor to a blesser, *so that* you can focus on building a life and legacy you're proud of. It's about gaining the things money can't buy, but that money problems *can* hold you back from: peace, patience, self-control, freedom, margin, options, and joy.

But here's what you've got to understand: The gap between financial stress and financial peace is *littered* with traps, myths, distractions, and slick marketing designed to keep you brainwashed and broke.

Maybe you've felt buried by some of those myths and a lack of financial literacy, with no understanding of how to dig out from the pile. Maybe you've been your own biggest obstacle, sabotaging your progress with excuses, justifications, and impulse spending for as long as you can remember. Maybe your life has been filled with legitimate challenges and hardships that have left you cleaning up a mess you didn't choose to make. Maybe, like me, it was a *poo*-pourri of all the above. What really matters isn't what got you here, but what you can do, starting today, to get to the *good* side of the gap, where money stress is just a memory.

Whether you believe it or not, *you* are your best shot at bridging the gap. And over the next 16 chapters, we'll tackle your best excuses and the worst myths head-on, building that bridge with truth, knowledge, and hope.

On the other side of that gap is the life you never thought would be possible. Where you own every blade of dead grass in the yard. Where the car drives differently because it doesn't have a payment weighing it down. Where your kid's education *and* your retirement are locked and loaded. Where you get to take vacations you always dreamed of and help others the way you always wished you could. And best of all, where you wake up every morning knowing you're free and clear, owing nobody anything.

That's a future worth fighting for. It's go time.

1

Chained to the System

It is hard to free fools from the chains they revere.
–VOLTAIRE

T*he little man can't get ahead.*

That's been the subconscious, Eeyore-esque mantra of the average American for a long time now. And as a man of below-average stature, I take moderate offense to it.

Here's what's behind that old trope: Money stress and money problems have caused most non-millionaires out there to feel like they're in a financial chokehold of hopelessness. Ramsey Research uncovered some sobering stats in their recent "State of Personal Finance" report:

- 37 percent of the people surveyed said they're struggling or in crisis with their finances.
- 43 percent said they have a hard time paying their bills.
- 50 percent said they struggle to pay their rent, and 38 percent struggle to pay their mortgage.

- 25 percent said they rely on credit cards to make ends meet.
- Nearly 4 in 10 have $0 in savings.
- 51 percent said they worry about their personal finances daily.
- 40 percent said they have cried or had a panic attack over their money in the past few months.[2]

That's bleak stuff. Maybe a few of those stats hit close to home for you.

Now, there are a whole bunch of reasons for this grim reality. For those of you looking to point some fingers, you could blame . . .

- Inflation, which had its largest increase in 40 years in 2022, making it painful to fill our gas tanks and our bellies.
- The housing market, with home values rising almost 50 percent over the past decade.[3]
- The cost of higher education, which has increased by almost 400 percent since the 1980s.[4]

---

[2] "The State of Personal Finance in America Q1 2023," Ramsey Solutions, June 21, 2023, https://www.ramseysolutions.com/budgeting/state-of-personal-finance.

[3] Lucas Jones, "Projecting the value of homes in the U.S. in 2030 and analyzing the impact of COVID-19," RenoFi, May 25, 2023, https://www.renofi.com/learn/projecting-the-value-of-homes-in-the-us-in-2030-analyzing-the-impact-of-covid-19/.

[4] Melanie Hanson, "Average Cost of College by Year," Education Data.org, January 9, 2022, https://educationdata.org/average-cost-of-college-by-year.

- The Fed, for raising interest rates, making credit card debt, auto loans, and mortgage loans more expensive and more crippling than ever.
- The president, whoever it is by the time you read this, and for whatever reason you think they're ruining everything.
- Our Congress, who can't balance a budget to save their lives, and the lobbyists who fight dirty with blank checks to keep screwing you over.
- Big, bad corporations that put profits over people and shareholders over consumers.
- Elder generations like the baby boomers, who yell at youngsters to get off their lawns from the comfort of a home they paid $30,000 for back in 1973.
- News and media outlets that use clickbait and fearmongering headlines to keep us feeling anxious and out of control.
- A toxic money culture that preys on our wallets through psychological manipulation, slick advertising, false promises, and our own discontentment.

Okay, that's enough. I'm sure you're riled up by now. Although, I've got to say, that was a bit cathartic too.

Now that we've got that out of our system, let's look at the *one* factor you can control in this whole mess: *you*. More specifically, the way *you* handle *your* money.

BORN (BROKE) IN THE USA

As a recovering pessimist, I have high hopes that you can still achieve the American Dream, whatever that phrase means to you. For a lot of people, the current American Dream is simply debt freedom. For others, it's the classic dream of homeownership. Maybe it's *time* freedom so you can travel, explore the world, and lean into passion projects and hobbies. Whatever that dream is—it's going to take money, or at least getting control of it.

Here's the mind-boggling part of all of this: We live in the most advanced society in history and yet we have *less* time and *less* money than ever before. How the heck did that happen? I have a theory. It all started when you were a wee little lad (or lass).

- You were never taught financial literacy in school, so you had no clue about debt, budgeting, taxes, or investing. (But hey, at least you remember what year the War of 1812 happened.)
- You grew up in a house where money wasn't really talked about, or when it *was* talked about, it was stressful. Things looked good to the outside world, but all the bills and financial worries took a serious toll on the family.
- Your parents didn't have the ability or foresight to save for college—or to have an honest conversation about how you would afford it without a full-ride scholarship miracle.
- You were told college was a necessary, unquestionable path to upward mobility, and therefore taking out unlimited student loans was simply an "investment" in your future.
- You financed your way through college with that magic monopoly money. Little did you know you were signing on the dotted line for terms that would potentially cause you decades of debt and stress. You had no clue about the post-graduation weight of five- or six-figure loans or how the interest worked. (Spoiler: It worked *against* you.)
- You were told that building your credit score was crucial for financial success as an adult, and that opening a credit card was the best way to do it. So you signed up for a card

from some rep on campus who lured you in with a free T-shirt and a pizza.

- You started out using credit cards for small purchases like gas and food, telling yourself you'd pay them off every month in full. When the credit card company sent you an email about how special you were and how they wanted to give you a bigger line of credit, you took it . . . and spent more. Then life happened, and maybe you missed a payment or couldn't afford the balance in full, triggering insane interest rates.
- After graduation, you were faced with the harsh reality of a tough job market and ended up taking a gig that probably paid less than the fairy-tale number you had in your head.
- You felt the "need" for nicer wheels. You justified why you deserved something shiny and new, and the salespeople were happy to "work with you" on the monthly payment. Before you knew it, you were tied to a car loan that lasted longer than your first job, and *way* longer than your last relationship (hey, the red flags were there—we tried to tell you).
- As you settled into adulthood and a more stable career, you were told that renting is a massive waste of money and that owning a home is the smart thing to do. Thanks to all those home renovation shows, too much Zillow-ing, and seeing your friends on Instagram post with new house keys and big smiles, you had your sights set on an aesthetic and price that you really couldn't afford yet. And maybe you did it anyway, taking on a 30-year mortgage with very little down, with the bank loaning you way more than should be legal.
- These decisions left you financially tapped, trapped, strapped, capped, and zapped.

A WHOLE NEW WORLD (THAT'S WHERE YOU'LL BE)

This is the story of how debt becomes "normal" in our lives and how the normalization of debt over time robs us of margin, freedom, options, and joy. It's a story of how people get screwed by a system that's designed to trap them in debt and keep them reliant on it.

But the story doesn't have to end this way. With the right plan, the right habits, and a big ol' paradigm shift, you can break free from this backward system and live a life of financial freedom you never thought possible.

How do we do that? Well, first, we need to unpack why today's money culture is so toxic and how it's not only holding you back but also leaving you completely exhausted. The problem isn't just in the different financial industries or types of debt that exist. Money myths, societal pressures, economic shifts, modern financing traps, technological advances, and psychological mind games have all led us to this place of extreme stress and frustration.

Over the next several chapters, we're going to explore the underbelly and common tactics of:

- Credit scores
- Credit cards
- Student loans
- Car loans
- Mortgages
- Investing
- Marketing and consumerism

Now, that all might sound relatively harmless, but fair warning: The stuff I'm going to share with you will be jarring, angering, and even downright offensive at times. You may get enough *ick* from each chapter that you'll feel like you need a shower. That's not a bad thing. (And a shower never hurt anyone.)

At times, you will disagree. Strongly. That's fine; we can still be friends. But there is one thing I ask of you as we uncover the truths and tenets of this toxic money culture: *Keep an open mind.* For real.

I'm fully aware that each of us is coming at this money stuff from 47 different angles. Different backgrounds, experiences, setbacks, upbringings, geographical locations, education levels, income levels, and walks of life. When you feel yourself getting riled up, ask yourself: "Where is this feeling coming from?" Is it from your own guilt, embarrassment, discontentment, or mistakes? Is it from anxiety, past trauma, shattered dreams, or scarred relationships? Is it from deep-seated beliefs, misinformation, things you've read, exceptions you've known, or maybe that TikTok advice you stumbled upon that was really just clickbait horse crap?

Regardless of what you feel as you read through the next seven chapters, I hope you won't shut the book early. Because in the remaining chapters is where hope and light begin to spill into the dark, dusty places. Once we've been inside the belly of the beast and made it out in one piece, we'll get to the good stuff. I'll lay out a proven plan to break free from the chains of each part of the financial system so you can make the most of your money *and* your life.

My confidence in this plan isn't *just* because it worked for me. It's also because it's worked for more than *10 million people,* for over *30 years.* I don't know how many people it takes to impress you, but 10 million is plenty of social proof for me. Following this plan, they've paid off debt, socked away an emergency fund, built wealth, and become more generous than ever before. If that weren't enough, Ramsey Research found that the people who follow this plan are exponentially more confident about budgeting, getting out of debt, and achieving their money goals. They are also way more focused and organized with their money.[5]

In the final third of the book, I'll lay out this plan in more colorful detail. But for the sake of common ground, let's briefly cover the tactical steps that have helped so many people break free from this system. Dave Ramsey coined them "the Baby Steps," and they outline seven principles in a specific order:

The Ramsey Baby Steps

Baby Step 1: Save $1,000 for your starter emergency fund.
Baby Step 2: Pay off all debt (except the house) using the Debt Snowball.
Baby Step 3: Save 3–6 months of expenses in a fully funded emergency fund.
Baby Step 4: Invest 15 percent of your household income in retirement.
Baby Step 5: Save for your children's college fund.
Baby Step 6: Pay off your home early.
Baby Step 7: Build wealth and give.

There it is. Cat's out of the money bag. Later, we'll dive into the "why" behind each step and offer some zesty takes on these timeless principles. The goal is for you to walk away realizing that debt is a dirty little thief, that budgeting doesn't have to suck, that savings are a wonderfully cushy cushion, that investing isn't just for Wall Street bros, and that generosity is the most fun you can have with money.

---

[5] "State of Personal Finance in America Q1 2023," Ramsey Solutions.

WHO SAYS YOU CAN'T BE FREE?

This book isn't *just* for broke people or smart people, white people or black people, Gen Xers or millennials, or liberals or conservatives. But there is a certain *type* of person this book *is* for: The person who is sick and tired of being sick and tired. Who feels like they work too hard to feel this broke. Who is worn out from running on an existential treadmill of bills and stress. Who wants to change their family tree and leave a legacy they're proud of.

This entire plan hinges on one thing: a paradigm shift. It's a tough one to make. And the first part of this book will help you make that shift by revealing how the system is designed to screw you. How it's designed to steal your money, your margin, your options, and your peace. How it's carefully crafted and marketed to feed you lies and myths, driving you to debt and discontentment.

It's a terrible drive. And yet millions of Americans have become passengers in this Uber ride from hell, where the music is terrible, red lights are ignored, and they're dropped off at a destination they never wanted to reach. Yikes. Zero stars. No tip. Would not recommend.

The system's time in the driver's seat of your life is up. It's time you grab the wheel and decide where *you* want to go with your life, your money, your legacy. You can't keep living like the average American Eeyore—in a cycle of debt, anxiety, and cynicism, hoping and waiting for the next occupant of the White House to fix your life. That plan sucks. That's no plan at all. Be better, do better. You *can* learn how to stand up for yourself financially, get above this toxic culture, and breathe the fresh mountain air of financial margin in your life, where you get to do the things you want to do without clingy lenders ruining all your fun.

We're about to go on this beautiful ride together. One where you'll experience the rock 'n' roll joy that comes with getting control of your money. At times, it may feel like you're up against Goliath. Which is good news because that means you're *David.* And you know how that story goes. The little guy wins against the big, bad bully in the end.

So get your financial sling ready, because we're about to bust some heads and take some names. It's on like Donkey Kong.

TAKE THE FIRST STEP TO WINNING WITH MONEY

You can't *win* with money if you're not *paying attention* to your money—by doing a budget. I know, I know. I used to think budgeting was for broke people and Excel-lovers. Turns out I was broke *until* I started doing a monthly budget using the EveryDollar budgeting app. It was the key that helped me go from broke to millionaire in 10 years. And to this day, my budget helps me spend, save, and give with intentionality and freedom. As my gift to you for reading this book, you get three months of access to EveryDollar and all its premium features—on me. Redeem your offer code and start your budget today at georgekamel.com/resources.

2

Credit Scores

A rat in a maze is free to go anywhere,
as long as it stays inside the maze.
–MARGARET ATWOOD

I've always been fascinated by the story of Sisyphus in Greek mythology. Sisyphus was a king who was punished by the gods for his deceitfulness (apparently the dude cheated death twice!). As punishment, he was forced to roll a heavy boulder up a hill, only to have it roll back down again every time he got close to the top. This task was supposed to last for eternity, so of course, Sisyphus was never able to complete it.

There are lots of hot takes about the meaning behind this downer of a tale. In 1942, French philosopher Albert Camus wrote an essay titled *The Myth of Sisyphus*, and his take was that Sisyphus personified the absurdity and futility of human life.

(Man, Albert must have been real fun at parties.) Yet Sisyphus was supposedly happy because the aspirational struggle toward the top of the hill is enough to fill someone's heart. *Yeesh.*

My response to that, quoting the great Randy Jackson: "It's gonna be a 'no' from me, dawg."

You might find that story to be a bit ridiculous, and yet sadly, most Americans live like a modern-day Sisyphus, in a never-ending cycle of money struggles, due to a different kind of myth: money myths.

The word *mythology* comes from the Greek word *mythos*, which means "sacred story or tale." Back in the day, these stories were associated with cultures and religions and often featured gods, heroes, or the supernatural. In the modern era, the word *myth* has been tweaked to mean a widely held belief or idea that is either false or unproven. In the context of money, it's shocking how many "sacred tales" and old myths we have come to believe as true.

One of the most sacred of money myths: the almighty credit score.

WHAT'S THE DEAL WITH CREDIT SCORES?

The only three-digit number Americans obsess over as much as their weight is their credit score. But unlike weight, they want that number to be as high as possible. And this number is living rent-free in their heads. According to "The State of Personal Finance" report by Ramsey Solutions, 83 million Americans were struggling or in crisis with their finances two years after the pandemic. That's a lot of stress. The study found that 46 percent of Americans say their finances have caused them to lose sleep, and

59 percent say they worry about their finances daily.[6] And at least some of that stress has to do with worrying about a credit score.

Why are they burning so many brain calories over this? The Ramsey research showed that 85 percent of adults say a high credit score is a sign of financial success. And 45 percent of adults are "Extremely/Very" worried about having a good credit score.[7] In fact, building credit is one of the top three reasons people said they use a credit card, right behind earning rewards and covering emergencies. Let's cover the basics before we go myth-busting.

What is a credit score?

Your credit score is like a grade that tells lenders how likely you are to pay back what you borrow. You've probably heard of the FICO score, which is the most widely used scoring model. It was developed in 1989 by the Fair Isaac Corporation (hence the cleverly named FICO) as a universal and objective tool for evaluating credit risk.

By 1991, the credit score became available from all three major US credit reporting agencies: Experian, Equifax, and TransUnion. (Pretty wild to think that humans survived just fine before the invention of the credit score in the late 1900s—or as you know them, the '90s.) Generally, the scores range from 300 to 850, with 850 being considered "perfect." And aiming for that perfection matters to a whole lot of people out there.

---

[6] "The State of Personal Finance 2022 Annual Report," Ramsey Solutions, February 25, 2022, https://www.ramseysolutions.com/budgeting/state-of-personal-finance-2022-annual-report.

[7] "State of Personal Finance in America Q1 2023," Ramsey Solutions.

Why does a credit score matter?

This score determines your creditworthiness. (What an unpleasant term. *Worthy of credit?* You're worth *so* much more than credit.) This creditworthiness affects whether you get approved for loans or credit cards, plus the interest rate and terms you're offered. On top of that, your credit score can impact job opportunities, insurance rates, and your ability to rent cars and housing. It's important to note that a low score *can* hurt you in all these areas, while having *no* score is . . . well, no biggie. More on that later.

How is my credit score calculated?

Lenders report the details of your payments—both positive and negative—to one of the three credit bureaus. Then, a credit scoring company like FICO or VantageScore takes that data and creates your magic number based on their own scoring model. When you apply for any new debt in the future, the potential lender does a "vibe check" with the credit bureaus and your credit score to decide whether to approve you or not.

While the exact mathematical algorithm remains a mystery, they do disclose the factors that make up your score:

- **Payment History (35%):** How consistently you've made on-time debt payments
- **Amount Owed (30%):** How much debt you owe and how much of your credit limit you're using, aka "utilization"
- **Length of Credit History (15%):** How long you've been in debt
- **New Credit (10%):** How often you apply for and acquire new debt
- **Credit Mix (10%):** How many types of debt you have (credit cards, auto loans, student loans, installment loans, mortgages, etc.)

You don't have to be the brightest crayon in the box to see a dark theme here. Everything used to calculate your score has to do with debt![8]

WHY A HIGH CREDIT SCORE DOESN'T EQUAL SUCCESS

As we've seen, most of us have been led to believe that a good credit score is a sign you're doing well financially. In reality, a high credit score means you're crushing it with *debt* management, not *money* management. Think about this:

Why do we want a credit score? To go into debt.

Why do we want to go into debt? For a higher credit score.

Why do we want a higher credit score? To have more access to debt.

Why do we want more access to debt? For a higher credit score.

If you really think this scheme makes sense, then I've got a bridge to sell you. Because the only way to achieve and maintain a high credit score is to go into debt, stay in debt, and continually pay your debt accounts "perfectly," without adding too much debt *or* paying too much off too soon.

What!? Just like Harry and Lloyd, this narrative starts dumb and gets even dumber.

Paid off your car loan? Awesome! Your score just dropped 15 points. Paid off your student loans early? Congrats! Your score just dropped 40 points. Closed your credit card account? Your score just dropped 10 points. *Make it make sense.*

---

[8] "What's in my FICO Scores?" MyFICO, accessed September 1, 2023, https://www.myfico.com/credit-education/whats-in-your-credit-score.

But wait! We're not done with the dumb, because your credit score has *nothing* to do with your income, your net worth, or how much money you have in the bank. If you get a huge raise, or you inherit a million dollars, it wouldn't impact your score one bit. A credit score *only* represents your relationship with debt.

It's really an "I love debt" score because all it tells you is how good you are at borrowing money and paying it back. That's it! It's based solely on how much you play kissy-face with lenders. (And to make matters worse, they have that elderly, mothball breath.)

Contrary to popular belief (and most money advice on social media), financial success is about what you have *in* the bank, not what you owe *to* the bank. In the wise words of my friend and fellow Ramsey Personality Rachel Cruze: "If your credit score is higher than your bank balance, you're headed in the wrong direction."

As it turns out, the credit score is just an ingenious way for lenders to lure you deeper into their web of debt while convincing you you're doing great with money.

If that riles you up, good! You should be riled! The mythology around credit scores has caused so many people to fall for debt traps—and held them back from building true wealth. And it leads us to a valid question: Is the credit-score game a necessary evil you have to play to live your financial life?

Short answer: No.

Longer answer: Keep reading.

HOW TO STOP THE ETERNAL CREDIT SCORE CYCLE

Are you sitting down? You probably are. I mean, most people read books sitting down. Are there people who stand up and read? I guess you could be listening to the audiobook while doing chores or working out. Or maybe you're one of those city slickers who hangs on to the subway poles with one hand and reads a book in the other. That always looks cool.

Anyway, here's a crazy truth about credit scores that may blow your mind: *You don't need one.*

Yep. I said it. I ain't scared. Come at me, bro.

You *don't* have to play the game. You can live without a credit score. In fact, living without it can help you build wealth *faster*. That's what happened to me.

When you decide to pay off all your consumer debt and cut up the credit cards, you'll take back control of your greatest wealth-building tool—your income. And with that comes the welcome disappearance of your credit score. Go with me here: If you're done with debt for good, then you don't need any more credit . . . which means you don't need a credit score!

After I paid off all my consumer debt years ago, my credit score soon became *indeterminable*, which is a $10 word for "she gone." You see, after six to twelve months with no debt, no loans, no credit history, and no open lines of credit, your score goes *poof.*

After becoming debt-free, I was *invisible* in the eyes of the Consumer Finance Protection Bureau, much like I was invisible to girls in high school. And while it was a lonely existence back then, I'm in good company these days with millions of other credit-invisible folks. In 2021, the CFPB reported that about 1 in 10 Americans (11 percent) are credit invisible, amounting to 32 million people.[9]

If you're ready to live in this cloak of invisibility, like Harry Potter, I've got just the spell for you. And there's no magic or

---

[9] "The Consumer Credit Card Market," Bureau of Consumer Financial Protection, September 2021, https://files.consumerfinance.gov/f/documents/cfpb_consumer-credit-card-market-report_2021.pdf.

wizardry involved (which is good, because my Arabic Baptist mother is *not* a fan of such things). This one just takes some old-fashioned effort and a little bit of time.

NO CREDIT VERSUS LOW CREDIT

Before we go any further, we need to pause here to talk about a misconception that having *no* credit score is dangerous to your financial life. Here's where the confusion lies. People mistake having no score with having a bad or a low score. Huge difference. *No* score? Rad. *Low* score? Bad.

> **No credit score:** This means you've avoided debt or gotten out for good. We celebrate this at Ramsey Solutions because debt is dumb. If you've zeroed out that credit score, congrats! You're on your way to building true wealth.
>
> **Bad credit (low credit score):** This means you've probably made money mistakes in the past: You've missed payments, racked up credit card debt, defaulted on a mortgage or car loan, or maybe even filed for bankruptcy. A bad credit score *will* make it harder for you to navigate situations like renting an apartment or getting a mortgage.

If you have a low credit score, avoid credit repair companies and credit "hacks" you see hyped on social media. Here's what to do instead: Catch up on all your debt payments, don't miss any more payments, don't get any new debt, pay off all your debts using the Debt Snowball method (which I'll explain in a later chapter), and close accounts as soon they're paid off. The ultimate hack to fix your credit score is to get rid of it completely.

LIVING LIFE WITHOUT A CREDIT SCORE

If you're ready to end the never-ending task of keeping up your credit score, then you've got to understand how to live your financial life without it. Let's cover the big fears and objections I know you have.

How do I buy a car without a credit score?

Remember, you only need a credit score to buy a car if you plan on going into debt for it. So, we're going to save up and pay for a car, in full, at the time of purchase . . . in cash! (Or at least with a debit card, cashier's check, or money order straight from your bank account.) I know it sounds like an insane concept if you've always had a car payment. But the simple answer to this question is: Pay cash for your cars, and you'll never need a car loan or a credit score to get one. We'll get to the nitty gritty on this in the "Car Loans" chapter.

How do I rent a car without a credit score?

This might blow your mind, but under the right circumstances, every car rental company I researched allows you to rent with a debit card, even if you have no credit score. I'm talking about companies like Alamo, Avis, Budget, Dollar, Enterprise, Hertz, National, and Thrifty. They each have a debit card policy, and the rules and restrictions vary by location. Here's the key to all of this: Do your due diligence. (Don't send me hate mail when you're stranded at the Boise airport because you didn't bother to take a few minutes to check the policy or call ahead.)

I've done this countless times with no issue, so let me walk you through a foolproof plan for a no-stress, no-credit-score rental car experience. It may be *way* easier than this, but these steps will cover all your bases:

1. **Choose a company and location that lets you rent with a debit card.** Call ahead and ask about their specific debit card policy.
2. **Research your vehicle options.** Some companies may limit you to economy, compact, intermediate, standard, and full-size cars. Do your homework if you need a specific type of vehicle.
3. **Bring a valid driver's license—and other forms of ID.** In addition to your driver's license, you may need to bring one of the following: an alternative debit card, passport, recent utility bill, or a store membership card (Costco or Sam's Club card if you're a wholesale hound like me).
4. **Be prepared for credit checks.** This is the big one you may be worried about. Don't worry. What they're *actually* looking for here is a bad/low score—which could mean a history of late payments or delinquent accounts. If you have *no* score, you'll be fine.
5. **Pay attention to travel-plan requirements.** This one is crucial. To pick up at airport locations, you might need to show a ticket or boarding pass as well as proof of a return flight. If you're trying to book a *one-way* rental, you may have to find alternative transportation. Again, research this ahead of time.
6. **Budget for extra holds or deposits.** Be sure to have some buffer in your checking account for authorization holds and security deposits, which could be $200–$500

depending on the company. Remember, you get this money back within a week or two after returning the car.

Aside from some vehicle restrictions and additional deposits, it's a nearly identical experience to renting with a credit score and credit card. Easy-peasy lemon squeezy. In the rare scenario where you're *not* able to rent a car, you're still not out of luck. You can always use ridesharing apps like Uber and Lyft to get around. There's also a newer option for renting with a debit card through car-sharing marketplaces like Turo or Zipcar.

Side note on rental car insurance: Check with your auto insurer to see if rental cars are already covered through your existing policy. That way you can firmly but politely deny all those last-minute extras and upsells they throw at you (especially when you're tired after traveling all day and waiting 37 minutes in line for your turn at the rental desk and desperately want to just be in a mediocre hotel bed getting some shut-eye).

How do I rent an apartment or house without a credit score?

You've probably heard people staunchly declare, "You can't rent an apartment or house without a credit score!" And yet there is simply no evidence to back this up. Again, a *bad* score can hurt your chances, or at least hurt the terms, but not having a score *at all* is completely different and widely accepted.

I've never run into issues trying to rent apartments or houses without a credit score. And to prove that my experience or locale has nothing to do with it, I called several rentals across the country in my narrative podcast series, *The Fine Print*. Specifically, Episode 7: "The Dirty Truth about Credit Scores."

Here's a conversation I had with an apartment complex in Austin, Texas.

Me: I'm just doing some apartment research right now, but I don't have a credit score. Is it worth applying with you guys still?

Them: You don't have a credit score?

Me: Yeah. I just don't have any debt, so it leaves me with an indeterminable credit score.

Them: Got it. I mean, it really just depends. It could clear you or it could approve you with an additional deposit.

Me: Okay. So, you're saying either it goes through just fine or I can get through, but it might require an additional deposit?

Them: Correct. If we're just going based off the credit. But, it is based off income, credit, and then criminal background as well.

Me: Cool. What would the deposit be?

Them: It would range anywhere from $500–$1,000.

Me: And I'd get that back as long as there's no damage when I leave the apartment?

Them: Correct.

Here's another answer from the landlord of a house for rent in Franklin, Tennessee.

Me: Do you take applications if I don't have a credit score?

Them: Uh, sure.

Me: I don't have any debt. And, you know, some places require you to submit that as part of the process. But because I don't have any debt, it makes things a little more complicated, funny enough.

Them: Yeah. I mean, as long as you have the income to produce it, and a clear background check, I'm willing to work with you.

Me: So, as long as I have a job and I'm not a criminal, you're like, "All right, cool."

Them: Pretty much. Yeah.

And *just* in case you're not convinced yet, I called an apartment complex in the quaint suburb of Greenfield, Indiana.

Me: I'm wondering if I can apply if I don't have a credit score?

Them: If you don't have a credit score?

Me: Yeah. Is that something you guys check for in the application process?

Them: We do. Are you employed?

Me: Yes.

Them: Okay, you should be fine. It just might come up with a little higher deposit, based on the fact that you have no tradelines.

Me: Yes, that makes sense. Okay. I had heard a myth from friends that you needed a high credit score to rent an apartment and all this stuff. But I don't do debt, so I didn't know if I could still rent with you guys.

Them: Smart man.

Me: Do you know what that higher deposit is?

Them: It would probably be $1,000. Our normal deposit on a complete pass is $500. But with no tradelines, they look at it as being a little bit higher of a risk, because there's no credit out there, so it would come back conditional with an additional $500 deposit.

Me: So, if I'm hearing you right, I would pay $500 more than someone who had a credit score.

Them: Um, yes, the deposit would come back to you as long as there were no damages to the apartment.

That's it. Kind of anticlimactic, to be honest. I was hoping to put up a fight. Make a stink about it. Raise some heck. I'm just glad we can officially debunk this myth once and for all. The big takeaway is that you just need to be employed, pass a background check, and have enough money to cover a potentially higher security deposit (which you get back when you move out). Big whoop.

How will I get through the job application process without a credit score?

This one is straight bunk. People think they won't land a job without a credit score. According to a report from HR.com, 95 percent of companies conduct some type of background check on potential employees, but only 16 percent pull credit or financial checks on *all* job candidates and just 31 percent do credit checks on *some* candidates.[10] But here's the wild part: Employers can't see your credit score! Potential employers only see your credit *report*.

What they're looking for here are signs of financial irresponsibility and poor money management (things like bankruptcies, delinquencies, and judgments). Having no score at all is a totally different scenario—and won't hurt your chances of landing the job.

---

[10] "How Human Resource Professionals View the Use and Effectiveness of Background Screening Methods," HR.com, July 13, 2018, https://pubs.thepbsa.org/pub.cfm?id=9E5ED85F-C257-C289-9E8E-A7C7A8C58D00.

How do I get good insurance rates without a credit score?

You may have heard that a great credit score will get you great rates on insurance. That tidbit is true. Many insurance providers (especially auto, but also homeowner's and other types) use something called "insurance scores" to rate how risky of a consumer you are. And while they don't share a lot of details about how the scores work, we *do* know your debt load is part of the calculation.

Since insurance providers use those ratings to decide how much to charge you for coverage, the sucky news is that having no debt *can* drive up your premium. In a debt-based economy like ours, mind-numbingly dumb stuff like this happens. But don't despair—while credit scores *do* influence your auto insurance premiums, they're not the only factor. Insurers in most states also consider:

Age—Boomers get the goldmine, Gen Z gets the . . . (mine) shaft. In other words, more-experienced drivers are less risky than younger drivers with fewer miles under their belts.

Location—High-population areas have more drivers and higher costs, while rural areas tend to see lower premiums. Makes sense.

History of claims—The more accidents you've had, the more you'll be paying. At least for a while. But remember that, over time, you can request forgiveness for past accidents (basically, dropping them off your record). Asking can't hurt, and it just might help.

Here are some simple ways you can still get a great, competitive rate on your insurance premiums:

Pay your bills on time. Timely payments carry more weight than the debt nonsense. If avoiding late penalties isn't motive enough, getting a break on your premiums should inspire you to pay your bills on time.

Bundle auto insurance with homeowner's. You can probably save 15–20 percent each year on your insurance premiums just by bundling auto and homeowner's insurance. Easy win.

Raise your deductible. When you raise your deductible, you lower your premium. Once you have a full emergency fund in place and you've mastered the fine art of budgeting, you're able to handle a little more of the risk. Raise it a notch, watch those premiums sink, and live in the peace of knowing you can cover your share with that big ol' emergency fund.

Shop with an independent insurance agent. Your old college buddy who works for fill-in-the-blank insurance company? He's called a "captive agent" because he only can sell you insurance from . . . you guessed it: *that* insurance company. Instead, work with an independent insurance broker who can get quotes from a variety of top-rated companies to get you the best deal.

PS: We have a network of insurance pros that are Ramsey-Trusted who can find you the best coverage at the best price. They've taken care of me and my family for years, and I know they'll take good care of you. Get the insurance party started at georgekamel.com/resources.

How do I buy a house without a credit score?

This is the big kahuna. The dream of homeownership is the biggest objection people have to letting go of their precious score. (Cue Gollum: "My precious!") And I get it. Credit scores are a big deal to lenders when it comes to six-figure loans for the largest purchase of your life.

The good news here: You have options to be a homeowner without the prerequisite of a credit score.

One option is the *100 percent down* plan. That's right. Pay cash like a baller. Now, before you throw this book at a wall and yell unkind things at me, just remember—I can't hear you. Also, I'm not saying this is the route you have to go. It's just . . . an option. It may sound wild and out of touch for most Americans in today's housing market, but I've heard some incredible stories from people who were able to pay cash for their home by:

- Buying in a low-cost-of-living area
- Buying a fixer-upper and cashflowing the renovations and repairs
- Taking equity from a current home sale and using the proceeds to pay cash for their next home

This is a really cool goal to have. And if you can save up aggressively for a few years, it's the ultimate way to buy a house. No payments. Total freedom.

The second, more common option is to buy a house with a *no-score loan*. Don't believe me? Well . . . believe me. Because *I did it*. Back in 2019, my wife and I had no credit scores, had worked our tails off to save up a big down payment, bought a townhome in the Nashville area, and got a 15-year fixed-rate conventional no-score loan with well over 20 percent down.

What's the difference between normal loans and no-score loans? Manual underwriting.

These days, to save time and money, most lenders use *automated* underwriting through advanced artificial intelligence (AI) technology to analyze a credit report and grant the mortgage.

Manual underwriting, on the other hand, involves *a real person* (the underwriter) reviewing your financial situation to approve you for a loan. What a concept.

Remember, the FICO score has only been a thing since the 1990s. People bought houses long before AI or credit scores. The manual underwriting process *can* take a little bit longer since it's, you know, *manual*. But don't let that deter you. If you're prepared with all the documents required, it'll be a breeze.

You may be thinking, *No lender does this anymore!* Well, it's your American right to be wrong. There *are* lenders across the country that still do manual underwriting and no-score loans. And the number-one lender specializing in these no-score loans is Churchill Mortgage. They've been a partner with *The Ramsey Show* for decades—and they're currently licensed to lend in forty-nine states. They've helped thousands of our fans go through this process and become homeowners without a credit score.

Let's walk through what it takes to get a mortgage without a credit score.

Proof of payments. The first hoop will be documentation. Here's what you'll need:

- Verification of income for the past 12–24 months (aka tax returns)
- Rental payment history (12 months of documented, on-time payments)
- 12-month history of savings/bank statements

- *And* one or more regular monthly expenses as an alternative tradeline. They'll give you their list of options, but this could be anything from utility bills in your name to insurance payments or childcare payments. Basically, they want to see that you have a history of making on-time monthly payments on other bills.

A solid down payment. Normally, we recommend a minimum down payment of 5 percent if you're a first-time homebuyer and 10–20 percent for everyone else. But if you have no credit score, you'll need a minimum of 10 percent down, and ideally, 20 percent or more since it reduces the lender's risk, eliminates that pesky PMI (Private Mortgage Insurance), and demonstrates your ability to handle money responsibly. Yes, this may take longer to save up, but it's worth it to move into the biggest purchase of your life with a little bit of equity and a whole lot of peace.

Choose a 15-year fixed-rate conventional mortgage. There are a lot of crappy mortgage types out there, which we'll cover in-depth in the "Mortgages" chapter. Spoiler alert: Nothing beats a good ol' 15-year fixed-rate conventional mortgage. It's the only type I recommend. For a lot of reasons. But in this case, it will give you the best interest rate possible for your no-score loan.

Will my interest rate be sky-high on a no-score loan?

A common objection to the no-score loan is that naysayers think your interest rate gets jacked up. That's another myth that I'm tired of busting, considering I got a great interest rate on my mortgage back in 2019. I even had a loan specialist at Churchill Mortgage run estimates to get at the facts, and here's what they found: If you go with the 15-year fixed-rate loan with a minimum of 10 percent down, you'll receive the same interest rate as someone with "excellent" credit. So if you follow the advice above, you don't have to worry about a sky-high interest rate.

Won't getting a mortgage create a credit score? What's the point of the zero score then?

Yes, getting a mortgage will give you a credit score . . . again. But that doesn't mean much at this point. You see, it was never *just* about having a zero credit score. It was about what the zero score *represented*: a line you drew in the sand where you said, "I'm done playing the debt games that keep me trapped and broke."

And if you're following the Ramsey Baby Steps, which I highly recommend you do, you're *going* to pay this mortgage off in under 15 years. In fact, on average, people following the Ramsey Baby Steps end up paying their mortgage off in about seven years!

LIVING A BETTER LIFE

Like Sisyphus, our culture is trapped in a cycle of improving credit scores to borrow more, only leading to more debt. We're programmed to repeat this task for all eternity, trying to keep up with the demands of the lending gods while worshiping at the altar of FICO. It's an absurd game, but one that many people play, nonetheless.

But you can't unsee the absurdity now. From this point on, you know that chasing a high credit score is ridiculous. It makes the banks richer and richer and pushes you further and further from your goals.

At the same time, you've seen that it's possible to live without a credit score. And not just live, but live *better*. Or for my Taco Bell fans/Spanish AP readers . . . *live más*. No more apps needed to help you keep tabs on your score. No more social media hacks to try and improve your credit. With some intentionality and good financial standing, you *can* do all the things you thought you couldn't do, without a three-digit number for validation. Will it take a little more effort? Sure. But it's a heck of a lot better than owing other people money for the rest of your life.

When you choose to rise above the system designed to keep you broke, you'll no longer be a Sisyphus, endlessly pushing a boulder of debt up the hill to appease the FICO gods. You'll be something so much more, and so much better: You'll be free.

3

Credit Cards

The credit card is the cigarette of the financial world.
–DAVE RAMSEY

There's something special about a rite of passage. School picture day, your first kiss, getting your driver's license, your first paycheck, high school graduation, and of course . . . your first credit card.

For me, it was a Discover® Cashback credit card. When I saw the subject line on that email—*You've been approved*—I felt so seen and loved. I guess 22 years of seeking approval from others had trained me to gladly accept the dopamine hit.

But that first credit card was just a gateway drug that steered me into a debt-filled ditch. Later that year, I got approved for the American Express Gold Delta Skymiles® credit card. (That's gold, Jerry! Gold!) In my mind, only rich people had AmEx cards, so I, of course, felt rich regardless of what my bank account balance had to say about it.

Those cards made me feel *good* about spending money, thanks to all the cash back, miles, and points, oh my! And how freakin' genius of me to build my credit score while I was at it! I felt like I was winning. Heck, they *told* me I was with emails like, *"We're happy to inform you that we have increased your credit line on your Discover® card."*

Looking back now, I can totally see why they were happy to inform me that I could go further into debt with their money. And I can totally see how I got sucked in. I believed I was being *rewarded*. After all, that was the word they kept using.

That was then.

In 2013, I was going through *Financial Peace University* and learned about how these cards and companies were intentionally funneling me and just about everyone I knew into a toxic financial system. As I shared earlier, it was a little scary performing plastic surgery on my credit cards during that second FPU class. Those cards had been my rewards getters, my credit score builders, my fraud protectors, my online purchasers, my hotel bookers, and my security blankie saviors. But after going $4,000 into credit card debt trying to play the game, I figured out quickly that these credit companies invented a game where they don't lose. Getting 2 percent cash back while paying double-digit interest meant I wasn't winning. They were.

AMERICA RUNS ON DUMB THIN (PIECES OF PLASTIC)

Much like the Kardashians, it's fascinating how thin, shiny pieces of plastic can quickly become part of the fabric of American culture. Statistically, 80 percent of you reading this right now have at *least* one credit card in your wallet.[11] Or if you're fancy, it's loaded into your smartphone or watch. Sadly, however, almost half of you (48 percent) don't know what your interest rate is on those credit cards.[12]

And of course, there's always another card, another perk, or another incentive waiting for you. A special card for Amazon; one for gas; an airline card (with concierge travel services) for flights; a 0 percent interest offer card for balance transfers; an AmEx card with a $700 annual fee so you can get a "free" meal at an airport lounge a few times a year; and, for kicks and giggles, an Apple card made of titanium because, for some reason, you think having a heavy, metal card will impress your friends. (If you really want to impress your friends with heavy metal, go blast some Metallica.)

So now you have 14 different cards in your George Costanza-sized wallet, and you're standing in a checkout line doing the mental math of which card will help you maximize rewards for this purchase—convinced that you're in control and "beating the system."

Are you starting to see how insane this is?

You open all these cards promising yourself, "I'll never carry a balance. I'll pay it off in full every month, get my rewards, and stick it to the credit card man! No brainer." Oh, how idealistic that promise was, considering that 49 percent of people are unable to

---

[11] "Economic Well-Being of U.S. Households in 2021," Federal Reserve, May 2022, https://www.federalreserve.gov/publications/files/2021-report-economic-well-being-us-households-202205.pdf.

[12] "State of Personal Finance in America Q1 2023," Ramsey Solutions.

pay off their credit card bills every month.[13] This means there's a coin-flip chance that you're lying to yourself when you open that card. (Truth bomb: Nobody lies to you more than *you* lie to you.)

All those false promises have made credit companies *real* rich. In 2020 alone, credit card companies made a cool $106 billion.[14] That explains how they can afford to spend billions of dollars on TV and digital ads, direct marketing in your snail mail, big buildings downtown, and stadium sponsorships. Give yourself a pat on the back, credit card users—you paid for that!

And things aren't slowing down either. In 2023, outstanding credit card debt hit a record high of $1 trillion.[15] For reference, that's *one thousand billion.* And it's spread out among 55 million households, with each household balance averaging over $14,000.[16] That debt has become harder to pay off too, thanks

---

[13] "Economic Well-Being of U.S. Households in 2021," Federal Reserve.

[14] "FinHealth Spend Report 2022," Financial Health Network, April 28, 2022, https://finhealthnetwork.org/research/finhealth-spend-report-2022/#creditservices.

[15] "Total Household Debt Reaches $17.06 Trillion in Q2 2023; Credit Card Debt Hits One Trillion," Federal Reserve Bank of New York Center for Microeconomic Data, August 8, 2023, https://www.newyorkfed.org/microeconomics/hhdc.

[16] "Changes in U.S. Family Finances from 2016 to 2019: Evidence from the Survey of Consumer Finances," Federal Reserve, September 2020, https://www.federalreserve.gov/publications/files/scf20.pdf and "Households and Families; American Community Survey," United States Census Bureau, accessed September 1, 2023, https://data.census.gov/table?q=household+and+family&tid=ACSDP1Y2019.DP02.

to insane interest rates which, as of 2023, average 22 percent.[17] All of this makes credit cards one of the highest-interest debts a consumer can get, second only to scum-of-the-earth payday loans.

IN NEW YORK (CONCRETE JUNGLE WHERE CREDIT'S MADE OF)

It's weird to think about, since they seem like such a normal part of life these days, but credit cards have only been around as long as hula hoops, TV remotes, non-stick pans, and superglue. How did we even live before then? Our pans were always sticky, and our glue wasn't sticky enough. And to add a layer of inconvenience, we apparently had to just, like, pay for stuff with our own money . . . instantly.

That all changed in 1950, when the first multipurpose credit card was created.

As the legend goes, New York City businessman Frank McNamara was out for dinner when he realized he'd forgotten his wallet at home. His wife had to come bail him out and pay the tab, and he was so embarrassed by the situation, he vowed, *Never again*. McNamara bounced around the idea of "credit" with the restaurant owner, and soon after, Diners Club International was born. (Fun fact: The original Diners Club card was made of cardboard. Not *quite* the flex of a titanium card.) It didn't take long for Americans to start saying, "Put it on my tab." Within the first year, Diners Club had 42,000 users.[18]

---

[17] "Consumer Credit—G.19," Board of Governors of the Federal Reserve System, August 7, 2023, https://www.federalreserve.gov/releases/g19/hist/cc_hist_tc_levels.html.

[18] "Diners Club History," Diners Club International, accessed August 29, 2023, https://www.dinersclub.com/about-us/history/.

In 1958, the American Express Company created a new major credit card that charged users an annual fee and sent monthly bills. Businesses that accepted these cards had to pay a service charge ranging from 4–7 percent of their total billings.[19] Around the same time, Bank of America began offering the BankAmericard in California. It was rolled out to other states in 1966 and then renamed Visa in 1976. Other banks jumped on the bankcard bandwagon, leading to the creation of Mastercard, Discover, and others. Retailers took note of the profits to be had and started creating their own store cards.

Fast-forward to today and 8 in 10 Americans have a credit card.[20] Based on some napkin math, that amounts to more than 260 million adults playing the credit card game.[21] So who's actually winning this game? Well, ask anybody who pays their card off every month, and they'll instantly brag about their free flights, cash back, and how they've "never paid a cent in interest!" But how does it all work? How are these companies making so much profit if all these users claim they're *also* coming out ahead?

I have the answers, and they ain't pretty.

---

[19] Editors of Encyclopaedia Britannica, "credit card," *Encyclopaedia Brittanica*, updated September 2, 2023, https://www.britannica.com/money/topic/credit-card.

[20] "The State of Personal Finance 2021 Q1," Ramsey Solutions, August 29, 2022, https://www.ramseysolutions.com/debt/state-of-personal-finance-2021-q1-research.

[21] Stella U. Ogunwole, Megan A. Rabe, Andrew W. Roberts, and Zoe Caplan, "Population Under Age 18 Declined Last Decade," United States Census Bureau, August 12, 2021, https://www.census.gov/library/stories/2021/08/united-states-adult-population-grew-faster-than-nations-total-population-from-2010-to-2020.html.

HOW THE (CREDIT CARD REVENUE) SAUSAGE IS MADE

At a basic level, we all understand that credit card companies are not charities. They make billions of dollars in revenue and pass on a teensy, tiny bit of the profits to credit card users, who are overjoyed to get those crumbs from the table. The companies make their money from three sources: interest fees, consumer fees, and interchange fees.

If you're wondering how much revenue those sources create, wonder no more. In 2019, the largest US banks reported that credit card revenue generated $89.7 billion from interest, $9.9 billion from consumer fees, and $41.3 billion from interchange fees.[22] Let's break it down.

Interest Fees

Interest is the price you pay to borrow a lender's money. For credit cards, that's labeled as an annual percentage rate, or APR. Carrying a balance from month to month triggers the interest fee. As of this writing, the average credit card interest rate is around 22 percent.[23] The Consumer Financial Protection Bureau estimates that the average American household with credit card debt pays

---

[22] Sumit Agarwal, Andrea Presbitero, André F. Silva, and Carlo Wix, "Who Pays For Your Rewards? Redistribution in the Credit Card Market," Finance and Economics Discussion Series 2023-007, Federal Reserve, accessed August 30, 2023, https://www.federalreserve.gov/econres/feds/files/2023007pap.pdf.

[23] "Consumer Credit—G.19," Board of Governors of the Federal Reserve System.

around $1,000 in interest annually. That adds up to $120 billion in credit card interest and fees paid each year![24]

Consumer Fees

Credit cards have so many potential fees, they make Ticketmaster look like the good guys. If you're a credit card user, I *dare* you to go read the fine print of your favorite card. You won't believe all the fees they can ding you with. Here are a few of them (okay, more than a few):

> *Annual Fee:* Not all credit cards have an annual fee, and sometimes it will be waived for the first year as an incentive. But once it kicks in, that yearly fee can be anywhere from $25 to $700 (or more), depending on the card. That means even if you pay your card off perfectly, you'll have to spend a lot of money to gain enough in rewards just to break even after the annual fee. (By the way, credit card companies *love* that you're psychologically and financially incentivized to spend enough to make up for that fee.)

> *Late Fee:* This is a charge for not delivering your payment on time—and it's usually pretty hefty, sometimes higher than your monthly minimum payment amount. In addition, when you don't pay the monthly balance in full, you've just

---

[24] Ashwin Vasan and Wei Zhang, "Americans pay $120 billion in credit card interest and fees each year," Consumer Financial Protection Bureau, January 19, 2022, https://www.consumerfinance.gov/about-us/blog/americans-pay-120-billion-in-credit-card-interest-and-fees-each-year/.

triggered a world of hurt through double-digit interest. Translation: They get you comin' and goin'.

Balance Transfer Fee: This is what it costs you to move debt from one card to another, generally to a 0 percent introductory APR card. You'll generally be charged anywhere from 3–5 percent of the transfer amount. Side note: That 0 percent introductory rate doesn't last long and doesn't solve the root problem, the debt.

Cash Advance Fee: You'll get dinged with this 2–5 percent fee for using your credit card to get cash from a bank or an ATM. You could also get hit with ATM fees *plus* a higher interest rate on the withdrawal. It's a very expensive way to turn their monopoly money into real money.

Expedited Payment Fee: Afraid you'll miss your payment date? You can fork over a fee to make sure your funds get applied on the day you send them, avoiding the costlier late charge. (But it'll still cost you.) It's like dishing out extra for expedited shipping—but for debt.

Foreign Transaction Fee: You could be charged anywhere from 1–4 percent (depending on the card) when you're traveling outside the US *or* buying something from a company based outside the US.[25]

---

[25] Odysseas Papadimitriou, "4 Tips for Using Credit Cards Overseas," Investopedia, May 18, 2023, https://www.investopedia.com/articles/pf/11/using-credit-cards-in-other-countries.asp.

Interchange Fees

Interchange fees, aka swipe fees, are charged to merchants anytime you swipe a card instead of paying cash. It's kind of like a tax that businesses pay for the card issuers to accept, process, and authorize your transactions. The rates from Visa, Mastercard, and Discover range anywhere from 1.5 percent to 2.5 percent, while American Express can go up to 3.5 percent! Woof. It's no wonder you see businesses with signs that say, "We do not accept American Express."

Debit cards, on the other hand, have a *much* lower interchange fee of 0.5 percent. That means businesses pay a fee that's *three to seven times higher* when you use credit instead of debit! By the way, when you pay in cold, hard cash, there's no interchange fee—which is why some businesses offer a discount for doing so.

WHERE DID YOU COME FROM, WHERE DID YOU GO? WHERE DID YOU COME FROM, CASHBACK DOUGH?

Maybe learning how the credit card sausage is made has you contemplating going financially vegan. But we're not quite done with the sausage talk. Because even though we know *how* these companies make money, we're still left wondering *where* the rewards come from. Credit card companies aren't exactly an open book when it comes to which pile of profits your free flights or cash back are taken from.

The more research I do, and the further I delve into the belly of this credit beast, the grosser it gets. You see, most credit card users assume their rewards are paid for by interchange fees, *not* by people struggling with credit card debt and paying exorbitant interest fees. But much like Shakira's hips, these numbers don't lie. I present to you Exhibit A . . . Capital One's 2022 Earnings Report:[26]

***Total net revenue from credit card products:* $22.35 billion**

- *Net interest income from credit cards:* $16.58 billion
- *Net non-interest income from interchange fees:* $4.6 billion

This means only 20 percent of their revenue came from interchange fees charged to businesses, while almost *75 percent* came from interest fees! Well, that hits different. (And don't miss that they made $4.6 billion in a year just from people swiping credit cards to buy things.)

Turns out credit card companies like Capital One are making *most* of their money from people who are struggling to pay their bills each month. They turn around and offer a *tiny* portion of that struggle-money back to you—so you can enjoy your free flight and some cashback, feeling like you beat the system.

Now, before you give me the ol' "Yeah, well, you know, that's just like, your opinion, man," we are *way* beyond opinions here. It's now a well-researched *fact*, thanks to a 2023 study by the Federal Reserve. They set out to determine who, exactly, pays for credit card rewards. The results, though expected, are alarming. In their report, the Fed said, "We estimate an aggregate annual redistribution of $15 billion from less to more educated, poorer

---

[26] "Capital One Reports Fourth Quarter 2022 Net Income of $1.2 billion, or $3.03 per share," Capital One, January 24, 2023, https://investor.capitalone.com/news-releases/news-release-details/capital-one-reports-fourth-quarter-2022-net-income-12-billion-or.

to richer, and high to low minority areas, widening existing disparities."[27] Wow.

Digging deeper, families with household incomes below $40,000 are less likely to even qualify for a reward card of any type, while being *more* likely to pay late fees and additional interest. Families making above $100,000 were more likely to have access to reward cards and reward programs—and *less* likely to pay late fees and interest.

Here's what that amounts to: Lower-income cardholders paid $4.14 billion in fees, while those with higher incomes raked in $1.26 billion in rewards. But get this. That leaves a gap of $2.88 billion. Where did that go? You guessed it, to the credit card companies. That's how they're able to sponsor the Taylor Swift tour, while we can't even afford a *ticket* to the Taylor Swift tour. It's a painful reminder we know all too well—that we're the foolish ones for being enchanted by these mastermind companies.

So let's recap what's going on here. Lower-income consumers barely see a dime from rewards programs, while shelling out *more* dimes for the same goods, which amounts to $15 billion redistributed every year to the well-off credit consumers.

What you do with all this information is up to you. But you should at least know who's *really* paying for your perks and how. Because it sure ain't the credit card companies.

WE ARE NEVER EVER GETTING BACK TOGETHER (GEORGE'S VERSION)

In just a few decades, we've gone from a society that rarely used credit cards (and hardly understood the concept), to one that's *so*

[27] Agarwal, et al., "Who Pays for Your Rewards?"

dependent on credit, we can't imagine life without it. And that's exactly where the credit card companies want us. They make a *killing* on how easy it is for us to swipe to get what we want. And yet they're killing *us*, based on the $1 trillion in credit card debt Americans are in right now.

If you're one of those people carrying credit card debt, there's hope that you can get rid of it once and for all. Later, in the "Debt Is a Thief" chapter, we'll cover a proven and foolproof way to get out of debt once and for all.

Maybe you don't have credit card debt, but you still have credit cards. I urge you to do something crazy and countercultural: Cut them up and close the accounts . . . forever. I know, I know, breaking up with your credit cards may trigger memories of your first breakup in high school (and that emo playlist you made). But just like opening your credit card account was a rite of passage, I think closing your account is an even *better* rite of passage.

How will you survive without one? Stick to debit cards and cash. Let me say it again, since that short and sweet sentence may have exploded your brain a little. *Stick to debit cards and cash.*

Since cutting up and closing my credit cards back in 2013, I've survived—nay, *thrived*—without them. Are you impressed? Confused? Shocked? I can hear you interjecting already: "But what about . . . ?" I get it. Let's go ahead and address the most common objections to surviving—sorry, *thriving*—without a credit card.

THE TOP 8 REASONS WHY PEOPLE WON'T DITCH CREDIT CARDS

Doing what I do for a living, I hear *all* the reasons for using a credit card. One of my favorite questions to ask is, "What's the biggest thing holding you back from getting rid of your credit cards?" I get some valid responses, some less-valid excuses, some passionate objections, and some wild justifications as to why a person refuses to let go of that rubber crutch—or in this case, a plastic crutch. Here are the top eight reasons I've heard, which I've bucketed into personality archetypes for your reading pleasure.

1. THE PERFECT SPENDER

The Reason: "I pay off my card on time and in full every month! I never pay a dime in interest! I treat it *just* like a debit card!"

The Reality: Even if you pay it off perfectly, *every* study shows that you spend more when you use a credit card.

Let's assume you're one of the 48 percent of people who statistically pay off your card balance every month. You're still lying to yourself if you believe you don't spend a *dime* more by using credit.

In 2021, researchers at MIT conducted a unique study using fMRI technology to examine brain activity during the moment of purchase.[28] They focused on the reward center of the brain, called the striatum, which releases dopamine. This is the same part of the brain that is triggered by addictive drugs like cocaine and amphetamines.

Here's what's wild. Research had already proven that credit cards reduce the pain of purchase, but this new study adds *another* layer. Not only do credit cards "release the brakes" on spending, but they also cause our brain to "step on the gas," driving us to spend even more! Citing additional studies, this research concluded, "Shoppers with credit cards are willing to spend more

---

[28] Drazen Prelec and Sachin Banker, "How credit cards activate the reward center of our brains and drive spending," MIT Management Sloan School, June 9, 2021, https://mitsloan.mit.edu/experts/how-credit-cards-activate-reward-center-our-brains-and-drive-spending.

on items, check out with bigger baskets, focus on and remember more product benefits rather than costs, and make more indulgent and unplanned purchase choices."[29]

To sum it up: When it hurts less, it costs more. Spending *your* own money, right *now*, causes more pain than borrowing *someone else's* money and paying it back *later*. Which is what's happening every time you swipe that credit card. America's addiction to convenience and comfort has made us flabby, stressed out, and broke. It's time to intentionally bring *back* some friction, some discomfort, and some pain into our life—so we can regain control of it.

2. THE REWARDS REDEEMER

The Reason: "I never pay for flights, I get free hotel stays, and the cash back more than pays for my annual fee!"

The Reality: Credit card companies run thousands of experiments on consumers every year to get them to chase the carrot of rewards through more spending.

Over 90 percent of *all* money spent on credit cards is on rewards cards.[30] America is *obsessed* with those perks. In fact, rewards and cash back are the top reason people keep their credit cards.[31]

---

[29] Sachin Banker, Derek Dunfield, Alex Huang, and Drazen Prelec, "Neural mechanisms of credt card spending," Nature, February 18, 2021, https://www.nature.com/articles/s41598-021-83488-3.

[30] "The Consumer Credit Card Market," Bureau of Consumer Financial Protection, September 2021, https://files.consumerfinance.gov/f/documents/cfpb_consumer-credit-card-market-report_2021.pdf.

[31] "The State of Personal Finance in America Q1 2023," Ramsey Solutions.

I get it. Who doesn't love "free" stuff like flights, hotels, gift cards, and cash back? While we've already covered the repulsive underbelly of who's really paying for these rewards, there's even more slime and grime where that came from.

Sumit Agarwal, a finance professor and economist who has done extensive research on credit cards, had this to say about the rewards game: "We have created an ecosystem where we have kind of essentially been giving a drug to the consumer, which is these rewards cards. And the reason we keep giving this drug is we know it's highly profitable and we know the consumer is addicted to it."[32]

I covered this topic in my narrative podcast series, *The Fine Print*, in an episode titled "The True Cost of Credit Card Rewards." I interviewed an ex-Capital One employee who was in senior management, and she spilled more tea than the colonists in the Boston Harbor. Here are the SparkNotes from the podcast interview.

She told me that credit card companies create these reward programs in a way that incentivizes people to spend more than anticipated, trapping them in a vicious cycle of debt. Once you're hooked, they can pull the ol' bait and switch, completely revoking your rewards if you miss a payment. Rewards can be devalued at any time, making them worth less and causing you to spend *more* for the same perk—much like inflation.

These companies intentionally incorporate complex pricing structures, confusing point systems, and tiny, fine-print terms that all exist for *their* bottom line and benefit. Not yours.

For someone to truly "beat the system," she explained that they'd almost have to make it a full-time job. *Geez.* Do you know what else can pay for flights and earn you some cash? An actual . . . full-time job.

---

[32] Agarwal, et al., "Who Pays for Your Rewards?"

Think about the math on this. For every dollar you spend (aka borrow), you're *hoping* to get a 2 percent reward, with the very real *risk* of paying 22 percent interest. You play with snakes, you get bit. You play stupid games, you win stupid prizes.

And for a good chunk of the population, these rewards are going to waste. A recent survey found that 23 percent of people didn't redeem their rewards in the past 12 months.[33]

Remember, credit card companies are not your friend—they don't care about you. They're also smarter than you. They understand your behavior better than you do, and they know exactly how to persuade you to spend more (and get you into debt). If you think you're going to beat them at their own game, they will happily let you think that. When you're the mouse in a giant laboratory maze, making it to the cheese seems like victory . . . But you're still a rodent, stuck in someone else's science experiment.

3. THE FRAUD PROTECTOR

The Reason: "Credit cards are so much safer than debit cards!"

The Reality: Debit cards have nearly the same fraud and liability protections as credit cards.

Out of all the reasons people keep their cards around, I have the most sympathy for this one. Our security gland can flare up when it comes to money—especially when it comes to losing it. And to give credit where it's due, credit cards *do* have solid protection thanks to the Fair Credit Billing Act, which frees you from any responsibility for charges that happen after you report a stolen

---

[33] Poonkulali Thangavelu, "Poll: 23 percent of cardholders have unused credit card rewards," Creditcards.com, March 20, 2023, https://www.creditcards.com/statistics/unused-credit-card-rewards-poll/.

card.[34] On top of that, most major credit cards have zero-liability policies, meaning you won't owe a thing for any purchase made by someone else. So I can see how there's some legit peace of mind with these cards, especially in a digital age riddled with scams, shams, hackers, and frauds.

But here's a little-known fact that should be better known: While debit cards aren't covered by the Fair Credit Billing Act, they *are* covered through the Electronic Fund Transfer Act.[35] This law gives you 60 days (from the day you get your statement) to report any unauthorized transactions to your bank.

If your *physical* card is lost or stolen, your max liability is $50 (as long as you report it within two days). If your card *number* is stolen, you have zero liability (as long as it's reported within 60 days).[36] For some additional good news that might convince you to switch from the dark side over to the debit side: More and more card issuers are offering the same zero-liability protection on *debit*

[34] Louis DeNicola, "What Is the Fair Credit Billing Act?" Experian, April 11, 2021, https://www.experian.com/blogs/ask-experian/what-is-the-fair-credit-billing-act.

[35] "Electronic Fund Transfer Act," Federal Trade Commission, accessed August 30, 2023, https://www.ftc.gov/enforcement/statutes/electronic-fund-transfer-act.

[36] "How do I get my money back after I discover an unauthorized transaction or money missing from my bank account?" Consumer Financial Protection Bureau, August 28, 2023, https://www.consumerfinance.gov/ask-cfpb/how-do-i-get-my-money-back-after-i-discovered-an-unauthorized-transaction-or-money-missing-from-my-bank-account-en-1017/.

cards. If your debit card has a Visa or Mastercard logo, you're covered by their zero-liability policies![37]

Now, you might be saying, "Yeah, but it still takes time for fraud to get resolved, and if it's my debit card, it's *my* own money on the line. With a credit card, it's their money and their problem!" Fair point. Allow me to counterpoint.

First, most banks will quickly issue a provisional credit while the fraud is investigated (thanks to Regulation E). Second, your debit card probably has a daily purchase limit, which prevents your account from getting wiped out. Third, I always recommend having an emergency fund in a *separate* savings account, which means you have access to other money while the mess gets sorted out.

Use these other pro tips to help you live your safest debit card life:

- Disable overdraft protection (to avoid overdraft fees and charges beyond your account balance).
- Use Apple Pay or contactless payment methods (which encrypt your card number, keeping it safe).
- Monitor your bank statements and subscribe to transaction text alerts (so you're immediately aware of charges to your card).
- Turn on two-factor authorization (to protect online accounts that include your banking info).
- Don't save your debit card info with retailers. (Bonus: You'll be less tempted to spend.)

---

[37] "Speed, security and safety with debit Mastercard®," Mastercard, accessed August 31, 2023, https://www.mastercard.us/en-us/personal/find-a-card/standard-mastercard-debit.html.

- Pay with virtual cards that hide your real card info (using a tool like Privacy.com).
- Keep your PIN private (and guard it with your whole heart).
- Exercise common sense: Avoid public Wi-Fi for banking, use strong, unique passwords, inform your bank about your travels, and store your card safely.

There you have it. Between legal protections, zero-liability policies, a solid bank, a separate emergency fund, and some common sense, a credit card doesn't have much protection over a debit card. One more reason to cut it up.

4. THE WORLD TRAVELER

The Reason: "I need a credit card for travel, rental cars, and hotels!"

The Reality: A debit card can handle all those things—without debt.

As I said in the previous chapter, my debit card has *never* stopped me from gallivanting around the globe. I'm able to book flights with my debit card just fine. (Shockingly, airlines are happy to take my money in any electronic form.) I'm able to rent cars and hotel rooms with a debit card.

Aside from the myths around booking with a debit card, you might still be hooked to the idea of free flights and hotels with your rewards. Let's talk about how this works.

You can collect points or miles based on how far (or how often) you fly and how much you spend on your credit card. For most cards, every dollar you spend will earn you one "mile" or point. I put *mile* in quotes because we're not talking about actual distance here. They call them *miles* to make it sound like you're getting more than you are. Ten thousand flight miles doesn't get you 10,000 miles away from home. It gets you to Boise if you're lucky (and you should be so lucky).

So when you make a purchase, it takes about one dollar to earn a mile. But when you try to *redeem* those miles, each one is only worth about one-and-a-half cents, depending on the kind of card you have.[38] (That'll get you about a foot down the runway.) If you're doing the math at home, that means you'd have to spend *$50,000* to earn 50,000 miles, which then gets you a "free" flight that would have cost about $750 out of pocket. *My debit card could buy a whole lot of flights for $50,000!* And don't forget to add on taxes and fees—because your rewards don't cover those either. Suddenly, that "free" flight is starting to feel a whole lot less . . . *free.*

But let's dream big. Let's say you get *two* miles for every dollar you spend. Great! Now you're livin' large. That $750 plane ticket only cost you $25,000 in other spending. Still insane. And like I mentioned earlier, the issuers of your miles and points for flights and hotels can change the value at any time, along with blackout dates and limited options.

Some of you may be in a job where your company reimburses you for these expenses, and it's even more enticing because, in a sense, you're spending *their* money to get these rewards. But it's still *your* name on that card . . . and there's still the temptation to overspend, the risk of carrying a balance (negating any rewards), the hassle of redemption, and the chance of devaluation. Not worth it.

---

[38] Holly Johnson, "How Much Are American Airlines Miles Worth?" *Time,* May 31, 2023, https://time.com/personal-finance/article/american-airlines-miles/.

If you pay attention to airline sales, use travel apps, and do some research, you can find better deals and pay cash without being beholden to a certain airline or points goal. If you have the income to support all this credit card spending, then you surely have the income to simply save and budget for travel.

5. THE CONVENIENCE SHOPPER

The Reason: "I love the convenience of a credit card!"

The Reality: Debit cards are just as convenient—with the added convenience of never going into debt.

Convenience can mean a lot of things here. For some people, they're comparing the convenience of a credit card to cash. They don't like the hassle or danger of carrying around a bunch of cash, which is fine. But at that point, a debit card is just as convenient. For others, convenience is making online purchases easily and securely. (We've already covered how debit cards do this too.) But what most people are talking about with "convenience" is that they don't have to use their own money right now to buy the things they want. They can go into debt now and *hope* they have the money to pay for it later. That's a terrible financial plan.

With a debit card, you're using money you *actually* have in your bank account to buy things you can *actually* afford. The transaction happens immediately without the hassle of being surprised by your credit card bill and having to pay that debt next month . . . and the month after that . . . and the month after that. Cash has similar benefits, with the bonus that it doesn't require any technology or the potential concerns about data breaches. That's pretty dang convenient too.

Simply put, using debit cards and cash will help remove the temptation to go into debt. You'll also spend less and be more intentional about your purchases.

If you can't afford it, *don't buy it.* If you don't have the money right now, *wait until you have the money.* Wild concepts, I know. Our grandparents used to call them common sense and delayed gratification. For real convenience, stick to debit cards and cash. Tried, true, and Grandma-approved.

6. THE EMERGENCY SHELTER

The Reason: "I need my credit card in case of emergencies!"

The Reality: That's what your emergency fund is for.

Broken HVACs, car trouble, sprained ankles—they're part of life. And when that part happens, it can be frustrating. One in four Americans with a credit card uses it to cover expenses they can't pay for in cash.[39] But charging an emergency to your credit card doesn't solve your problem—it just makes it worse . . . at 22 percent APR!

This one has a simple solution: You create your own (piggy) bank reserve called an emergency fund. Then, instead of relying on a credit card company to be your hero, *you* can be your hero, baby. (Enrique Iglesias fans, if you're still out there, that one was for you.)

If you have consumer debt, I recommend starting with a $1,000 baby emergency fund. Once you've paid off your consumer debt, continue saving up until that emergency fund is big enough

---

[39] "State of Personal Finance 2021 Q1," Ramsey Solutions.

to cover 3–6 months of expenses (we call that a *fully funded* emergency fund). The peace of mind that comes with having a big ol' pile of cash tucked away, just in case, is a gamechanger.

Keeping that little plastic card around like it's some sort of shield gives you the *illusion* of safety, but not a peaceful reality. So get that emergency fund in place ASAP—and cut up your weak plastic shelter.

7. THE FEAR TRANQUILIZER

The Reason: "Having a credit card makes me feel more secure!"

The Reality: Credit cards give you a false sense of peace while adding on more stress, anxiety, and risk.

Fear is a terrible financial advisor. And credit cards end up increasing that fear. The solution, then, is not to tranquilize yourself with credit cards, but to address the root cause of that fear. Did your family struggle to make ends meet growing up? Did a divorce leave you financially vulnerable? Did a health scare make you believe that no amount of money would ever be enough to cover you? Are you reading too many headlines about how the economy is going to crash and the apocalypse is near?

Once you figure out the root cause, address it with facts. My friend and Ramsey Personality Dr. John Delony says, "Facts are your friends." Focus on the facts instead of your fear. Actual friends, community, wise counsel, therapists, turning off the news—all of that can help too.

Personally and emotionally speaking, here's why credit cards are a terrible solution to fear: Using other people's money makes you feel *less* in control because your body is keeping score—it *knows* you're not truly safe when you borrow money or owe someone money. When you don't use debt, you have less risk, less stress, fewer payments, and more peace. Couple that with an emergency fund and sticking to debit cards and cash, and you'll be amazed at how quickly the grip of fear will begin to loosen.

8. THE CREDIT SCOREKEEPER

The Reason: "I need a credit card to build (and keep up) my credit score!"

The Reality: You don't need a credit score to live your financial life. And therefore, you don't need a credit card to keep it up.

As you now know, you can accomplish all your financial goals *without* a credit score. The credit score is an overhyped scam that keeps you playing the debt game forever. To *get* a credit score, you have to go into debt (yes, even if you pay it off every month). How do you get a higher score? More debt. Get off this miserable merry-go-round.

Once you pay off your debts and close the accounts, your score will eventually disappear. Living without a score isn't much different. For a refresher on how this all works, and how well it works, reread the previous chapter. And if you're holding onto credit cards for the stupid score, it's time to let go.

YOU SAY GOODBYE, I SAY HELLO (TO FREEDOM)

By now I hope you see how screwed up and scummy the credit card industry is. Do you see that playing their game isn't worth the perks, even if you play it perfectly? And that the reasons we hang onto our credit cards don't have as much merit and truth to them as we think? I hope I've convinced you that you can not only survive without one—but you can *thrive* without one.

I'm not on some moral high-horse trying to guilt you into cutting up your cards. You can still make it to heaven if you use credit cards. But it's worth asking yourself: *Is this the kind of system I want to be a part of (and benefit from)? Is this the game I really want to play for the rest of my life? Do I want this kind of poison in my financial waters?*

You may be silently screaming, "George, we have no choice! This is how the system works!" Yeah . . . but *no*. The truth is, you *do* have a choice. You can opt out of *this* particular system by simply using cash and debit cards. As someone who hasn't had a credit card in over a decade, I'll share my honest experience: I've found that bucking this credit card system has given me more perks and benefits than any company ever could.

Once I cut up my card, I weirdly built wealth *faster*, with more confidence and peace. I didn't miss the cash back or free flights because I learned how to take control of my money and simply save up and pay for things. Imagine that. Rewarding *yourself* instead of waiting on some "blessing" from a credit card company. I was able to budget, save up, and pay for flights to see my family at Christmas without worrying whether I had accrued enough airline miles. I was no longer subconsciously tempted to spend more on eating out or entertainment due to some rotating cashback reward. My budget told me how much I could spend, and using my *own* money caused me to make better decisions at every turn.

We've got to think bigger than points and rewards and perks. We've got to quit stepping over dollars to pick up pennies. Cut up the credit cards and pay for things with a debit card or cash. Quit the credit card rat race and start running your own race. One where you achieve your money goals on *your* terms—not theirs.

TAKE THE "NO CREDIT CARD" CHALLENGE

Hey, credit card users! I triple-dog dare you to take my No Credit Card Challenge. Here's how it works:

1. Stick your credit cards in a block of ice or lock them away somewhere you'll never see or think about them. Delete your credit card info from apps and sites you use. (Honor system here—don't let me down.)
2. For the next 30 days, stick to using a debit card or cash for all purchases.
3. Track your spending with a budgeting tool (I highly recommend and personally use EveryDollar).
4. After 30 days, compare the numbers from your previous credit card days. See if you spent less, were more intentional, got closer to your financial goals, and felt more in control and aware of your money.

My hunch is that it will feel more peaceful to not have to think about maximizing rewards, that it will feel a little more painful to see your own money disappear with every purchase, and that you'll end up cutting up the cards and never looking back. Best wishes on your credit card-free journey.

4

Student Loans

I began my education at a very early age; in fact, right after I left college.
–WINSTON CHURCHILL

Raise your proverbial hand if you experienced some version of this conversation:

Them: You need to go to school!
Us: Why?
Them: To get good grades!
Us: Why?
Them: To get into a good college!
Us: Why?
Them: To get a degree!
Us: Why?
Them: To get a better job!
Us: Why?
Them: To make better money!

Us: Why?
Them: To have a better life with less money stress!

And *that*, my friends, is how multiple generations fell for the trap of student loan debt. It's mind-boggling how easily and naively we all just . . . went with it.

RUNNIN' DOWN A DREAM (THAT WOULD NEVER COME TO ME)

The problem with this not-so-trivial pursuit? They left out the part where most of us went to college at all costs, and "all costs" turned out to be unlimited, seemingly free, and easy-to-get student loans that would take decades to pay off. And when we used student loans to fund this whole operation, we ended up frustrated, broke, with *lots of* money stress. Not less.

Here's how this plays out in reality. The *Chicago Sun-Times* interviewed some graduates for a piece on the student loan crisis.[40] One of them was Jessica. After graduating high school, she chose to save money by going to a community college for two years. *Alright, good start, good start.* Then she transferred to Loyola University of Chicago and graduated with a biology degree. She was the first college graduate in her family, and it took $100,000 in student loans to make it happen.

Even with her degree, she still couldn't land a good-paying job in her field. Turns out, only 41 percent of college graduates

---

[40] Rachel Hinton and Ashlee Rezin, "A generation of college grads buried in student debt," *Chicago Sun Times*, June 2, 2018, https://chicago.suntimes.com/2018/6/2/18527648/college-grads-buried-student-debt.

find full-time employment within the first year of graduating.[41] Unfortunately for Jessica, lenders don't give a rip about that. So six months after graduating, they came knocking. "Yo! Where's our money?"

Jessica picked up a job as a lab technician and customer service representative at a veterinarian's office. Three years later, she was considering going *back* to school to become a pharmacist because she couldn't find a job with her existing degree that paid above minimum wage. The catch is . . . well, she's broke. To go back to school, she would need to take out *more* loans!

She was quoted saying things like, "How am I going to ever be able to afford a house?" "Every day is a struggle just to afford living, getting to work, getting food and paying other bills, like gas or rent." "I'm the first college graduate in my family, and I'm worse off than my two siblings who didn't go to school."[42]

Sadly, this isn't a unique story. Millions are living this way: stuck between a rock (a job they didn't dream of) and a hard place (a degree they mostly regret). We all want our version of the American Dream—to be a homeowner, to start a family, to travel, and to live with financial stability instead of living paycheck to paycheck. But for decades now, we've been sold the lie that college is the one and only path, and that student loans are just the price of admission (literally) to this "dream."

Well, the data is clear. Student loan debt is *not* the answer. In fact, it's the *problem*. Student loans are *selling* the American Dream but *delivering* the American Nightmare.

---

[41] "First Destinations for the College Class of 2020," National Association of Colleges and Employers, accessed September 1, 2023, https://www.naceweb.org/job-market/graduate-outcomes/first-destination/class-of-2020/interactive-dashboard.

[42] Hinton and Rezin, "A generation of college grads."

AND IT BURNS, BURNS, BURNS (THE DUMPSTER FIRE)

Where do we stand today? As of this writing, 43 million Americans carry a total of $1.6 trillion in student loans.[43] Don't gloss over that. One trillion is one thousand *billion*. One billion is one thousand *million*. So it takes one million million, or one thousand billion, to get to a trillion. And we're *way* past that. I need an antacid after digesting those numbers.

Let's double-click on this folder of forgotten dreams to see what sadness lies within. The average student loan debt per borrower is almost $40,000.[44] At the average interest rate of 5.5 percent,[45] this amounts to a payment of about $393 a month. That's awful enough, but here's the kicker: It takes the average borrower anywhere from 17 to 23 years to pay off their loans![46]

Now, based on those numbers, let's do some math that will move you from sad to angry. If you pay $393 per month for 20 years, you will have paid more than *$94,000 in total payments.* On a loan that was . . . $40,000 at graduation. Are you punching

---

[43] "Federal Student Aid Portfolio Summary," Federal Student Aid, accessed September 1, 2023, https://studentaid.gov/sites/default/files/fsawg/datacenter/library/PortfolioSummary.xls.

[44] Chris Horymski, "Americans Shed More Than 10% of Total Student Loan Debt Since March 2020," Experian, August 25, 2023, https://www.experian.com/blogs/ask-experian/state-of-student-loan-debt/.

[45] "Interest Rates and Fees for Federal Student Loans," Federal Student Aid, accessed September 1, 2023, https://studentaid.gov/understand-aid/types/loans/interest-rates.

[46] Imed Bouchrika, "Average Time to Repay Student Loans: 2023 Statistics & Data," Research, July 28, 2023, https://research.com/education/average-time-to-repay-student-loans.

a hole in the wall yet? (Please don't. You can't afford the drywall repair—because of the student loans.)

You'd think by now we'd wise up to this student loan scam and stop getting fooled, right? *Hah!* Wrong. More than 2 million students will go to college this year. And about 1.3 million of those students will take out loans.[47] How did this become normal? How did we get here? Let's dig into this villainous Joker origin story.

WE DIDN'T START THE FIRE (THE GOVERNMENT DID)

To fully understand this student loan crisis, we've got to look at its roots. I'll try to make this history lesson painless and entertaining. Plus, who doesn't love a good timeline?

1957: The Soviet Union launches a beach ball-sized satellite named *Sputnik* into outer space. America gets insecure and decides that our students need more higher education to keep up with Russian rocket scientists.

1958: President Eisenhower creates a low-interest student loan program through the National Defense Education Act. This money comes *directly* from the government and is meant to make it easier for middle-class families to send their kids off to college.

---

[47] "Who Borrows and How Much do They Borrow?" State Council of Higher Education for Virginia, accessed September 1, 2023, https://research.schev.edu/info/Articles.Student-Debt-A-First-Look-at-Graduate-Debt.

1965: President Johnson wants to make loans and grants more accessible to lower-income students, so he signs the Higher Education Act. Now it's even *easier* to go to college, but it also changes the way these loans are funded: The money will come from banks instead of the government. The banks are jazzed because, at this point, student loans are a super low-risk investment. If students default and can't pay back the debt, the government *guarantees* it will foot the bill.

1972: President Nixon creates the Student Loan Marketing Association (SLMA). You know this rose by its thorny name . . . Sallie Mae. As a government-sponsored enterprise, they're designed to funnel money into the student loan program. They buy the loans from the banks, which gives the banks the cashflow to issue more loans. The best part (for them)? The government *guarantees* all that money, which really just shifts all the risk to taxpayers. Not cool, guys. Not cool.

1997–2004: The government decides to let Sallie Mae transition to a *private* organization while *still* guaranteeing their loans. This is where the student loan program goes from being a public good to a big-time, money-making scheme. It's not even a "program" anymore. It's a freaking industry with dozens of student loan companies. Because now, as a bona fide business, Sallie Mae can focus on generating massive profits, which they use to up their marketing game and crush the competition. They pay colleges to drop the government loan program and sign up with them instead. They sponsor cruises and trips for financial aid officers. They sneakily put Sallie Mae employees in university call centers to talk to students who *think* they're talking to college loan officers. What a bunch of scum burgers.

2005: Sallie Mae convinces Congress to make it really hard to get rid of private student loans through bankruptcy. This causes more people to default on their loans, accumulate lots of interest, and deal with never-ending repayment plans. How never-ending, you ask? Even if the borrower *dies*, the loans can still haunt the borrower's family.

2010: President Obama does away with the Federal Guaranteed Loan Program, which let private lenders offer student loans at low-interest rates. He thinks this will save money by cutting out the middleman and taking away the government burden to guarantee private loans. (Narrator: It did not, in fact, save money.) Instead, the Congressional Budget Office *increases* its 10-year forecast for the loan program's costs by 30 percent, which amounts to an extra $27 billion—much of it passed on to borrowers through higher interest, more loan fees, and fewer repayment options.

2019 BC (Before Covid): *The Wall Street Journal* interviews economist Alice Rivlin, who led the Johnson Administration task force that created the system of federally guaranteed loans. When asked what she thinks about the system after all this time, her response is, "We unleashed a monster." Hindsight is 20/20, Alice. Or in this case, $1.6 trillion.

This monster gives colleges and universities free rein to charge whatever the flip they want. And they do. Between 1977 and 2023, college tuition and fees shot up about 1,400 percent.[48] For

---

[48] "Digest of Education Statistics" and "Tuition costs of colleges and universities," National Center for Education Statistics, both accessed September 1, 2023, https://nces.ed.gov/programs/digest/d07/tables/dt07_320.asp and https://nces.ed.gov/fastfacts/display.asp?id=76.

comparison, that's more than 3.5 times the rate of inflation (415 percent) during that same period.

While tuition skyrockets, so does student loan debt. America's student loan debt grows from $240 billion to $1.6 trillion between 2003 and 2018. That's an increase of more than 550 percent, making it the fastest-growing portion of the total household debt in the US.[49] I think we can all agree that any debt growing that fast is a financial cancer to society.

Okay, let's recap. Over the past six decades, the government, with the help of banks and lenders, made student loan debt easier to get, while also inflating college tuition at a speed that would make Usain Bolt look slow. This was the catalyst for an entire nation to be duped into taking out student loans.

Along with a pile of debt, these decisions created an entire industry of bloodsucking student loan companies whose pockets are now overflowing with the money *your* future was supposed to be built on. And in the wake of their profits are multiple generations drowning in student loan debt, who took it on in hopes of making a better life for themselves.

This vicious cycle of debt and regret now begs the question: Is the college juice still worth the squeeze?

IS (COLLEGE) WORTH IT? LET ME WORK IT

When it comes to life after high school, there's no one-size-fits-all plan. I don't like *anything* that's one-size-fits-all. As a small-framed

---

[49] "Total Household Debt Reaches $17.06 Trillion in Q2 2023; Credit Card Debt Hits One Trillion," Federal Reserve Bank of New York Center for Microeconomic Data, August 8, 2023, https://www.newyorkfed.org/microeconomics/hhdc.

man, let me be the first to tell you that one size does *not,* in fact, fit all.

Simply assuming that college is the *only* answer and that student loans are the *only* way to get there is . . . well, you know what they say about assumptions.

Don't misunderstand. I am pro-education. I decided to go to college, and after some twists and turns, I graduated with a bachelor's degree in communication. (A solid choice considering I'm here right now . . . communicating.) That being said, whether you're helping your own kid grapple with this decision or you're weighing the options for yourself and the dreams you're pursuing, we have plenty of research and real-life scenarios out there proving that higher education (college, grad school, etc.) may not be the right next step for everyone. Let's cover why that is.

1. A four-year degree isn't quite the job requirement it used to be.

College degrees *can* open doors, but practical experience and networking are what get you through the door. The University of Washington found that 53 percent of college grads are unemployed or working jobs that don't require a degree.[50] And the employment rate for 25- to 34-year-olds without a degree is 78 percent, not far from the 86 percent rate for those *with* a degree.[51]

---

[50] "What can students do to improve their chances of finding employment after college?" University of Washington, April 9, 2021, https://www.washington.edu/doit/what-can-students-do-improve-their-chances-finding-employment-after-college.

[51] "Employment rates of young adults," National Center for Education Statistics, accessed September 1, 2023, https://nces.ed.gov/fastfacts/display.asp?id=561.

Looking toward the future, a recent report from Burning Glass Institute projects that an additional 1.4 million jobs could open up for workers without college degrees over the next five years.[52]

2. Not all degrees rake in the big bucks.

When it comes to salary, degrees are not created equal. A history degree might land you a $36,000 starting salary, while a mechanical engineering degree could earn you double that. So think about whether the cost of your degree is worth the potential income. Time and time again, my colleagues and I hear stories and take calls on *The Ramsey Show* from people who took out $100,000 or more in loans and are trying to pay the money back on a $40,000 salary. That's tough.

3. You might end up with regret.

A survey conducted by Ramsey Solutions revealed that 49 percent of those who took out student loans say they regret using student loans to pay for their education—and 33 percent didn't have a full understanding of how student loans worked before they took them.[53] The only thing that could add more regret is an unfortunately spelled "NO RAGRETS" tattoo. If you're unsure about your path after high school and whether you'll even need a degree, college could be a costly mistake.

---

[52] "The Emerging Degree Reset," The Burning Glass Institute, February 9, 2022, https://www.burningglassinstitute.org/research/the-emerging-degree-reset.

[53] "State of Personal Finance in America Q1 2023," Ramsey Solutions.

4. Graduation isn't a guarantee.

Just over 60 percent of recent high school graduates enrolled in college in October 2021.[54] But the National Center for Education Statistics reports that only 63 percent of college students finish their degree within six years. Put another way, for every ten students who graduate from high school, six will go to college, but only *four* will finish within six years. That means a whole bunch of people with college debt, minus the degree. And for a third of the students going to college, it might be the *wrong* next step.

Now let's look at the other side of the ol' college coin. Why might college be the *right* next step?

1. Some jobs require a college degree.

Not all careers do, but many (like teaching, nursing, engineering, and law) do. Even when it's not required, a degree *could* help you stand out during job hunts in a pile of digital résumés.

2. College grads usually earn more.

In 2021, the average college graduate earned $69,000 a year compared to $42,000 earned by someone with *only* a high school education.[55] The gap shrinks a bit for those with *some* college or an

---

[54] "61.8 percent of recent high school graduates enrolled in college in October 2021," U.S. Bureau of Labor Statistics, May 23, 2022, https://www.bls.gov/opub/ted/2022/61-8-percent-of-recent-high-school-graduates-enrolled-in-college-in-october-2021.htm.

[55] "Education pays, 2021," U.S. Bureau of Labor Statistics, May 2022, https://www.bls.gov/careeroutlook/2022/data-on-display/education-pays.htm.

associate's degree, but the data is clear: The lifetime earning potential of college grads is higher.

3. College teaches valuable skills and broadens perspectives.

Hopefully college helps train you in skills like problem-solving, critical thinking, teamwork, and organization. You also meet diverse people and understand different points of view. Is it worth a six-figure price tag? Heck no. You can do most of that by sending your kid on a six-month European adventure at a tenth of the cost. But to be fair, there is value beyond textbook knowledge.

4. College offers resources and opportunities.

Campuses have guidance counselors, career centers, job fairs, clubs, and volunteer opportunities. Internships, often available only to college students, provide on-the-job experience and potential job offers. On top of that, the networking and connections you gain through your college experience can lead to job opportunities you otherwise may not have had.

To sum it up, I'm reminded of my friend and Ramsey personality Ken Coleman's two-question filter:

1. Is it the only way?
2. Is it the best way?

If a four-year degree is truly the *only* way and the *best* way to do what you want to do in your career, then college is probably the right next step. But too many students are choosing college for the wrong reasons. And there are *lots* of wrong reasons.

RAGE AGAINST THE (MARKETING) MACHINE

Society at large has convinced students that a college degree is "priceless." That you should borrow whatever it takes; otherwise, you'll fall behind in the career rat race and never get ahead financially either. And nobody is cautioning students against it—not the government, the guidance counselors, the financial aid office, the admissions office, the teachers, or the parents. They're complicit in this crime under the guise of "good intentions," and in some cases, bad motives.

Now, it's fair to say that college isn't *just* about the education. Ask any high schooler, and they'll tell you it's largely about the *experience.* In 2019, I hosted a Ramsey Network podcast series on the student loan crisis titled *Borrowed Future* (which was developed into a feature-film documentary by the same name in 2021). In the podcast, I interviewed high schoolers, asking about their college dreams: where they wanted to go, why they wanted to go there, how much it would cost, what they wanted to study, and how much money they'd make with the resulting career. You would've thought it was a criminal interrogation by the way the blood drained from their faces. The answers ranged from clueless, to assumptive, to borderline arrogant. Most of the answers had very little to do with the classes and programs, and more to do with the *experience.*

You see, colleges realized that if they spruced up their campuses, more students would flock like street rats descending on a slice of New York pizza. It became a life hack for colleges to get higher rankings in *US News and World Report.* It was a snowball effect as their rankings climbed. Fancier amenities and savvy marketing produced more applicants, which increased tuition and profits. The football team, the landscaping, the world-class cafeteria, the luxury dorms, the waterpark—it all became the oil greasing the gears in the marketing engine. The ratchet kept on turning, and guess who was getting caught in the gears? The students taking out massive amounts of debt for the experience.

We've put colleges on such a high pedestal that opening the acceptance letter has become a viral video trend on social media. (Interestingly enough, they don't send the tuition info along with the acceptance letter.)

Another marketing tactic colleges use is brand association. Mom or Dad went to this school, and now as the alumni, they want their kid to go to their school. Parents, allow me to be blunt for a moment. I know your alma mater means a lot to you, and you have great memories of sorority rush, frat parties, and football games. But that same "experience" now costs 500 percent more. Stop pressuring your son or daughter to go to the same school you did 30 years ago so that *you* can feel good while he or she takes on debt for it. That's not okay.

Alma maters aside, parents tend to put way too much pressure on their kids to go to "famous" schools. Do you want to know why? Because parents have a harder time bragging to their friends about how their son or daughter goes to the community college down the road.

Stop it. There is dignity in *all* education. Your child's college choice isn't your chance to live vicariously through them. Quit using your kids as an emotional pillow to prop yourself up. I beg of you, parents: Swallow your freaking pride so that our kids aren't in chains when they graduate.

EVERY ROSE HAS ITS THORN (EVERY DEBTOR PAYS A SAD, SAD LOAN)

We frequently get calls on *The Ramsey Show* from people whose school loans are crushing them. They've got $50,000, $100,000,

$200,000, or even more, in student loan debt. They're emotionally overwhelmed, mentally paralyzed, and financially drowning. As a bystander, you might be thinking to yourself, *Well if they took out that much debt, they must have a good degree and a good job that allows them to pay it off. If they don't, it's their fault.* That's a myopic take at best, and cavalier at worst. Because as we've learned, the lie they were sold by this system doesn't match the reality they're experiencing.

We've talked about the villains that got us tangled up in this trillion-dollar knot. And hanging on to the end of that rope is the student who decided to take out these loans. They were unwitting accomplices in what feels like a crime—allowing a teenager to borrow virtually unlimited money with the guarantee of a better life later.

How did we convince millions of teenagers to do this? Two simple, paradoxical words: *good debt.*

There's something about the word *student* in front of the word *loan* that makes people see it differently. They see it as an "investment" instead of debt. But even then, any investment has risks. Sadly, we've gotten so starry-eyed over college as a status symbol that we've removed the risk factor in our brains. It's an insane set of assumptions:

- That you're automatically going to get a return on this investment.
- That you will get a degree and a job in a field that pays more than what you would have made had you *not* had the degree.
- That you *will* graduate.
- And that you'll be able to pay off the loans in due time.

It's easy to see why many people have stopped mentally categorizing student loans as debt—4 out of every 10 according to a

Ramsey Research study. To that I say, we have lost our ever-loving minds! Let me remind you exactly what debt is: owing *anything* to *anyone* for *any* reason. So student loans *are* debt. Simple as that.

When you pay for college with this so-called good debt, the future you were promised comes at an even higher price. And it's not just the tuition bill. It's delayed dreams.

In 2022, a survey of more than 5,000 adults with student loan debt revealed a tragic state of stunted growth:[56]

- 42 percent of young adults delay paying off other loans because of their student loans.
- 14 percent of young adults delay getting married because of student loans.
- 44 percent of young adults delay saving for retirement because of student loans.
- 33 percent of young adults delay buying a home (and often just live with their parents) because of student loans.
- 35 percent of young adults delay travel because of student loans.
- 16 percent of young adults delay having a baby because of student loans.

Anyone who still believes this is "good debt" needs a pulse check.

Student loan debt is now the second-highest consumer debt category—surpassed only by mortgage debt. And it's not just a millennial or Gen X problem anymore. According to the Federal Reserve Bank of New York, the number of student loan borrowers 60 and older increased by more than 500 percent between 2004 and 2021—and their total debt rose from $6.4 billion to

---

[56] Victoria Rodriguez, "CNBC/Momentive Poll: 'Invest in You'" Curiosity at Work, January 2022, https://www.surveymonkey.com/curiosity/cnbc-invest-in-you-jan-2022/.

$126.6 billion.[57] Today, tens of thousands of seniors are having their Social Security benefits snatched away because of defaulted student loans, leaving them in a serious financial bind.

Borrowers across the spectrum are drowning, and to add to the heartbreak, the number of people who can't make their student loan payments keeps growing. An average of 7 percent of borrowers default on their student loans—that's about 4 million students each year.[58] For federal student loans, you default if you miss full payments for nine months or more. At that point, a collection agency is coming after you. They can garnish your paycheck without permission and withhold your tax refund. The lender can even take you to court.

Do you know what doesn't help all this madness? The unethical practices of these sleazy student loan servicers. From misapplied payments to lost paperwork to misinformation from customer service reps, these companies are inept at best and malicious at worst.

In 2019, the Consumer Financial Protection Bureau sued Navient over allegations that they systematically encouraged student loan borrowers into forbearance. Forbearance is an agreement to postpone your loan payments while interest continues to grow. In the *Borrowed Future* documentary, a former employee of Navient's call center explained that when Navient put an account in forbearance, they were able to collect the interest. So they were collecting interest *on top of* interest. Good grief!

---

[57] "Total Balances by Age Group," 2022 Student Loan Update, Federal Reserve Bank of New York Center for Microeconomics, August 8, 2023, https://www.newyorkfed.org/microeconomics/databank.html.

[58] Melanie Hanson, "Student Loan Default Rate," EducationData.org, August 27, 2023, https://educationdata.org/student-loan-default-rate.

In a leaked internal strategy memo from 2010, a Navient executive described their battle cry as "forbear them, forbear them, make them relinquish the ball." The result of their strategy? Four billion dollars of unnecessary interest put onto the most vulnerable borrowers. Told you they were scum.

Thanks to the interest on these loans, only 38 percent of borrowers make any progress in paying down their balances while many (42.6 percent) actually see their total student loan debt balance *increase* in the first five years of their loan.[59] And it can take a lifetime to pay off. Twelve years after borrowing, the average borrower has barely made a dent in their student loans. That helps to explain why it takes the average borrower around *20 years* to pay off their student loan debt.

Another trap in the student loan world? Co-signing. When you (a parent or other caring adult) co-sign a student loan, your name is attached to the debt, which means you essentially just took on that debt yourself. If the student can't make their payments, you're 100 percent responsible to pay it back. About 93 percent of private undergrad student loans for the 2018–2019 academic year included a co-signer.[60]

For most federal loans, you don't need a co-signer, but when you *do* need one, it's called a Parent Plus loan, which means the parent is the primary borrower. These loans are a curse on families, and they can destroy relationships. Think about it. The reason

---

[59] Jillian Berman, "Student-loan interest is resuming. Here's why the government charges it," Morningstar, September 2, 2023, https://www.morningstar.com/news/marketwatch/20230902363/student-loan-interest-is-resuming-heres-why-the-government-charges-it.

[60] Donna Rosato, "5 Things to Do Before Co-Signing a Student Loan," Consumer Reports, April 19, 2019, https://www.consumerreports.org/student-loans/5-things-to-do-before-co-signing-a-student-loan/.

a co-signer was needed is because the lender didn't have faith in the student's ability to repay the loan. There's already more risk on your part. Finding out a collection company is coming after *you* because your kid stopped making payments can make Thanksgiving dinner extra awkward.

This student loan nightmare has led to a whole lot of bankruptcies. According to one study, 32 percent of consumers filing for Chapter 7 bankruptcy carried student loan debt.[61] Of that group, school debt took up 49 percent of their total debt on average. If you're doing the math at home, that means 1 in 3 people who filed for Chapter 7 bankruptcy had student loans taking up half of their debt load.

What's wild is that many people who qualify for bankruptcy *still* won't qualify for their student loans to be discharged, thanks to super strict laws (see Sallie Mae's heinous move in 2005 in the timeline, pages 75–77). When I interviewed a student loan lawyer, she offered up an example of a man who experienced just how strict these laws were. He was diabetic, blind in one eye, and had a prosthetic (glass) eye in the other. He was on kidney dialysis, needed a liver transplant, and was in the hospital. He filed for bankruptcy to discharge student loan debt. The judge basically said, "Ah, you know what? You *could* get better and pay this off, so I'm not going to discharge it because you haven't shown 'undue hardship.'" Wow.

In other words, while you *technically* can get student loans discharged through bankruptcy . . . good freakin' luck.

Are you starting to understand my hatred for student loans and the lenders who dish them out? This "good debt" is the worst

---

[61] Mike Brown, "Study: For Those Filing For Bankruptcy, Student Loan Debt Still Lingers On," LendEDU, April 5, 2023, https://lendedu.com/blog/student-loans-bankruptcy/.

debt. I will die on this hill (unlike federal student loans, which only die when you do).

SO WE KEEP WAITING (WAITING ON STUDENT LOAN FORGIVENESS)

If you currently have student loans, I'm guessing at some point in this chapter you've thought, *Ha! I'm not worried, George. I'm banking on student loan forgiveness to wipe out my debt!* You're seriously banking on the *government* to get this done? Have you met . . . the *government*? Their track record on this isn't exactly faith-inspiring. Let's break down why.

The success rate of the Public Service Loan Forgiveness (PSLF) program is straight-up *embarrassing*. In 2017, 890,516 people had their employment and loans certified as eligible and 19,321 people applied for PSLF. Only 55 were approved. That's a 0.28 percent success rate. Or on the flip side, a 99.72 percent fail rate.[62]

Fast-forward to June of 2022 and the numbers weren't any better—even with looser eligibility requirements. A total of more than a million-and-a-half combined PSLF forms were submitted, and only about 12,500 were approved—that's a failure rate of 99.26 percent and a success rate of 0.74 percent.[63] Cue Lloyd Christmas: "So you're telling me there's a chance!"

---

[62] "Public Service Loan Forgiveness: Education Needs to Provide Better Information for the Loan Servicer and Borrowers," U.S. Government Accountability Office, September 27, 2018, https://www.gao.gov/products/gao-18-547.

[63] "Combined Public Service Loan Forgiveness (PSLF) Form Report," Federal Student Aid, June 2022, https://studentaid.gov/sites/default/files/fsawg/datacenter/library/pslf-jun2022.xls.

Let's look at the Temporary Expanded Public Service Loan Forgiveness (TEPSLF) program that was intended to give people another shot at this. As of June 2022, almost 3.6 percent of those applications met the requirements for forgiveness.[64] So, uh . . . *slightly* better than PSLF . . . but the bar was so low, any number would look impressive by comparison.

Suffice it to say, the current student loan forgiveness program is an epic failure. And while politicians will continue to make big promises and campaign on the issue of widespread forgiveness, the outlook is not looking good. In June of 2023, this headline demolished the dreams of 43 million Americans: "Supreme Court strikes down Biden student loan forgiveness program."[65] So quit holding your breath. If the resolution on this is anything like the last episode of the TV show *Lost*, it's going take a whole lot of time to get there and leave you sorely disappointed.

YEAH, I'M (DEBT-) FREE-FALLIN'

Okay, I'll be the first to admit that this was a depressing chapter. How about we end on a high note?

First, let's address the parents and students who are facing the college decision and have now decided to do it without debt. I'm *so* proud of you. You're setting yourself up for a brighter future, even if it means more sacrifice now. You *can* go to college completely debt-free. Here's how to pay for college without student loans:

---

[64] "Combined PSLF Report," Federal Student Aid.

[65] Devin Dwyer and Alexandra Hutzler, "Supreme Court strikes down Biden student loan forgivenss program," ABC News, June 30, 2023, https://abcnews.go.com/Politics/supreme-court-strikes-biden-student-loan-debt-forgiveness/story?id=99231423.

1. Take debt off the table. No matter what it takes, *you're going to college without debt.* This decision will help you make other decisions. You'll realize you don't *need* to go to that dream school because of its fancy cafeteria or the football team that you love. You'll realize you don't *need* to go to the school where your parents went so that you can join the same frat or sorority and make them feel warm, fuzzy feelings of nostalgia.

2. Open a college savings account. I recommend two options: an Education Savings Account (ESA) and a 529 Plan. You invest after-tax dollars, your money grows tax-deferred, and withdrawals are tax-free for education expenses. ESAs offer virtually unlimited investment options (similar to a Roth IRA), but they *do* have income limits. The 529 Plans are typically specific to each state, but you can also invest in plans from other states. By investing $167 a month ($2,000 a year) from age 0 to 18, assuming a 10 percent average return, you could have $100,000 tax-free for college! Investing wisely to avoid student loan debt in the future is a noble goal. Aim for it.

PS: Investing for college can be intimidating. If you need some guidance, one of the best things you can do is get an investing pro in your corner. They can help you figure out your best path to save for college and craft a strategy for your goals. Learn more about getting investing guidance at georgekamel.com/resources.

3. Choose an affordable school. College choice is the life hack to graduating college debt free. Opting for an in-state school rather than out-of-state will generally be a much more affordable option (barring full rides and scholarships). And fun fact: About 30 states offer free tuition at community colleges—take advantage of that! Knock out your prerequisites and transfer after two years. The quality of education at community colleges has drastically improved over the years, shrinking the gap with four-year schools.

Allow me to nerd out on the numbers. The average cost of attending a four-year public in-state college was more than $23,000 a year (for the 2022–23 school year). The average cost of attending a four-year private college was more than $53,000. Now let's compare that to the average cost of attending a community college and living at home: $3,860 a year.[66] That means a community college cost 86 percent less than a public in-state school and 93 percent less than a private school. And *that* means . . . if college was a breakfast cereal for a private name-brand like Fruity Pebbles, you'd be paying the equivalent of $20 a box—instead of just $1.49 for the generic brand, Far-Out Fruities. Why pay 93 percent more when they both accomplish the goal of a delicious, sugary breakfast?

4. Apply for scholarships and grants. You've heard about the Free Application for Federal Student Aid (FAFSA). With it, students provide information to their potential college choices, which the colleges then use to determine which federal grants and work-study programs, state aid, and school aid they'll offer. But here's the problem—the FAFSA also sneakily includes student loans! So tread with caution and avoid any debt that's cosplaying as "aid."

Next up, scholarships. Make searching for scholarships a part-time job, and don't overlook the little guys. If a student spends

---

[66] "Trends in College Pricing and Student Aid 2022," College Board, October 2022, https://research.collegeboard.org/media/pdf/trends-in-college-pricing-student-aid-2022.pdf.

five hours researching and applying for scholarships and gets even $1,000 in scholarships, they essentially made $200 an hour with that five-hour investment of time!

Once you're in college, don't stop applying for scholarships. Keep looking every single semester. Each year, over $3 billion of grant money and $100 million in scholarship money goes unclaimed by incoming freshmen.[67] Go claim it!

5. Work smarter and harder while in school. This might mean living at home, and it definitely means living on a budget. While you're in college, you've got to make a plan for any dollars coming in. And if at all possible, pick up a part-time job—to make sure dollars are coming in. Studies show that students who work 15–20 hours a week while taking classes have a higher GPA than those who don't. Makes sense. They have more discipline, more focus, and they're trying to graduate in four years or less because they're actually paying for it!

So there you go. You *can* go to college debt-free. The real question is, will you do *what it takes* to make it happen?

Are you willing to talk to your parents (or kids) early on and develop a game plan to avoid debt? Spend some nights hustling

---

[67] Raymond AlQaisi, "NCAN Report: In 2022, High School Seniors Left $3.58 Billion on the Table in Pell Grants," National College Attainment Network, January 31, 2023, https://www.ncan.org/news/629039/NCAN-Report-In-2022-High-School-Seniors-Left-3.58-Billion-on-the-Table-in-Pell-Grants.htm and Mark C. Perna, "$100 Million In Scholarship Money Goes Unclaimed Every Year. Does It Have To?", *Forbes*, November 1, 2021, https://www.forbes.com/sites/markcperna/2021/11/01/100-million-in-scholarship-money-goes-unclaimed-every-year-does-it-have-to/?sh=f55798e3b6ff.

on scholarship applications? Go to that community college for two years because it's the more affordable option?

Will you ignore other people's opinions and pressures of what your future is supposed to look like? Will you forgo the glitz and the glam of the famous school that your parents or older sibling went to? Will you go get that part-time job while you're in school? I hope the answers are a resounding *yes*.

It's that simple, and it's that hard. While I've heard devastating stories of student loan debt, I've also been inspired by countless people who were able to get a debt-free degree thanks to the principles I just laid out for you. It's 1,000 percent worth swimming upstream to avoid the Niagara Falls of student loan debt.

ANOTHER (STUDENT LOAN) BITES THE DUST

If you're one of the 43 million carrying student loan debt, this part is for you. You're not carrying this debt much longer if I've got anything to say about it. You're going to pay that bad boy off.

Most people who follow the money plan in this book pay off their debt in 18 to 24 months. I was able to pay off $36,000 in student loan debt in 18 months using the Debt Snowball method. We'll get into the specifics of that in the "Debt Is a Thief" chapter. In the meantime, stay angry and motivated to destroy your student loan debt ASAP!

There are only two paths to choose now. You could be like most of America and continue to

- wait in frustration for someone to do something about this.
- put yourself or your kids in chains by taking out student loan debt.

- stay in debt, allowing scummy lenders to steal your paycheck and your joy.
- delay your dreams of homeownership, getting married, starting a family, starting a business, traveling the world, and even retiring with dignity.

That's a bummer of a life.

Here's a better picture of what *could be* if you rise above this toxic system, stay out of student loan debt, or get out of student loan debt. You could:

- live life on your terms, achieving your goals and dreams.
- graduate and get on with your career without the pressure/worry of student loan payments.
- pay off your school loans in the next few years.
- be your own hero rather than hoping the government will rescue you.
- take control of your future.

Now we're talkin'. You see, a college degree is *not* the secret sauce to your success. *You* are. Your tenacity, grit, sacrifice, discipline, critical-thinking skills, people skills, knowledge base, real-world experience, and willingness to learn. That's the sure route to being fulfilled and doing work you love.

If it takes a diploma to get there, great. But don't forget what this is really about: freedom. When you do it the hard way the first time, you earn the freedom to decide what you're going to do next. And that freedom is worth way more than any piece of paper.

PS: I highly encourage you to go watch the *Borrowed Future* documentary (and with your parents or kids) as a next step.

Consider it the video accompaniment to this chapter, further uncovering the dark side of the student loan industry and exposing how the system works against you. It will spark conversations and inspire you to graduate debt-free or destroy your student loan. Start watching for free at georgekamel.com/resources.

5

Car Loans

If you think nobody cares if you're alive,
try missing a couple of car payments.
—EARL WILSON

If I were to create an alphabet based on the most American things I can think of, my list would start like this:

Apple pie
Bald eagles
Car payments
Diners (Drive-Ins and Dives)
Elvis
Football

Honestly, it was tough to choose between Elvis or Easy Cheese, but I wanted to stay classy for America's sake. I'm not here, however, to talk about America's favorite science-defying, processed cheese spread in a can. I'm here to talk about something even more troubling: car payments.

Assuming you're like most people, it's been ingrained into your brain that car payments are a way of life. Then again, most people are broke.

Think about this. Buying a car is one of the largest purchases you'll ever make, most likely in second or third place behind a college education and a home. Getting a return on your investment with a home purchase is likely, thanks to the long-term appreciation of real estate as an asset. Getting an ROI on your education? Possible, as we discussed in the previous chapter. But cars? That's what we call a "depreciating asset."

For you to go $30,000 into credit card debt to buy "stuff" and pay the minimum every month with interest is, we would all agree, tomfoolery. But going 30 grand into debt for a *car* and paying the minimum every month with interest—nobody bats an eyelash.

Americans may be obsessed with driving nice cars that also flaunt their façade of wealth and success, but it's costing them big-time—$1.58 trillion worth of car loans, to be exact. That means for the first time in history, car loan debt has taken the lead over student loan debt, which currently sits at $1.57 trillion.[68] Unlike student loans, nobody would even attempt to call a car loan "good debt." It's unequivocally bad. Like the Rotten Tomatoes score for the 2003 rom-com *Gigli*, featuring Ben Affleck and J-Lo, which is

---

[68] "Total Household Debt Reaches $17.06 Trillion in Q2 2023; Credit Card Debt Hits One Trillion," Federal Reserve Bank of New York Center for Microeconomic Data, August 8, 2023, https://www.newyorkfed.org/microeconomics/hhdc.

sittin' ugly at 6 percent. If 6 percent is a box-office bomb, $1.58 trillion is a financial nuclear disaster.

CARMAGEDDON BY THE NUMBERS

Yes, I gave this auto loan crisis the snappy name *Carmageddon*. And yes, I'm aware that Carmageddon was also a PC game released in 1997. Unfortunately, this isn't a game. As of this writing, here's Carmageddon by the numbers:

SALES PRICE

- Average transaction price of a new car: $48,344[69]
- Average transaction price of a used car: $32,811[70]

LOAN AMOUNT

- Average amount financed on a new car: $40,356[71]
- Average amount financed on a used car: $29,665
- Average loan term: 68.5 months

---

[69] "Auto Market Weekly Summary: August 7," Cox Automotive, August 7, 2023, https://www.coxautoinc.com/market-insights/auto-market-weekly-summary-august-7/.

[70] "Electric Vehicle Prices Collapse Even As Overall Used Car Market Stabilizes," ISeeCars, July 10, 2023, https://www.iseecars.com/used-car-prices-study.

[71] Statistics for all remaining bullets in "Loan Amount" and "Monthly Payment" are from "Car Shoppers Feel the Heat from Scorching Financing Costs in Q2," Edmunds, July 3, 2023, https://www.edmunds.com/industry/press/car-shoppers-feel-the-heat-from-scorching-financing-costs-in-q2-according-to-edmunds.html.

MONTHLY PAYMENT

- Average monthly payment on a new car: $733
- Average monthly payment on a used car: $569
- Consumers with monthly payments of $1,000 or more: 17.1 percent

What in tarnation? This is *madness*! And whether you're a part of these stats or not, you've got to be wondering what caused the insanity.

One reason for the price surge is supply and demand. You see, when global supply chains shut down during the pandemic, it caused years of production backlog and economic chaos. That chaos decreased the supply of cars while demand was still high. In February 2021, there were 2.6 million unsold used cars on dealer lots. Fast-forward two years to February 2023, and there are only 2 million used cars for sale.[72] That's a decrease of 21 percent in two years. In short, fewer cars and higher demand equals increased prices—and higher levels of auto loan debt.

We saw this same thing happen with the housing market, causing an insane spike in home prices for a few years. Record-low interest rates by the end of 2021, combined with a shortage of supply, drove prices up—which meant bigger mortgages. The tides have turned more recently, with auto loan interest rates climbing to the highest levels since 2008. Will that cool off the dumpster fire of Carmageddon? Only time will tell.

Arguably, the most important reason for this crisis is that we live in a progressive society. And by that I mean, people are getting progressively stupider. Remember how student loans got out of

---

[72] "Spring Selling Season Kicks Off Early With Used-Vehicle Supply Low," Cox Automotive, March 17, 2023, https://www.coxautoinc.com/market-insights/used-vehicle-inventory-february-2023/.

control and colleges kept raising tuition and people just took out *more* student loans to compensate for the price gouging? Yeah, it's kind of like that, but with cars.

A DEPRESSING DEPICTION OF DEPRECIATION

The problem with buying motorized joyrides comes down to one word: *depreciation*. And when you mix payments with depreciating assets, you add insult to auto injury.

Simply put, depreciation is the difference between how much your car was worth when you bought it and what it's worth when you sell it. Here's the kicker for you new-car lovers: New cars depreciate *much faster* than used cars do. How much faster? Grab a barf bag and buckle up, buttercup.

- **After One Minute:** A brand-new car loses *9–11 percent* of its value the *moment* you drive off the lot.[73] So, with a $40,000 new vehicle, you're basically throwing $4,000 out the car window as you drive the car home for the first time! *Ouchie.* I guess Sheryl Crow was right: The first cut *is* the deepest.
- **After One Year:** After a single orbit around the sun, your car is probably worth about *20 percent* less than what you bought it for.
- **After Five Years:** That new car will depreciate by another *15–25 percent* every year until it turns five years old. And here's the birthday gift: Your now-used car has lost around *60 percent* of its value.

---

[73] All car depreciation stats are from Rick Popely, "Car Depreciation: How Much Value Does a Car Lose Per Year?" Carfax, February 3, 2021, https://www.carfax.com/blog/car-depreciation.

New Car Purchase Price	**$40,000**
New Car Value After . . .	
1 minute (–10%)	$36,000
1 year (–20%)	$32,000
2 years (–32%)	$27,200
3 years (–42%)	$23,120
4 years (–51%)	$19,650
5 years (–60%)	$16,000

You heard that right: A brand-new car will lose *60 percent* of its value within the first five years. And yet you continue to pay the same monthly payment for the entire length of the loan term (which on average is now *longer* than five years), while your car drops in value like a freakin' rock.

Let's recap. After 70 months of payments, you've got a paid-off car that you *bought* for $40,000, that ended up *costing* you $50,000 (thanks to interest), that's now only *worth* $16,000 (thanks to depreciation). So, as astronomically stupid as that is, why are people still buying new cars on payments? Or worse, leasing them?

THE BASS-ACKWARDS LOGIC THAT'S BREAKING YOUR BANK

As a cohost of *The Ramsey Show*, I've heard a carload of arguments, situations, predicaments, and justifications from callers when it comes to their car decisions. Here's a sampling.

"You'll always have a car payment."

No, you won't. The only way you'll always have a car payment is if you continually buy cars you can't afford. Buying used cars with cash and upgrading over time is the only way out of this cycle.

In 2017, I bought a 2009 Honda Civic for $6,000. In 2020, we bought my wife a 2010 Mazda CX-7 for $8,000. In both instances, I paid cash. I've done a lot of dumb things with money, but I'm proud to say I've *never* had a car payment.

Do you know how many people I impressed with these cars? Close to zero. Do you know how much I cared about impressing people with these cars? Even closer to zero. What did leave an impression (on *me*) was how not having a car payment freed me up to do other things—like save up to upgrade those cars, invest in retirement, and pay off my mortgage early.

"As long as I can afford the monthly payment, who cares?"

I care. I care about you becoming wealthy, being outrageously generous, and living a life unencumbered by debt. By having a car payment, you're actively saying, "I don't want to be wealthy. I'd rather *look* wealthy but stay broke." Broke people ask, "How much down, how much a month?" Wealthy people ask, "How much?" That's it. That should be where the question ends. If you can't afford it in full, today, you shouldn't buy it.

This is why the salespeople at dealerships never start by asking how much car you can *afford*. They instead ask: "What kind of payment are you looking for?" They *know* they can milk you for more if they can just get you thinking in monthly terms.

Let's look at exactly what that payment, and this short-term thinking, is costing you. What if instead of sending that $700 "you can afford" to lenders every month, you were investing it in mutual funds with an annual average return of 11 percent (which, by the way, is the historical track record of the S&P 500 from its inception in 1928)?[74] Investing a $700 car payment from age 22 to 62 could amount to *more than $6 million.* In your pocket. Hope you like the freakin' car! Heck, even if I'm half-wrong, you'd still have $3 million. Cry me a river and wipe your tears with $100 bills.

"I need a new car because it's safer and more reliable. It'll be cheaper than a used car in the long run."

This one grinds my gears because it assumes all used cars are death traps that could spontaneously combust on the interstate. Let me remind you that the moment you drive a *new* car off the lot, it becomes a *used* car. There are plenty of used cars that are just as safe, reliable, and much more affordable. Plus, with vehicle history reports, you'll have peace of mind about a used car's past life.

Turning the tables, some newer cars (especially models in their first year of production) are among the *least* reliable cars you can drive.[75] From faulty air conditioners to bunk transmissions, even newer-model cars can wind up in the shop regularly or be recalled by manufacturers.[76]

---

[74] "Historical Returns on Stocks, Bonds, and Bills: 1928–2022," Stern/New York University, January 2023, https://pages.stern.nyu.edu/~adamodar/New_Home_Page/datafile/histretSP.html.

[75] Keith Barry, "New Cars Aren't Always More Reliable, Despite What Buyers Think," Consumer Reports, June 28, 2018, https://www.consumerreports.org/buying-a-car/new-cars-arent-always-more-reliable-survey-a1097859269/.

[76] Patrick Masterson, "The 10 Biggest Recalls in 2018," Cars.com, January 7, 2019, https://www.cars.com/articles/the-10-biggest-recalls-in-2018-1420756943863/.

Now let's talk about those assumed cost savings of a new car being "cheaper" in the long run. According to AAA, the average cost of repairs, maintenance, and tires for a new car is $121 a month. As a personal-finance nerd who drives used cars, I keep track of my vehicle expenses and found that my average cost was actually *less* than $100 a month. So don't believe the myth that used cars will cost you more to maintain.

And the other factor you're leaving out? Insurance. New cars are more expensive to insure than older ones since they cost more to repair or replace. You might be thinking, *But I get a discount on MY insurance for my newer safety features!* While it's true that safety features *can* lower insurance costs, the higher premiums you pay to cover all the gadgets and tech often outweigh the discount.

The average American now pays $1,529 per year for car insurance. But if you choose to drive a five-year-old vehicle, it would be about 27 percent less expensive to insure than the zero-year-old version. And a nine-year-old vehicle is even less expensive to insure![77] With those cost savings, you can set that freed-up money aside to cover future repairs and maintenance without losing any sleep.

"I can get a better deal on a new car than a used car."

Where do you go to buy a brand-new car? That's right: dealerships. Let's talk about dealerships and how this "better deal" *actually* works. (Hint: in their favor, not yours.)

Dealerships often make more profit from the *method* of your purchase rather than the car sale itself—specifically, in the financing options, add-ons, and upsells. That's because they're not so

---

[77] "2022 The State of Auto Insurance," The Zebra, 2022, https://www.thezebra.com/state-of-insurance/auto/2022/.

much in the car business as they are in the lending business. If you've watched the TV show *Breaking Bad*, you know that the chicken restaurant, Los Pollos Hermanos, is just a front for Gus Fring's meth operation. The fried chicken is simply a *vehicle* for the real moneymaker: drugs. For dealerships, cars are just the vehicle (literally) for the real moneymaker: debt.

To be clear, dealerships don't give you the loan themselves—they just link you with a lender they work with. In return, they either get a flat fee from the lender *or* they jack up your interest rate as a fee for playing the middleman (it's called *dealer reserve* or *dealer markup*). You may be thinking, *Yeah but I can negotiate the payment on a new car!* Sure, they can lower your monthly payment, but to make it happen, they extend the loan term. What that really means: Your payment hangs around longer, and you end up paying more for the car in the long run through interest. (Win-win for them, lose-lose for you.)

What about "zero down" and "zero interest" loans? They're tactics to get you in the door. Don't fall for this trap. "Zero down" just means "no down payment," which means borrowing *more* money for the car. And 0 percent financing? It is a thing, but it's incredibly difficult to qualify for. Dealers draw you in—and when you don't qualify, you're hit with a high interest rate. Also, most 0 percent financing "deals" are only offered on cars selling at *full* price. That means no discounts, no negotiating. Some dealerships even mark up the price to make up for their loss on the interest.

On top of all that, they'll aggressively try to tack on extras like paint or fabric protection, gap insurance, extended warranties, and service plans to make some profit. These upsells get added to your loan and keep you coming back to their dealership for service. As soon as you have to pay for any replacement part or work beyond those warranties, you'll be paying the dealership's inflated prices for those things too. Hard pass.

Anytime you walk away from a car lot convinced that you got a "deal"—you just got screwed. Don't be a sucker.

"Why not lease a new car every few years with low monthly payments?"

Never lease a car. *Never.* The fact that dealerships bend over backward to talk you into leases should be the first of many red flags.

Leases look sexy from afar because the monthly payments are generally lower than a car loan, and you're not paying for repairs. But as you get closer, you realize you got straight-up punk'd. Here's why: Leasing a car is *the most expensive way to operate a vehicle.* Let's talk about how it's the biggest scam in the auto world.

A car lease is a contract where you make monthly payments to drive a car for a certain period of time (usually two or three years). Your payments are calculated by totaling up the expected depreciation plus tax and additional fees, then dividing that total by the number of months in the lease.[78] That's right, depreciation is built *into* your lease payments. And since cars lose the most value in the first two to three years, you're stupidly picking up that tab.

When the lease is up, you'll fork over even more for backend charges like a disposition fee (the cost of cleaning up and selling the car) and any excessive mileage or wear-and-tear fees. Straight-up highway robbery. What stings is the fact that you'll likely have paid more than the car's actual depreciation during the lease period. And at the end of all that, *you still don't even own a car*—you have to give it back to the dealer after paying the worst of the depreciation!

---

[78] "Financing or Leasing a Car," Federal Trade Commission, July 2022, https://www.consumer.ftc.gov/articles/0056-financing-or-leasing-car.

Let's take this to the streets. If you paid $16,000 over the life of the lease, and the vehicle went down $10,000 in value, then it cost *you* an extra $6,000 to lease the car for that period. If you're the leasing company, that's called profit. If you're the person leasing the car, that's called *stupid tax*.

What makes car leases extra sketchy is that the interest rates aren't disclosed. Why not? The Federal Trade Commission doesn't define a lease as a "debt," so there's no federal disclosure required. That works out wonderfully for the leasing company, which gets to bake those terrible interest rates into your monthly payment.

What if you want to be released from your contract or you can't pay anymore? Well, there are three ways out (if the leasing company even allows this), and none of them are pretty.

The first option is *early lease termination*, which involves a whole bunch of fees.

The second option is a *lease transfer*, which involves finding *someone else* to take over your lease agreement. That's almost as rough as trying to find someone to buy your timeshare.

The third option is a *lease buyout*, where you pay the difference between the lease payoff amount and the current value of the car (which could amount to several thousand dollars).

No matter which option you choose, be ready for extra charges and fees. Guaranteed, they will get you for every dollar they can. The best way to keep their hands off your money is to not lease at all.

HOW TO BUY A CAR THE RIGHT WAY

Now that you're informed and ready to never make a dumb car decision ever again, it's time to cover how to buy a car with no remorse.

You've probably guessed by now, but the *best* way is to save up and purchase a reliable used car with cash. The *only* time you should even think about buying a brand-new car is if you have a net worth of at least $1 million. I know that sounds crazy. But you know what's crazier? Taking a 60 percent hit on depreciation when you don't have the wealth to stomach it. If you're a millionaire, though, and you want to buy a new car that costs a *very* small percentage of your net worth, then go for it. At that point, the punch of depreciation will feel more like a pinch. Until you hit millionaire status, a reliable used car will do just fine.

In the National Study of Millionaires (the largest study of millionaires ever done in North America), Ramsey Solutions found that the average millionaire drives a four-year-old car with 41,000 miles on it. And 8 out of 10 millionaire car buyers pay in full, up front, and drive away without a car payment. Just think, if you follow this advice, you're closer to living like a millionaire than you imagined!

Here's the step-by-step guide to buy your next car the right way.

1. Set your budget

Figure out exactly how much you're able and willing to spend. If you're wondering what that amount is, here's a good rule of thumb: The total value of all your vehicles shouldn't add up to more than half your income.

Let's say you make $50,000 a year. The total of *everything* you own with a motor and wheels (vehicles, boats, RVs) shouldn't exceed $25,000. The reason is simple: You never want half of your income tied up in things going *down* in value. That's how you become middle-class fancy and *stay* middle-class fancy. Your budget dictates what kind of a car you can get—not the other way around.

2. Save up

Once you've set the budget, start saving up. The best way to do this is with a sinking fund. A sinking fund is a strategic way to save money for a specific purchase by setting aside a little bit each month. You're saving up small amounts over a longer time frame instead of having to come up with a big chunk all at once.

Let's say you budget $12,000 for a new-to-you car. You currently have no debt, a fully funded emergency fund, and you want to make this car purchase within 12 months. You would need to save $1,000 per month for a total of 12 months to get there. Remember, you'll also have the proceeds from the sale of your current car, which will help. Should you want the car sooner, your choices are to either save more each month or lower your budget and expectations.

What if you need a car way sooner and don't have the money? You'll have to lower your budget and expectations. Remember, *you don't buy stuff you can't afford.* And if you can't pay cash in full—today—you don't buy it today. Set a specific savings goal, a time limit, and make a line item in your budget for that car. My favorite budgeting app for sinking funds is EveryDollar, which makes it super easy to set these up and keep track.

3. Find your ideal car

With your budget in hand, you can find your ideal car. Not your *dream* car. Your *ideal* car. The one that best fits your lifestyle and your budget—right now. As you begin the search, remember: You're not buying to impress anyone. Even yourself. Cars, while a fun representation of your identity and personality, are a terribly expensive way to show that off. No car will make you like yourself—or make others like you. Therapy would be a much better use of the money you overspent on a car.

Now, before you declare your loyalty to your favorite make or model, step back and take a look at the *kinds* of vehicles and what each was designed to do. Trucks, for instance, were designed to carry heavy stuff. So unless you're frequently hauling heavy cargo (you know—gravel, timber, bricks), don't buy a truck. Most people just need a good, fuel-efficient commuter vehicle, like a sedan, hatchback, or hybrid. Narrow down your choices with this quick checklist, picking the three that apply to your situation the most.

I want a vehicle . . .

- ❑ with plenty of cargo space.
- ❑ that can fit more people.
- ❑ with better fuel economy.
- ❑ that's easy to get in and out of.
- ❑ with great safety features.
- ❑ to carry heavy cargo.
- ❑ that I can take off-road or over rough terrain.
- ❑ that is compact for city parking.
- ❑ with towing capacities.
- ❑ with newer tech features.

Remember, you'll have to make some sacrifices too. You won't find a vehicle that does *everything*. Just prepare your heart for that. And . . . you might have to settle for some basic (uh, I mean "classic") features too, like manual locks and windows instead of those newfangled, automatic doohickeys. Be honest with yourself about distinguishing between your wants and your needs. By embracing simplicity and utility, you'll not only find a car that gets you from *A* to *B*, but you'll also keep your wallet full of a whole lot more *C*—cash.

4. Research, research, research

Now that you have a budget, savings plan, and ideal car in mind, it's time to start the hunt. Here are some of the best places to look:

Independent Used-Car Dealerships. Shopping at a used-car dealership means you won't be tempted by or sold on the newer, sleeker cars on the lot. Dealerships and used-car salespeople can get a bad rap, but there are plenty of service-oriented, non-slimy ones out there. If you've done your homework beforehand and have the willpower to walk away if necessary, you can have a great experience at a reputable dealership.

Private Sellers. Yes, it *can* be riskier to buy a car through a private seller. But you'll have the best chance at negotiating a great deal if you're prepared and take the right precautions. You can find hundreds of cars for sale in your area on sites like eBay Motors, Cars.com, CarGurus, Autotrader, Craigslist, and Facebook Marketplace. Always be on alert for scams, sketchy profiles, and too-good-to-be-true prices (usually with stories like "My brother is shipping out on assignment" or "My elderly mom moved to Montana and wants me to sell her car"). And only meet during daylight hours in safe, public locations to inspect and test drive the car. Never hurts to bring a friend along either.

Online Car Retailers. Places like Carvana and CarMax have a huge online inventory, and their cars go through a detailed inspection process. The downside is, their prices are higher than private sellers—and there's no wiggle room to negotiate. You're basically paying more dollar to skip the hassle, but that can be its own perk.

5. Check the car's value

Kelley Blue Book (KBB) uses data from actual sales transactions and auction prices to give you an accurate price range on vehicles. This can keep you from paying too much for the car you have in mind when it's time to negotiate. You'll also want to get an idea of how much you'll spend to maintain the car and what long-term repairs you should expect for the make and model you're thinking about buying. Sites like ConsumerReports.org and Edmunds.com can be super helpful for this research.

6. Do a test drive

Nobody wants to get duped and buy a lemon. You can avoid that by inspecting and driving the car yourself. Compare its condition with what was shown in the listing.

Next, take that baby for a test drive. The car should drive smoothly on flat roads. Keep an ear out for any strange noises like engine rattles. When braking, the car should remain straight on the road. It's important to test it on a road or interstate where you can go over 60 miles per hour—this is often where you'll notice problems. Smell anything funny? It better be you and not the car.

Assuming everything seems fine, consider buying a vehicle history report (VHR) if it's not provided. Services like CARFAX, AutoCheck, and VinCheckUp can give you the details on a car's ownership history, accident history, title status, and mileage.

7. Get a pre-purchase inspection

Always have a mechanic of your choice inspect a used car, no matter the condition. A good mechanic will be able to tell if you're about to buy a dreamboat of a used car or a nightmare on wheels. Use the inspection results to decide if the car is worth purchasing or to negotiate a lower price. You can get a standard vehicle inspection for about $150 these days. Worth every red cent.

8. Negotiate and agree on the price

At this point, you should know more about the car than the seller or salesperson. Your confidence and knowledge will let them know that you didn't come to play—you came to win. Don't be nervous and don't act desperate. Play it cool. Take your time to shop around and visit a few locations, and don't get pressured if they say the car has had "lots of interest" and "won't last long." Be kind but firm. Be decisive but patient.

If the salesperson at a dealership asks, "How do you plan on paying?", they're really trying to see if you plan to finance the car. You have no moral or legal obligation to tell them you're paying cash at this stage. Just say, "I'd rather not talk finances until we've landed on the price."

The one number you're focused on here is the *out-the-door price*. This includes the sale price, sales tax, and the registration, title, and documentation fees. If they try to tack on extended warranties, service plans, insurance products, nitrogen-filled tires, window etching, paint protection, fabric protection, market adjustment, or anything else that looks sketchy, push back and be ready to walk away from the deal. If they're rude and slimy, tell 'em to kick rocks and pound sand, and peace out of there.

On the other hand, if you land an out-the-door price you're satisfied with, and you've read the paperwork and fees closely, it's time to close the deal.

9. Pay with cash

Once you've agreed on an out-the-door price, now is the time to let them know that you're paying cash. The simplest way to do this is with a debit card, personal check, or cashier's check. Be sure to call your bank ahead of time to raise your limit for the day and let them know how big the transaction might be.

Congratulations! You just bought a car the best way possible: with no debt and a whole lot of confidence.

Do not forget this one last thing: Lock in your auto insurance ASAP. I recommend using Zander Insurance since they shop the top-rated companies to find you the best coverage at the best price. They've been a RamseyTrusted provider for years, and I've used them for a decade now for all my insurance needs. Get a quote today at georgekamel.com/resources.

THE CROSSROADS OF FREEDOM AND . . . FREE TO BE DUMB

You've learned about the insanity of the car market, the reality of depreciation, the stupidity of car payments, and the beauty of buying a car the right way. You're at a crossroads now. You can continue making car payments for the rest of your life because it's what most people do. *Or* you could drive in the complete opposite direction and head out on the highway of financial freedom.

Don't fall for the instant-gratification trap. Don't be swayed by marketing gimmicks or the social pressure. Don't buy a car to make a fashion statement, political statement, or tribal statement. (Nobody in your life gives a rip about what you drive. If they do, you need better friends.) It just never pays to get emotionally attached to an overpriced appliance on wheels. Because every vehicle on planet Earth, no matter how wonderful, gets hit, worn out, scratched and dented, or traded for another.

Matthew 6:19–20 says, "Don't store up treasures here on earth, where moths eat them and rust destroys them, and where thieves break in and steal. Store your treasures in heaven, where moths and rust cannot destroy, and thieves do not break in and steal" (NLT). Do you hear that? The Bible knows our treasured vehicles will get destroyed by rust (if not something else). It knows we desire a bunch of toys that don't really matter. Can you own nice stuff? Sure. Just don't let your nice stuff own you. Buy a vehicle that suits your needs, that's safe and reliable, in cash. And the next time you're itching for a car upgrade, try this instead of going car-shopping: Drop $100 on a thorough detailing. You might just fall back in love with your ride.

If you want to win with money, you've got to learn to live like no one else, so later you get to live like no one else. And in this case, you've got to *drive* like no one else, then later, you get to drive like *no one else.*

PS: We have a free car-buying guide that walks you through this stuff and so much more. Check it out at georgekamel.com/resources.

6

Mortgages

The paid-off home mortgage has taken the place of the BMW as the status symbol of choice.
–DAVE RAMSEY

Americans have a "thing" for homeownership. Alright, maybe it's more than a thing. For the past hundred years or so, homeownership has been a cornerstone of the American Dream.

I get it. Not only is owning a home an aspirational goal to set, a milestone to achieve, and a status symbol to acquire, but it has some undeniably awesome financial benefits. It's like putting your money in a giant piggy bank that you get to live in. With every mortgage payment, you have a forced savings plan that builds this magical thing called equity. Simultaneously, your house value is climbing over time—turning your home into a huge net-worth booster. (Thanks, appreciation. It's time someone appreciated *you.*) And that value grows virtually tax-free due to current law, which allows you a *tax-free* gain of up to $250,000 if you're single or $500,000 if you're married filing jointly when you go to sell. (Caveat: It has to be the main home you've lived in for at least two of the past five years.) This is one of the rare times I'll say, "Thanks, IRS!"

Since real estate prices tend to rise during inflationary periods, homeownership is like a hedge shielding your financial garden from the thorny branches of inflation. And let's not forget the sense of stability, belonging, community, and pride that comes with having your own place. You can paint the walls Agreeable Gray (or the less popular choice, Disagreeable Gray). You can adopt that adorable pup you saw at the shelter. Heck, maybe you can build a Par 3 in the backyard to keep your golf game strong—but good luck getting past those HOA CC&Rs. They sure love an abbreviation.

On the flip side, owning a home isn't *all* rainbows, sunshine, and backyard barbecues. Between property taxes, insurance, maintenance, and surprise repairs, it can be a wildly expensive asset to keep up with. Not to mention the six-figure elephant in the three-bedroom: a mortgage.

Mortgages are *secured* debts, meaning your house is collateral for the debt. If you can't keep up with the repayments, the lender can take your house through a foreclosure. We saw a whole bunch of those in 2008, which, in combination with some other key economic factors, created a domino effect that led to the collapse of the housing market and the biggest financial crisis since the Great Depression.

Luckily, a lot has changed since then as far as regulation and risky mortgage lending go. One thing that *hasn't* changed, though, is America's willingness to take out a loan for a home. By the end of 2022, Americans held $12 trillion in mortgage debt. For perspective, here's what those digits look like: $12,000,000,000,000.

That larger-than-life number makes up more than 70 percent of *total* household debt in America.[79]

While mortgages may seem less haunting than other types of debt, they have a dark past. The word *mortgage* is derived from Old French and literally translates to "death pledge." That sure puts things in focus. The only one who should hear the words "'til death do us part" is your spouse.

Suffice to say, homeownership can be a huge blessing in your life . . . or it can be a curse if done the wrong way. On *The Ramsey Show*, we get lots of calls from people who are in real crisis because they did real estate the wrong way. They rushed into buying a home before they were financially ready, they bought or sold poorly, or they fell for one of the many mortgage traps. The general narrative with these calls is that FOMO turned into impulse, which turned into regret and financial despair. But it's avoidable with the right knowledge and the right financial choices.

In this chapter, we're going to unpack which mortgages to stay away from, which one you should go with, and the *best* way to buy a home. It's about to be a mortgage battle royale. Let's get ready to rumble!

LOOKIN' FOR LOANS IN ALL THE WRONG PLACES

A mortgage is generally the largest and longest debt you will ever carry. But getting the *wrong* type could cost you tens of thousands of dollars and decades of debt. And getting *too much* mortgage

[79] "Total Household Debt Reaches $17.06 Trillion in Q2 2023; Credit Card Debt Hits One Trillion," Federal Reserve Bank of New York Center for Microeconomic Data, August 2023, https://www.newyorkfed.org/microeconomics/hhdc.

could cost you your peace, your retirement, your relationships, and your freedom. Nothing is worth that.

There are about as many mortgage types as there are seasons of *Grey's Anatomy*. In other words, too many. And just like *Grey's Anatomy*, mortgages can last for decades, with seemingly no end or closure in sight. So let's cover the most common mortgage types to understand who these are aimed at and how to avoid being the next target. I'll explain why each type can *seem* attractive, and then I'll reveal the ugly truth behind the curtain.

CONVENTIONAL MORTGAGES

A conventional loan is the most common type of mortgage—making up more than 76 percent of all mortgages.[80] Since conventional loans are privately insured against default and not backed by the government, lenders tend to require a higher down payment (at least 3 percent) compared to unconventional loans (which we'll cover in a minute).

This type of loan also requires you to pay private mortgage insurance (or PMI, for short) if your down payment is less than 20 percent of the home's value. Mortgage insurance protects the lender (not you) if you stop making payments on your loan. It's a "riskier borrower" fee that gets added to your monthly mortgage payment. While there are a whole bunch of conventional loan types, the popular kids at the conventional loan table are the 15-year and 30-year fixed-rate mortgages. And unlike the high school cafeteria, it's easy to join their clique without having to be athletic or a mean girl.

---

[80] "New Houses Sold by Type of Financing (Table Q7)," U.S. Census Bureau, July 26, 2023, https://www.census.gov/construction/nrs/pdf/quarterly_sales.pdf.

15-Year Fixed-Rate Mortgages

This is a type of home loan where the borrower agrees to repay the loan amount over 15 years, with an interest rate that never changes.

Why They're Attractive: A 15-year mortgage gets you out of debt faster and typically has a lower interest rate compared to longer-term loans. Not only do you pay off the house way faster, but you also save potentially six-figures-worth of interest payments compared to a 30-year loan.

Why They're Ugly: A 15-year loan will have a higher monthly payment compared to a 30-year loan. That's just math: A shorter time frame for the same loan amount equals a bigger monthly payment. But remember, that higher payment means a quicker payoff and less interest paid!

30-Year Fixed-Rate Mortgages

These mortgages are the same concept as a 15-year fixed-rate mortgage, but the payoff period is twice as long.

Why They're Attractive: A lower monthly payment compared to a 15-year loan. (If you've been tracking so far, you know that *low* payments are *never* the goal. *No* payments are the goal.)

Why They're Ugly: A 30-year loan will have a higher interest rate compared to a 15-year loan and take *twice* as long to pay off. Not only does that mean you're in debt for 15 years longer—it also means you'll pay *more than double* the interest compared to a 15-year mortgage. That blows.

Adjustable-Rate Mortgages (ARMs)

This type of loan has an interest rate that fluctuates based on market conditions. For example, a 5/1 ARM locks in the rate for the first five years and adjusts annually for the remaining 25 years. A 5/5 ARM keeps the rate fixed for five years before adjusting every five years. Although these technically fit in the conventional loan category, they're a bit less traditional compared to your standard fixed-rate mortgages.

Why They're Attractive: The interest rates start lower for an initial period, making payments more affordable . . . for now.

Why They're Ugly: While the initial low rate may seem enticing, ARMs transfer the risk of higher rates *off* the bank and *onto* you. This can lead to higher monthly payments and create financial stress if the rates go up or your life circumstances change. You don't have to be the lead singer of Creed to know that with ARMs, you're *wide open*—to risk.

GOVERNMENT-BACKED LOANS

Government-backed loans are considered *unconventional* loans since they don't meet the guidelines from Fannie Mae and Freddie Mac. They march to the beat of their own government drum and set their own underwriting guidelines.

If the loan meets these guidelines, the government agency agrees to buy the house if the lender forecloses on the home. This protects the lender and guarantees they won't lose money if a borrower stops paying. (Remember how the government created the federally backed student loan program, promising the student loan companies that if borrowers defaulted, they would cover the loan? Yeah, it's kind of like that, but with mortgages.) Let's cover the big three government loan programs.

FHA Loans

The Federal Housing Administration (FHA) designed this loan to allow people who don't qualify for a conventional mortgage to still become homeowners.

Why They're Attractive: FHA loans allow you to get a mortgage with as little as 3.5 percent down. They also have more lenient credit requirements and allow a higher debt-to-income ratio.

Why They're Ugly: Borrowers are required to pay an upfront mortgage insurance premium (MIP) of 1.75 percent *and* an annual premium between 0.15 percent and 0.75 percent for the life of the loan. The only way to remove MIP is to put down more than 10 percent—but even then, you'll still have to pay it for 11 years![81]

VA Loans

The US Department of Veterans Affairs designed the VA loan as a benefit for military veterans to buy a house.

[81] "Mortgagee Letter 2023-05," U.S. Department of Housing and Urban Development, February 22, 2023, https://www.hud.gov/sites/dfiles/OCHCO/documents/2023-05hsgml.pdf.

Why They're Attractive: Virtually no down payment, no PMI, and no minimum credit score required. However, most lenders issuing these loans want to see a FICO score of at least 620.

Why They're Ugly: There's a funding fee (as of 2023) between 1.25 and 3.3 percent of the loan amount, making your monthly payments and overall interest higher.[82] The property requirements are also strict. And, by putting nothing down, you won't start with any equity in your home, which is risky. Note: Some vets with service-connected disabilities can get the fee waived, which *can* make this a decent option under the right financial circumstances.

USDA/RHS Loans

The United States Department of Agriculture (USDA) loan program, managed by the Rural Housing Service (RHS), allows people who live in rural areas with low or modest incomes to buy a home.

Why They're Attractive: No down payment is required, and these loans sometimes have below-market interest rates.

Why They're Ugly: USDA loans include additional premiums with an initial fee of 1 percent *and* a 0.35 percent annual

---

[82] "VA funding fee and loan closing costs," U.S. Department of Veterans Affairs, April 7, 2023, https://www.va.gov/housing-assistance/home-loans/funding-fee-and-closing-costs/.

fee after that.[83] The location criteria and income requirements are also super strict, making it difficult to qualify.

OTHER MORTGAGE LOAN TYPES

Aside from your conventional loans and government-backed loans, there are several more you should know about.

Construction Loans

These are short-term, high-interest loans that can help pay for a plot of land, home construction, or major renovations to an existing home.

Why They're Attractive: Construction loans provide the means to build your dream home from the ground up, tailored to your specific vision, timeline, and needs.

Why They're Ugly: Complex financing mixed with the potential of project complications make these a risky, and often more-costly-than-planned, choice. You've also got to deal with strict requirements, higher lender fees, and higher interest rates. To add to the stress and expenses, you'll most likely pay three sets of closing costs: the purchase of the land, the construction loan, *and* your final mortgage loan. That's a triple threat worth avoiding.

---

[83] "Upfront Guarantee Fee & Annual Fee," United States Department of Agriculture, accessed September 5, 2023, https://www.rd.usda.gov/files/RD-SFH-UpfrontFee1.pdf.

Subprime Mortgages

Subprime mortgages have more lenient criteria to qualify, allowing people with no money and bad credit to buy a house.

Why They're Attractive: They allow borrowers with lower credit scores, limited income history, or higher debt levels to access financing and become homeowners.

Why They're Ugly: Lenders know there's a big risk in loaning money to people who have no money—go figure. That's the reason these mortgages come with *terrible* terms like high interest rates and stiff prepayment penalties. The right move is never subprime. I like to keep things *prime*—whether it's numbers, steaks, ministers, or Amazon purchases.

Interest-Only Mortgages

These loans allow borrowers to *only* pay interest on the loan for a period. They can have an adjustable rate or a fixed rate.

Why They're Attractive: Interest-only mortgages have lower payments because you're *only* paying the interest portion.

Why They're Ugly: Your monthly payment doesn't reduce your loan balance, which means you're making *zero* progress on the loan while *still* paying interest. Once the interest-only period ends, payments are way higher than they would have been if you had just gone with a conventional loan from the start. Avoid these—and not just because they remind me of trying to get a prom date in high school (you know, interest-only, with no real date).

ALTERNATIVE FINANCING FOR CURRENT HOMEOWNERS

Even current homeowners aren't insulated from doing stupid. These mortgage products have been aggressively marketed as homeowners have gained more equity than ever thanks to massive appreciation these past few years.

Reverse Mortgages

A reverse mortgage allows homeowners ages 62 and up to borrow part of their home's equity as tax-free income. You essentially own less of your house over time in exchange for monthly payments or a lump sum.

Why They're Attractive: These loans can give older people a source of income without having to sell their homes or make monthly mortgage payments.

Why They're Ugly: They put your home at risk by adding more debt to your name later in life. The interest and fees can reduce your equity further, and if you don't meet the loan obligations (property maintenance and property taxes), you could lose your home in foreclosure—after you've already paid it off! Worst reverse UNO card ever.

Refinance

Refinancing is the process of replacing your existing mortgage with a new loan, but with different terms.

Why It's Attractive: You can switch to a shorter loan term, drop down to a lower or fixed interest rate, eliminate PMI if you have enough equity, or consolidate a hefty second mortgage.

Why It's Ugly: Refinancing comes with closing costs that could erase the savings benefit. And "no closing cost" refinancing usually comes with higher interest and extra fees baked into your loan balance. Do a break-even analysis to figure out how long you need to stay in your home to make it worth paying the closing costs. Let's say your closing costs are $4,000, and refinancing saves you $200 a month. You'd need to stay in the house for at least 20 months to break even. Month 21 is when you'd start actually saving money.

Cash-Out Refinance

A cash-out refinance allows homeowners to tap into their home equity by trading in their current mortgage for a larger loan. After they've paid off the current mortgage from that loan, the leftover money (the equity that gets "cashed out") can be used for home improvements, debt consolidation, or other financial goals unrelated to the house.

Why It's Attractive: It lets you access the "piggy bank" of your home equity at a typically lower interest rate than a personal loan. Plus, in sticky situations like a divorce, a cash-out refinance can come in handy for smoothing out financial settlements without having to sell your home.

Why It's Ugly: You're turning your home equity into more debt, keeping you in debt longer. Plus, a bigger loan brings a bigger risk of losing your house. If you're thinking of using the cash-out to buy stuff you can't afford, like that $7,000 massage chair with zero-gravity SL track, 4-D heating elements, neck, shoulder, back, calf, toe, foot, and ankle rollers, chromo-therapy lighting, and HD Bluetooth speakers—please don't. If you're wanting to use it to pay off other consumer debt, it doesn't fix the habits that got you into debt in the first place. It just inflates your mortgage and delays your wealth-building journey. The goal is to get *out* of debt, not go further into it.

Home Equity Lines of Credit (HELOC)

A HELOC is a secured loan and revolving credit line that allows you to borrow against the current value of your home. It's like a credit card tied to your home equity that can be used to cover all kinds of expenses.

Why They're Attractive: People tend to treat a HELOC as a financial parachute in case of emergency. It's just another way that these loans are like a credit card. (Side note: You're way better off having an emergency fund saved up to cover the unexpected.)

Why They're Ugly: HELOCs have a variable interest rate, which means these loans can increase in any given month. If you miss a payment and default on a HELOC, the bank could take your house. You could also pay transaction fees, minimum withdrawal fees, inactivity fees, or early termination fees, in addition to having required balances.

Home Equity Loans (HEL)

A home equity loan (HEL) is a second mortgage that allows borrowers to take a full lump sum against their home equity.

Why They're Attractive: Unlike the charge-as-you-go method of the HELOC, you get a lump sum with this type of loan—usually with a fixed interest rate and more predictable payments.

Why They're Ugly: If you don't make payments, you, of course, risk losing your home through foreclosure. On top of that, you'll have a higher interest rate than a primary mortgage, along with closing costs and other fees. Using your house like an ATM moves you in the wrong direction financially.

THE ANSWER TO YOUR MORTGAGE PROBLEMS

You've probably seen a theme by now. Most of the mortgage products out there exist to get people into homes even if they're not financially ready. They're also riddled with fees that make homeownership even more expensive over the long haul. Home equity products and cash-out refinancing keep people broke by making them *think* they've solved a problem—when all they did was moonwalk further into debt. These mortgage "solutions" all involve lots of risks and could lead to foreclosure down the line if life happens and you can't pay.

If you don't have the money to cover home improvements, vacations, cars, or education—you need to push pause, save up, and cashflow those things when you do have the money. Getting on a budget, slashing your expenses, aggressively paying off consumer debt, and increasing your income are just some of the ways to do that. Heck, some people even sell their *house* and downsize or rent to give themselves financial breathing room. Bottom line: If you want to pay off debt (or pay for anything for that matter), tapping into your home equity is not the move. Taking out *more* debt to pay off debt sounds insane because it is insane. Use the Debt Snowball method for debt payoff instead. We'll cover that later.

For those of you who *don't* have a mortgage yet, stick to a 15-year fixed-rate mortgage when you're ready for it. If you already have one of the other types of mortgages I mentioned, do a break-even analysis and figure out when the time might be right to refinance to a 15-year fixed-rate mortgage. It's the best bang for your buck with the least amount of interest of any conventional loan—especially if you're able to put 20 percent down to avoid that pesky PMI.

HOW TO BUY A HOUSE THE RIGHT WAY

We've covered lots of mortgage options, but there's a non-mortgage option that takes the cake for the best way to buy a house: the 100 percent down plan. That's right, I'm talking about paying cash outright. Before you laugh me off, hear me say that I understand this is unrealistic for most people and many areas of the country. But I've heard from plenty of buyers who avoided consumer debt, got their income up, lived frugally, saved up for years, bought a modest home, and proudly wrote a big fat check to own it free and clear.

Maybe going all-in with cash isn't in the cards for you right now. That's okay. Just don't settle for the "normal" plan of a 30-year loan with a tiny down payment. If you *must* take out a mortgage, here's the rule of thumb: **Stick with a 15-year fixed-rate conventional mortgage where the monthly payment is no more than 25 percent of your take-home pay.**

Note: By take-home pay, I'm talking about your after-tax income, but *before* any other paycheck deductions like retirement contributions or healthcare premiums. That means if you have a gross household income of $90,000, and your after-tax monthly income is around $6,000, then your mortgage payment (principal, interest, property taxes, homeowner's insurance, plus any extra fees like PMI or HOA) should be no more than $1,500 per month. If the math ain't mathing for you, then pause your house search so you can:

- save up a higher down payment
- increase your income
- adjust the house type and budget, and/or
- look at a more affordable area

I know that's easier said than done, but if homeownership is worth doing, it's worth doing right. Don't bite off more house than you can financially chew—you'll choke. And there's no Heimlich for homeownership outside of a foreclosure or short sale.

AN OVERVIEW OF THE HOME-BUYING PROCESS

Since there's so much that goes into making a home purchase, let's break it down and make it digestible. Consider this your cheat sheet to refer to as you navigate each step along the way.

1. **Decide you're ready to buy.** Being ready to buy means you're completely debt-free and have an emergency fund saved of 3–6 months of expenses. You've got to get your financial house in order before you get an *actual* house.
2. **Figure out how much house you can afford.** Your monthly house payment should be no more than 25 percent of your after-tax monthly income. Use our free mortgage calculator to help you do the math at georgekamel.com/resources.

3. **Save for a down payment (and more).** Ideally, you'll want at least 20 percent of the home price. For first-time home buyers, it's okay to only put 5–10 percent down. But remember that will add the expense of private mortgage insurance, aka PMI. Also, don't forget to save up for closing costs (3–4 percent of the purchase price) and furniture and moving expenses.
4. **Get preapproved for a mortgage.** This is where a lender verifies your finances and gives you a letter to show sellers that you're a serious, credible buyer who can close the deal. If you're following the Ramsey plan and have no credit score after getting out of debt, go check out my step-by-step walkthrough in the Credit Scores chapter on how to get approved for a "no score" mortgage loan! Connect with a RamseyTrusted mortgage provider and get the preapproval party started at georgekamel.com/resources.
5. **Find an expert real estate agent.** You want one who cares about your financial goals, who offers guidance at every step of the home-buying process . . . and who sells lots of houses and knows how to get the deal done. I know just the type. Locate a RamseyTrusted real estate agent in your area at georgekamel.com/resources.
6. **Go house hunting.** This is the only kind of hunting I enjoy. Create a list of your must-haves and discuss them with your agent. Be realistic and be ready to compromise—it may not look like the one you saw on HGTV. Most buyers search for a couple of months and look at *lots* of homes before they find the right fit.
7. **Make an offer.** Once you find an affordable home you love, trust your real estate agent to help you make a competitive offer and negotiate with the seller for the best

price. After your offer is accepted, you'll put down a deposit called earnest money (usually 1-3 percent of the purchase price). Don't worry, it's not really an extra cost. It typically goes toward your down payment or closing costs at the end of the deal.

8. **Get a home inspection and appraisal.** A home inspection will protect you from a nightmare of repairs, and an appraisal will protect you from overpaying. *Never* skip the inspection—those short-term savings are not worth the long-term risks.
9. **Be patient as your lender finalizes your loan documents.** A ton of paperwork goes into getting a mortgage. There's just no getting around it. On average, it takes a month or two to close on a loan.[84] That makes the DMV look like a NASCAR pit crew. But time is money—and homeownership takes a whole lot of both.
10. **Close on your home—finally!** Review all your closing costs, sign a mountain of paperwork, and bring the money. Oh, and get your keys! Closing day is when you officially become a new homeowner. Time to send out the housewarming invites and break out the charcuterie board.
11. **Bonus Step: Pay off your home early!** That's Baby Step 6. Make it a goal to pay extra toward the principal on your mortgage payments as soon and as often as you can. Every month would be ideal. Set a goal for how much extra you can throw at the mortgage, and how long it will take. The plan here is to free up your greatest wealth-building tool—your income. Once you do that, you'll be in Baby Step 7, with the ability to build wealth and give like never before.

[84] "Trusted expertise and a streamlined workflow," ICE Mortgage Technology, accessed September 5, 2023, https://www.icemortgagetechnology.com/.

PS: For more practical tips and guidance on your quest for homeownership, check out our free Home Buyers Guide at georgekamel.com/resources.

HOUSE OF THE RISING SON (OF A GUN THOSE PRICES ARE HIGH)

If you're not currently a homeowner, my guess is you'd like to be one someday, though *someday* may feel like a Tasmanian devil-level moving target thanks to increasing home prices. The post-pandemic-induced inflation is enough to throw any renter into a low-grade depression. As of July 2023, the national median home price was $440,000,[85] while the median household income in 2022 was just under $71,000.[86] Here's the sad math on that: The median home price is now *six* times the median income.

To put that in perspective, between 1973 and 1975, home prices were about *two* times the average income.[87] *Oof.* But we can't just sit here and wallow in misery. As the adage goes, "The best time to plant a tree was 30 years ago. The next-best time is now." In this case, the best time to buy a house was 50 years ago.

---

[85] "July 2023 Monthly Housing Market Trends Report," Realtor.com, 2023, https://www.realtor.com/research/july-2023-data/.

[86] "Median Household Income," United States Census Bureau, September 13, 2022, https://www.census.gov/library/visualizations/2022/comm/median-household-income.html.

[87] Alexander Hermann, "Price-To-Income Ratios Are Nearing Historic Highs," Joint Center for Housing Studies of Harvard University, September 13, 2018, https://www.jchs.harvard.edu/blog/price-to-income-ratios-are-nearing-historic-highs.

The next-best time is now. If history tells us anything, houses will be *more* expensive five years from now than they are today. So the sooner you're financially ready to buy a home and lock in that price, the better. Key words: *financially ready*.

I know you feel the pressure and the FOMO. It may seem like you're behind compared to some of your friends, and your family may be judging you with comments like, "You're throwing away money on rent!" But guess what. Those people don't pay your bills. That means they don't get a vote in the biggest financial purchase of your life.

Not caring what other people think is a *superpower* in today's world. If you can harness that, you'll have more joy and peace, and less stress and anxiety, than almost anyone you know. Until you're out of debt and have built up your emergency fund, renting is the way to go.

Don't let anyone fool you into thinking otherwise. Renting shows patience and responsibility as you get your financial house in order and save up for that down payment. You can't compare monthly rent to monthly mortgage—it's not apples to apples. Home maintenance, repairs, more expensive insurance, increasing taxes, and (often) pricey HOA fees make homeownership a huge financial burden if you're not prepared.

Rent is the *most* you'll pay, while leaving you with less risk and more flexibility. The mortgage is only the *beginning* of what you'll pay, due to all the expenses I mentioned above. I'm a big fan of homeownership, but I beg of you, *do not* buy a home before you're ready. (Steps off soapbox.)

THE BURDEN OF HOMEOWNERSHIP

We take heartbreaking calls all the time on *The Ramsey Show* where people are in a real bind because they bought a house before they were ready. Undoing that decision is a difficult and expensive one. If your mortgage is 35 or 40 or 50 percent of your take-home pay, you're not going to be able to pay the bills; save for retirement, vacations, or college; or pay off the house early.

Getting into a crappy mortgage (which is most of them) means you'll pay thousands and thousands more over the life of the loan thanks to interest and fees. And if you're in debt or don't have an emergency fund, and suddenly have to replace the HVAC or a roof, it could set you back into dangerous levels of debt that might take years to get out of.

THE BLESSING OF HOMEOWNERSHIP

Let me give you another picture. What if you bought a home the *right* way? Where you take the time and sacrifice to become debt-free first, then save up a fully funded emergency fund, then work hard to save up a solid down payment, and then select a 15-year fixed-rate mortgage that's 25 percent of your take-home pay? Here's what happens: less stress and more peace for you, and you pay off your home—*worst case*—in 15 years.

The data is clear. In our National Study of Millionaires, we found that the average millionaire pays off their home in 10.2 years. And those following the Ramsey Baby Steps end up paying off their homes *even faster*—in about seven years! I see these stories shared all the time in our Ramsey Baby Steps Community on Facebook. Danita and her husband paid off more than $193,000 in mortgage debt in just 54 months. Here's what she had to say in her post: "We've experienced so much personal growth, an improved marriage, and an anything's possible outlook on the world. I used to tell everyone that I'll have to work until noon on the day of my funeral. Not my motto anymore! Yes. It's hard. But keep going. It's worth it."

Imagine that—no payments in the world . . .

Owning a home is so much more than just a status symbol. When you buy a house the right way and pay it off early, it's a huge milestone on the road to building wealth.

This is your chance to break free from the "death pledge" and create a life on your terms. Where buying a home truly becomes *ownership*. If the American Dream is all about freedom and opportunity, you'll have every opportunity to freely live and give like no one else. That's a dream worth running down. Now go out there and make it happen.

7

Investing Traps

Greedy people try to get rich quick but don't realize they're headed for poverty.
–PROVERBS 28:22 NLT

Allow me to regale you with a tale of two bros: Lee and Chase. At 22 years old, they graduated college and landed great jobs in their fields making $70,000 per year.

Chase had fallen for some money traps, graduating with student loans and a car loan. Despite his incredible salary, he was living paycheck to paycheck. Feeling strapped by payments, inflation, and his lifestyle, Chase decided he needed more money—fast. He started day trading single stocks, gambling on cryptocurrencies, and opened an indexed universal life insurance policy that his buddy from college sold him as a "wealth hack." He'd occasionally play the lottery and try his hand at sports betting apps. Even though he almost always lost money on these schemes, the recurring mantra was: "It'll be different this time!"

Lee, on the other hand, was a bit more leisurely with his investing strategy. Between a 529 Savings Plan and working part-time during college, he was able to graduate debt-free with savings in the bank. Living on less than he made allowed him to take full advantage of his company's Roth 401(k), where he consistently invested 15 percent of his income into mutual funds. By sticking to a monthly budget, he was also able to save up and pay cash for a car and a couple of vacations a year.

As the years went by, Chase lost his lunch on the ups and downs of his roller coaster of wealth. Occasionally he'd be up and feeling good, but most of the time, he'd lose big and land back at square one. His net worth moved at a snail's pace, thanks to a 401(k) loan he took out for a home down payment and, later, a line of credit on his home equity that he used to finance a pool. After giving up hope that the government would forgive his student loans, he *finally* paid them off at 32 years old. He then started investing 3 percent of his income in his company's 401(k) to get the employer match, banking on Social Security to cover the rest of his retirement.

Decades passed, and Chase and Lee found themselves at the ripe retirement age of 62. Lee had been slow and steady (some would say "boring"), staying consistent with his wealth-building strategy and putting compound growth to work. He now had a million-dollar, paid-for house and $7 million sitting in his Roth 401(k). Chase, on the other hand, was *still* paying off his mortgage and had only half a million in his 401(k). Bummer.

Moral of the story: Be like Lee. Be the tortoise in a world full of hares.

TRAPS, TRENDS, AND TIPS

I've said it before and I'll say it again: *If you follow the trends, you'll fall for the traps.* And nowhere does that ring truer than investing.

Building wealth is like a reverse Reese's Cup—there *is* a wrong way to do it. Lots of wrong ways, in fact. Instead of being the old guy yelling at you to get off my lawn, allow me to be the younger guy using my indoor voice to steer you away from costly mistakes. Note: While *some* of these strategies you shouldn't touch with a 39-and-a-half-foot pole, not *all* of them are "bad" per se. There may be a time and place where you utilize a few of these along your wealth-building journey. The crash course starts now.

Cryptocurrency

Cryptocurrency is a virtual currency (technically a "store of value") that can be traded instantly, peer-to-peer, worldwide, 24/7, with few to no fees. It is decentralized, which means it's not controlled by any one entity. Instead, the currency is stored on a digital ledger called the blockchain, which validates transactions and keeps track of who owns what. Once a transaction is added to the blockchain, it becomes permanent, and the information stored on the blockchain can't be modified or erased. It's as complex and confusing as it sounds, and yet somehow that's simpler than any crypto bro would explain it.

THE HOT TAKE | *Cryptocurrency is just Mary Kay for young men.*

Let's compare the multilevel marketing (MLM) fangirls and the crypto fanboys.

First, the people who are into these money-making schemes are *obsessed*. It's all they talk about, post about, and if you're not on board, you "just don't get it." Go to any Bitcoin lover's Twitter profile, and I bet you a hundred Dogecoin (about $7 currently) that their bio includes #Bitcoin. If my Twitter profile started with #MutualFunds, you would think I'm a psychopath.

Second, the product and profit are hype-driven. Both MLM and crypto involve high hopes of making big bucks. But it's all about recruiting and sales—and less about the value of the product sold. Warren Buffet, one of the greatest investors of all time, said, "If you told me you own all of the Bitcoin in the world and you offered it to me for $25, I wouldn't take it because what would I do with it? I'd have to sell it back to you one way or another. It isn't going to do anything."[88] With mutual funds, *real* company shares are represented. And we're rooting for those companies to make a profit, which in turn causes our account balances to grow. Crypto largely uses tactics like scarcity and hype to grow in value.

Third, the business model heavily relies on new recruits. With crypto and MLMs, profits are largely based on how many more suckers you can get to buy in. Without those people, the whole thing falls apart like a house of cards. We saw that happen at the end of 2022 when FTX, one of the biggest cryptocurrency exchanges at the time, completely collapsed, losing billions and filing for bankruptcy.

As dead-set as you may be on dabbling in crypto, know that it's not *investing*. You're speculating, gambling, or betting on crypto. You're playing virtual roulette. If you're debt-free, have a fully funded emergency fund, and you're *already* investing 15 percent into tax-advantaged retirement accounts—then and *only* then would it be okay to bet some of your fun money on crypto. But never bet on crypto (or an MLM, for that matter) to provide your retirement income.

---

[88] Tanya Macheel, "Warren Buffett gives his most expansive explanation for why he doesn't believe in bitcoin," CNBC, April 30, 2022, https://www.cnbc.com/2022/04/30/warren-buffett-gives-his-most-expansive-explanation-for-why-he-doesnt-believe-in-bitcoin.html.

NFTs

Ever seen those ads where you can buy a star in the galaxy? Non-fungible tokens, aka NFTs, are kind of like that. With NFTs, you get a unique digital token (basically a URL) that serves as a certificate of digital ownership and lives on the blockchain permanently to prove that *you* are the verified owner of that code sequence. Each token represents a unique asset (like a piece of art, digital content, or media). A creator "mints" the media as an NFT, hoping someone buys it to claim bragging rights to that specific digital asset.

By making the purchase, you end up with bragging rights to a link to a picture that anyone can then screenshot and enjoy for free . . . *na-na na-na boo boo!* Essentially, you're buying an expensive treasure map (with little to no resale value) that points to the treasure. But you don't own the treasure! The creator does.

THE HOT TAKE | *NFTs are a useless flex of "ownership" with the illusion of an investment.*

Fans of NFTs have described this as a "sense of ownership." That's code for "you own nothing." Funny enough, that's exactly how timeshares are pitched. At least you can *physically* go to a timeshare. What's next? Timeshare NFTs? That would be like a sense of ownership of . . . a sense of ownership. *Bazinga!*

The only reason you would buy an NFT is: (a) you love burning money on virtual collectibles, or (b) you hope another sucker comes along who is willing to pay more than you did for the asset, making you a profit. Just about the only people making money with NFTs are the creators selling them. It's no wonder NFT value and popularity has plummeted faster than 3D TVs and HD DVDs. Don't waste your money on this stuff, unless you just enjoy wasting money.

Permanent Life Insurance

You may be surprised to see life insurance in a chapter on investment traps, but it's become a popular trend thanks to phony financial gurus on social media. The main types of permanent life insurance are whole life, universal life, indexed universal life, and variable universal life. What they have in common is that, in addition to the death benefit, there's a cash-value portion, which insurance agents promote as an investment.

THE HOT TAKE | *Permanent life insurance as a "wealth-building tool" is a legal scam peddled by insurance agents posing as financial advisors. It gives them fat commissions and locks you into a lifetime of stupid tax.*

Here's a quick rundown of the different types of permanent life insurance:

- *Whole Life:* Fixed premiums, guaranteed death benefit, and growing cash value.
- *Universal Life:* Flexible premiums and death benefit, with cash-value growth based on a minimum interest rate.
- *Indexed Universal Life (IUL):* Same as universal life, but the cash-value growth is tied to a stock market index, with a minimum interest rate and capped returns.
- *Variable Universal Life (VUL):* Flexibility of universal life plus cash-value investment in stocks, bonds, or mutual funds.

Insurance agents will often use a title like "tax-free wealth strategist" to lure investors into these policies. But the only "wealth strategy" involved is them lining *their* pockets with *your* money. Permanent life insurance is, at best, a bad investment. It locks you in for *years* with high costs and commissions. If you stop paying, your cash value and insurance vanish. And with most policies, your family won't get the cash value when you die—it goes to the insurance company! Call it a parting gift. Or a rip-off.

Instead, choose *term* life insurance to replace your income if you die. It's a fraction of the cost and keeps your insurance separate from your wealth-building. My permanent opinion on permanent life insurance? It's hucksters selling to suckers. Insurance *is not* an investment. Don't fall for it. You're smarter than that.

Single Stocks

Single stocks represent shares (tiny pieces of ownership) of one company. When a company goes "public," it sells these shares to investors to pay for business-growth goals. Over time, the value of the stock hopefully grows and produces a return on your investment.

THE HOT TAKE | *Single stocks are like betting all your money on a single racehorse. Mutual funds let you own the racetrack.*

The value of a stock is tied to the performance of the company and how it's perceived by consumers. Because of that, single stocks can be super volatile, meaning that the price can rise and fall quickly. If the company goes south, for whatever reason, you could lose a bunch (or all) of the money you invested.

A lot of people who buy single stocks are hoping to time and beat the overall market. Their thinking is that if they can predict which company's share prices will go up, they can buy them at just the right time and make a big profit. That's a bad plan. Don't get me wrong, I'm a huge fan of the stock market. But there's a much better way to invest in stocks, and that's to diversify with giant groups of stocks called mutual funds. With mutual funds, a group of investors (people like you!) pool their money to buy stocks from 90–200 companies chosen by a professional fund manager. They're the type of investment where teamwork indeed makes the dream work.

Day Trading

Day trading is the act of buying and selling stocks within a very short window of time—like minutes or hours—with the hopes of making a bunch of small profits that add up to big gains. A day trader might buy a stock at 9:15 a.m., turn around and sell it at 3 p.m. that same day, and then do it all over again with another stock.

THE HOT TAKE | *Day trading is a great way to decrease your wealth and increase your anxiety.*

Think I'm exaggerating? One study found that *97 percent* of day traders who persisted for more than 300 days *lost* money![89] If you think you'll be the 3 percent, your risk meter is broken. Along with the risk, day trading often comes with high commissions and transaction fees.

Many day traders *borrow money* and go into debt to make their trades—they call this "buying on margin" or using "leverage" to obtain more stock than they can afford. I call it unbridled stupidity. Not only could you lose all the money you've *invested*, but you could also end up buried under a pile of debt. Never, under *any* circumstances, borrow money to invest.

---

[89] Fernando Chague, Rodrigo De-Losso, and Bruno Giovannetti, "Day Trading for a Living?" SSRN, June 15, 2020, https://papers.ssrn.com/sol3/papers.cfm?abstract_id=3423101.

We've taken some gut-wrenching calls on *The Ramsey Show* from people who have lost $30,000, $150,000, and even $300,000 through day trading. It breaks my heart every time I hear one of these stories.

Your goal should be to build wealth slowly—and keep it—while leaving your risk meter intact. Wealthy people *do not* day trade. And anyone who *says* they do probably has a bridge to sell you—and a get-rich-quick course to go along with it.

Investing Apps

Investing apps like Robinhood, M1 Finance, Cash App, Webull, and Acorns sit on your smartphone and make playing the financial markets as easy as swiping right on a dating app. But just like getting catfished on Tinder, these investing apps can leave you feeling duped. They simplify the investing game (which is partially good) but can lead users to make hasty decisions and lose money (which is completely bad).

THE HOT TAKE | *Investing apps are designed to take your money—not make you money.*

Do you know the purpose of apps? To get you to open them *again* and *again*. They do this through gamification, promos, and push notifications, constantly luring you back in for another trade, only to hit you with hidden fees and taxes. They might even tempt you with higher-risk investments (like margin trading) with very little guidance, which leaves you flying blind. Plus, their social features can trigger some serious FOMO, making you chase after the next hot stock like a cat after a laser pointer.

Rather than falling for the app trap, stick to tax-advantaged retirement investing and work with an investing pro. Skipping the urge to swipe into your next trade is going to save you stress and money.

Micro-Investing

Micro-investing is a strategy that allows people to invest small amounts of money regularly through mobile apps like Acorns, Stash, and Robinhood. Many of these apps will automatically round up your purchases and invest the spare change or make automatic transfers to investments.

THE HOT TAKE | *Investing spare change is like picking up spare change—it's not a bad habit, but you'll never build wealth doing it. Micro-investing leads to micro results.*

While micro-investing can be a stepping-stone toward an investing habit, the problem is that it makes you *think* you're doing something without really moving the needle. If that's a part of your wealth-building strategy, you'll be lucky to retire this century. You're far better off prioritizing consistent, larger contributions in tax-advantaged retirement accounts like 401(k)s and IRAs. (Go with a Roth account if it's available.)

Investing 15 percent of your income is a great place to start, once you're debt-free with a fully funded emergency fund of three to six months of expenses. That 15 percent will build a whole lot more wealth than your spare change.

Annuities

Annuities are contracts from insurance companies that promise a stream of income during retirement. You make a payment (or payments) to the issuing company, and, in return, they promise to grow that money and send you payments during retirement.

THE HOT TAKE | *Annuities prey on fears of market risks under the guise of "protecting" your nest egg. But they're less like a bank vault and more like a prison that you pay to be in.*

Annuities come in three different flavors: fixed, variable, and indexed. Here's a quick primer:

- *Fixed Annuities:* Offer a fixed interest rate (typically 5 percent or less) on your investment for a set period, and a fixed income stream during retirement.
- *Variable Annuities:* Allow you to invest in mutual fund subaccounts, making your income stream variable based on stock market performance.
- *Indexed Annuities:* A hybrid between fixed and variable that links returns to a market index like the S&P 500—but with caps on gains and protection against losses. The result? More moderate returns.

What are the pitfalls? Well, fixed annuities barely keep up with inflation. Variable annuities are one of the most expensive and complicated financial products out there. And indexed annuities suck for the same reasons as indexed universal life insurance—subpar returns and super high fees.

What's scary is that *anyone* with a life insurance license can sell annuities. That becomes a sneaky shortcut for life insurance agents to sell you mutual funds without the proper licensing. In other words, if you're being pitched annuities, it's by someone who hasn't been trained to sell mutual funds the right way. That's what my Gen Z friends would call "sus."

Riddle yourself this: Why do they need to push high-pressure sales seminars to convince you that they're such a great investment? Just like with MLM parties, timeshare presentations, and house-flipping workshops, you're about to get duped. I've just spared you the three-hour dinner and grueling pitch. My one caveat: If you're in Baby Step 7, and really want the guaranteed returns and estate-planning benefits, a *variable* annuity is the *only* type that would be Ramsey approved. Even then, I'm not a fan. For most people, annuities are terrible investments with massive surrender fees and commissions. Avoid them like dysentery on the Oregon Trail.

Bonds

Bonds are loans that corporations or governments sell to investors. Think of them as IOUs on a set schedule. Investors buy bonds and get their money back, plus some interest. Bonds are also called "debt securities" or "fixed-income securities," which is Wall Street talk for investments that pay fixed returns in the form of recurring interest payments. Since they're often backed by governments and guarantee a steady return, bonds are seen as a safe investment and attract people who get spooked by market volatility.

THE HOT TAKE | *Investing in bonds is like trying to run a marathon by crawling. Sure, you won't trip and fall, but moving that slow will hurt your chances of ever finishing.*

Another way to describe them is that bonds are the rice cakes of the investing world. The unexciting, safe choice. The problem is, over time, bonds have far lower returns compared to mutual funds. The bond market also has an inverse relationship to interest rates, so when interest rates rise, bond prices fall. That could result in a loss if you sell the bonds before maturity.

Bonds are not terrible or evil (don't you put that evil on me, Ricky Bobby!). In fact, many mutual funds include a small portion of bonds (4–6 percent in my current 401(k) portfolio) to help keep them stable. But there's a reason why most mutual funds are heavily weighted toward stocks: The returns you get from bonds aren't impressive and *barely* outpace inflation.

The goal of investing is to *grow* your money—not just keep up with inflation. Stick to mutual funds for long-term investing, and high-yield savings accounts for short-term goals, and your investment accounts will high-five you down the road with a bunch of zeroes on the end.

Money Market Accounts

Money market accounts (or MMAs if you want to sound cool) are interest-bearing deposit accounts offered by financial institutions. Think of them as the hybrid between a checking and a savings account. They keep your money safe and sound, have relatively higher interest than a normal savings account, and give you more access to the money, with checks and debit cards.

THE HOT TAKE | *Investing with money market accounts is like using a paddleboard in a yacht race. Sure, you'll stay afloat, but you'll never outpace the mega-yachts of inflation.*

As of this writing, the national average interest rate for savings accounts is just 0.43 percent, while money market accounts sit at

0.62 percent.[90] I'm falling asleep just saying that out loud. That's abysmal. Along with incremental returns, the interest earned on these accounts doesn't even come close to keeping up with inflation, which generally hovers around 2 percent (with a wild spike up to 7 percent in the early 2020s).[91] They can also have requirements for initial deposits or monthly balances.

A money market account is great as a temporary parking spot or to store your emergency fund, but for long-term investing, stick to the mutual funds in the stock market.

CDs

With Certificates of Deposit (CDs), offered by banks and credit unions, you deposit your money for a specific term, and in return, you earn a fixed interest rate until the term ends. This can range anywhere from three months to five years. These generally offer a higher interest rate than traditional savings accounts or money market accounts, but with more red tape.

THE HOT TAKE | *Investing in CDs is like locking your money away in a minimum-security financial prison just to get some free, mediocre cafeteria food.*

A real gear grinder with CDs is that most have limited liquidity, meaning you can't access the money without paying a withdrawal penalty. And like all other low-interest savings accounts,

---

[90] "National Rates and Rate Caps," FDIC.gov, October 16, 2023, https://www.fdic.gov/resources/bankers/national-rates/index.html.
[91] "Monetary Policy Report—March 2023," Federal Reserve System, March 3, 2023, https://www.federalreserve.gov/monetarypolicy/2023-03-mpr-summary.htm.

you're at the risk of trailing behind the rate of inflation. Like money market accounts, CDs are an okay parking spot temporarily, but a worse option thanks to restrictions and penalties.

You're better off putting that money in a high-yield savings account where you have penalty-free access to it at a similar interest rate. If you're investing for the long term (five-plus years), stick with mutual funds in tax-advantaged accounts.

Index Funds

Index funds are passively managed mutual funds designed to mirror the performance of the stock market. Some well-known stock market indices (that's the fancy plural of *index*) include the S&P 500, which tracks the performance of 500 large, established US companies; the Dow Jones Industrial Average, which tracks 30 major US companies; and the Nasdaq Composite, which focuses on tech and innovation-driven companies, mainly in the US.

THE HOT TAKE | *Index funds are the solid copycats of the stock market—settling for average—while actively managed mutual funds strive to be the top dog, fetching higher returns.*

The perks of index funds are diversification, low expense ratios, and predictability. But every investing rose has its thorn. For starters, index funds won't *beat* the market, which means you'll settle for average. (But hey, 10–12 percent average annual returns ain't half bad!) They're also not very flexible since the holdings only change when companies are dropped for others in that index. And lastly, while index fund crusaders hate on mutual fund lovers because of higher expense ratios, you still could pay a hefty maintenance fee—sometimes listed as a *12b-1* fee—to make up for it. And that can also hurt your returns in the long run.

Index funds can be great investments for a taxable brokerage account (outside of retirement), but the tried-and-true advice still stands: Invest 15 percent of your gross income for retirement in mutual funds that have a track record of strong returns that outperform their index fund counterparts.

ETFs

Exchange-traded funds (ETFs) are investment hybrids that combine the diversification of a mutual fund with the tradability of a stock. They generally track a particular index, sector, or asset class, with low fees and tax efficiency.

THE HOT TAKE | *ETFs are the edgier cousin of mutual funds. Younger, hipper, but more prone to rash decisions and regret.*

While ETFs and mutual funds share some qualities like diversification, pooled money from investors, and holding a wide variety of investments, there are some big differences.

ETFs are actively bought and sold throughout the day—whereas mutual funds are bought and sold *once* per day. Consequently, the price of ETFs may fluctuate at any time, whereas mutual fund prices only change after the market closes each day. Also, ETFs tend to be passively managed (meaning that investment pros pick the investments based on the index the fund is tracking). Mutual funds, on the other hand, are *actively* managed (meaning that investment pros hand-select the funds' holdings to try and beat the market index).

The major issue with ETFs is that *intraday pricing*, which can cause people to day trade ETFs like a stock. Remember, building wealth is a marathon, not a sprint. Any investment that allows you to sprint could land you flat on your face. ETFs are also newer on the scene, and there are lots of gimmicky, niche, unproven funds out there that could lure investors in and leave them broke.

ETFs, while not my first choice for investing, *could* have a place in your investing strategy. Let's say you've maxed out your 401(k)s and IRAs and still want to keep investing. In that situation, you could open a taxable brokerage account and invest in ETFs that mirror a stock market index. Just know that, unlike your retirement accounts, your taxable investment accounts are subject to capital gains taxes. But since a lot of stock ETFs have low turnover (meaning, the investments inside them aren't switched around as often), you'll usually pay less in capital gains. This can make them a tax-efficient way to invest outside of retirement accounts. As long as you hold on to your ETF shares just like you would a mutual fund for long-term growth, this is an option to consider.

REITs

Real estate investment trusts (REITs) are companies that own, operate, or finance income-producing real estate, allowing investors to earn returns from a diversified real estate portfolio without having to own any property. Think of it like mutual funds that buy real estate instead of stocks.

THE HOT TAKE | *REITs are the passive landlord's dream, with the risk of a rude awakening from a real estate roller coaster.*

These investments have some cool upsides. They pay no corporate tax, they help diversify your portfolio, they can offer higher dividends than other investments, and they're professionally managed. But it's not all real estate rainbows—there's some rain too.

They're sensitive to fluctuations in real estate markets, interest rates, and the economy. They're limited in growth potential since 90 percent of the profits must be paid in dividends to shareholders (which might leave less money for buying new properties). They're actively managed funds (which means fees can eat into your returns over time). They're hard to sell quickly (since they can't be sold on the open market). And lastly, you have no control or say when it comes to the properties that are selected (you're just along for the ride).

Real estate investment trusts run the spectrum from *sucks* to *awesome*, so you've got to do lots of homework before you invest in one. There are a bunch of types: equity REITs, mortgage REITs, non-traded REITs, private REITs, and hybrid REITs.

Mortgage REITs are the worst of the bunch since they rely heavily on debt. Equity REITs, on the other hand, are probably the best choice. They own and manage the properties inside the fund, they're registered with the Securities Exchange Commission (unlike private REITs), and they offer more transparency than non-traded REITs. You might find a handful that perform as well as good growth stock mutual funds.

If you go this route, you want to choose a fund with a history of strong returns that's run by a competent group of investors. That's where your homework comes into play.

You should only consider investing in REITs once you reach Baby Step 7 *and* you've maxed out your tax-advantaged retirement accounts—like your 401(k) and Roth IRA. Even then, your REIT investments should be no more than 10 percent of your net worth. Until you get to Baby Step 7, stick with growth stock mutual funds for retirement investing, which offer the most balanced growth over time.

Gambling

Gambling is betting money on a game of chance. The two most popular forms are the lottery and casinos. While gambling *does* not and *should* not fall under the header of *investing*, it's worth mentioning since so many people think it could be their ticket to wealth.

THE HOT TAKE | *As the saying goes in Vegas, "The house always wins." If you think you can outsmart the house, you're only bluffing yourself.*

Most casino games have a built-in house advantage (5.26 percent in American roulette), making it statistically more likely for players to lose.[92] The odds of winning a major lottery jackpot are astronomically low, like 1 in 292 million for Powerball.[93] And if you hear those numbers and you still play, thinking, *Well, someone's gotta win!* then as we say in the South, your cornbread ain't done in the middle.

According to the National Council on Problem Gambling, an estimated 2 million men and women in the US (1 percent of the adult population) have a gambling disorder—and another 2–3 percent would be considered problem gamblers.[94] That's sad and frightening.

The lottery isn't *only* a form of gambling. It also acts as a tax on the poor, because lower-income communities disproportionately

---

[92] "Casino house edge explained," Casino, accessed September 5, 2023, https://www.casino.org/features/house-edge/.

[93] "Prize Chart," Powerball, accessed September 5, 2023, https://www.powerball.com/powerball-prize-chart.

[94] "Gambling," Stark County Mental Health & Addiction Recovery, accessed September 5, 2023, https://starkmhar.org/topics/gambling/.

spend more income on lottery tickets, hoping for a life-changing win. Wealthy people don't buy scratch tickets or play Keno or Powerball. You'll just never *become* wealthy by wasting your time or money on those things.

All forms of gambling are not addictive, but out of all the "investing" traps I've mentioned thus far, gambling is by far the most dangerous for your mental health, your relationships, and your bank account.

If you or someone you know has a gambling addiction, you don't have to suffer alone. Get some people in your corner who can help you. Talk to a counselor, a pastor, or friends and family. Join a Gamblers Anonymous support group. And if you don't feel like you have anyone to talk to, you can always reach out to the confidential 24-hour national hotline. Just call or text 1-800-522-4700.

Sports Betting

Sports betting is exactly what it sounds like—except that this ain't your grandpa's Kentucky Derby wagers anymore. These days, you can place bets on just about any sport, from anywhere, now that sports betting apps have taken over.

THE HOT TAKE | *Sports betting is socially acceptable gambling disguised as entertainment. It's not fandom—it's financially dumb.*

You've seen the commercials all over TV and social media (hint: billions of advertising dollars means they're winning and you're not). Legalized sports gambling has skyrocketed due to a 2018 Supreme Court ruling that let states call the shots. That opened the floodgates. Now you can bet on an individual player's performance, like how many home runs they'll hit or touchdowns they'll score. Or you can bet on a team's performance, like how many rebounds or turnovers they'll have.

Take the already-addictive nature of gambling, combine it with the ease of mobile apps, add in some peer pressure from your sports-loving friends, throw in the odds stacked against you by a professional bookie, and that's a recipe for disaster (not unlike your Aunt Donna's green congealed salad).

On top of that, people's love for their team can cloud their judgment. Even if your team isn't great, it's tough to bet against them, or worse, *for* their rivals (I'm pretty sure that's a form of treason). All that emotion and loyalty, mixed with your dollars, is dangerous.

Your odds of making serious money through sports betting is seriously low. It takes a *huge* bankroll, and you'd have to bet hundreds of thousands of dollars a year to see real money from it. The bookies who figure out the odds are super intelligent people who do this professionally. As in . . . *for a living*. You can't beat them in the long run, so don't waste your time trying. If you want to keep both your team spirit *and* bank account balance high, don't dip into your funds—stick to the buffalo chicken dip.

Precious Metals

Precious metals are the rare and valuable ones (like gold, silver, and platinum) that investors buy as a hedge against inflation and currency devaluation.

THE HOT TAKE | *Precious metals are fear-based investments with poor returns, sold by opportunistic fearmongers.*

You've probably heard people on social media or TV saying, "Buy gold! It will save you during an economic collapse!" or

"Silver will hold its value even if the dollar collapses!" That sounds pretty good, right? An investment that does well even when the economy is in the toilet? I bet their snake oil works the same way.

How about we look at the hard numbers? Let's say you bought $1,000 worth of gold in the year 1989. That $1,000 would have bought 2.6 ounces of gold back then, and would now be worth over $5,000.[95] Not too shabby.

Now let's say you invested that same $1,000 in the S&P 500 the same year. You would've gotten about 3.5 shares for your money.[96] Today, those shares would be worth over $15,000! That's three times the return of gold!

Aside from the fact that precious metals aren't a great investment, the industry is rife with scams and fraud. This isn't rare. It happens enough that government agencies get involved. The Commodity Futures Trading Commission (CFTC) recently published a warning for people to beware of "tricky promises of easy profits from rising prices in precious metals."[97]

Listen, if the economy actually crashes, we would go back to the bartering system, trading for food, water, fuel, and ammunition. And as my friend Dave Ramsey says, "At no time has gold

---

[95] "Live Gold Price," Kitco, accessed September 5, 2023, https://www.kitco.com/charts/livegold.html.

[96] "S&P 500 Historical Prices by Year," Multpl, accessed September 5, 2023, https://www.multpl.com/s-p-500-historical-prices/table/by-year.

[97] "Fraud Advisory: Precious Metals Fraud," Commodity Futures Trading Commission, accessed September 5, 2023, https://www.cftc.gov/LearnAndProtect/AdvisoriesAndArticles/fraudadv_preciousmetals.html.

been used as a medium of exchange in a crashed economy since the Roman Empire."

In times of uncertainty, people flock to gold out of the false assumption that it'll be a safe bet. But anytime we make investment decisions based on fear, we end up poorer, not richer. Avoid precious metals *and* the people selling them.

Leveraged Real Estate

Leveraged real estate refers to buying investment property with borrowed money to generate income and build wealth. By using leverage, you get the property without immediately paying the whole cost.

THE HOT TAKE | *Leveraged real estate is financial Jenga. Stacking up too much debt can topple your wealth-building strategy.*

There are plenty of real estate moguls and financial influencers who will gladly tell you all about how real estate is the path to retiring to a tropical island in your twenties while passive income stacks up in your bank. Think Airbnb side hustles, duplex hacking, and nothing-down real estate videos on social media. But the reality is much different than whatever the heck these gurus are selling you in their online courses.

Leveraged real estate is a high-stakes gamble. The real estate market is volatile enough, with prices and rental demand influenced by fluctuating interest rates, employment rates, and inventory. Six-figure debt loads only amplify the risks. And missed payments or market downturns can quickly erode equity and lead to foreclosure. In fact, around 15 percent of mortgages in the US were in forbearance at some point during the pandemic.[98] Lastly, owning and managing rental properties requires time, effort, and expertise, with potential pitfalls such as tenant issues, maintenance costs, and legal liabilities.

Here's a wild idea. Instead of leveraging debt to get into real estate, save up more slowly and pay *cash* for investment properties. It will lower your risk and stress, and increase your cashflow and peace.

Real estate can be a wonderful blessing in your wealth-building strategy when done right, and a terrible curse when done wrong. Don't believe the hype from real estate influencers. Go slow, do your homework, and pay cash. I know it sounds crazy. But it's even crazier to be leveraged up to your eyeballs and hope that this tower of wobbly wealth doesn't come crashing down into a mess of wooden blocks.

THE THREE STOOGES OF WEALTH-BUILDING

We've covered a lot of ground. I hope those hot takes motivate you to give some of these trends the cold shoulder and opt for something timeless. The best investing advice I've heard is not from a business guru or financial mogul. It's from a guy named King Solomon, who penned these words around 900 BC in the book of Proverbs: "Wealth gained hastily will dwindle, but whoever gathers little by little will increase it" (13:11).

---

[98] Jonnelle Marte and Katanga Johnson, "Vulnerable U.S. homeowners face uncertainty as mortgage forbearance ends," Reuters, October 15, 2021, https://www.reuters.com/world/us/vulnerable-us-homeowners-face-uncertainty-mortgage-forbearance-ends-2021-10-15/.

That's some priceless investment wisdom right there. If it sounds too good to be true, it is. If it looks like easy money, you're about to learn a hard lesson. Run fast and run far from this crap.

At the root of wealth-building shortcuts and get-rich-quick schemes are three character traits that will wreak havoc on your life if left unchecked: greed, fear, and pride.

Greed: An intense and selfish desire for something, especially wealth.

Few would care to admit it, but those who have an insatiable desire for quick wealth are simply greedy. The Bible says, "The love of money is the root of all evil" (1 Timothy 6:10 KJV). Do you hear that? Money itself is *not* the problem—it's the *love* of money. That intense, selfish desire for fast money decreases your quality of life by narrowing your sights. You develop tunnel vision to make money at all costs, it damages relationships, and it affects your mental, emotional, physical, and spiritual health.

Luckily, there is a strong antidote for greed: generosity. Being generous with your resources, especially your money, turns you self*less* instead of self*ish*. Generosity increases your joy, keeps anxiety at bay, and helps you avoid self-destructive decisions.

Fear: A feeling of anxiety concerning the outcome of something.

So many get-rich-quick plans involve FOMO—the fear of missing out. I'm here to tell you that FOMO is real, but JOMO is . . . more real. What's JOMO, you ask? The *joy* of missing out. How do we get that joy? With an infusion of the antidote to fear: contentment. You see, I don't worry about missing out on the next hot stock or crypto coin when I'm content and confident in my investing strategy.

Anytime you can look in the mirror and be content with who you are, what you have, and where you are financially, it produces this amazing feeling called peace. Fear tends to have a real hard time hanging out in the company of contentment, joy, and peace.

Pride: An excessively high opinion of oneself or one's importance.

Ever heard of the seven deadly sins? Well, pride is considered the original and *worst* of them, and for good reason: Prideful investors tend to be the ones who get their butts handed to them. An ancient proverb says, "Pride goes before destruction, a haughty spirit before a fall" (Proverbs 16:18 NIV). Old-school wisdom, new-school sick burn.

These people will time the market because they think they can predict the future. They'll place a risky bet because they know better than the bookies. They'll put money in crypto instead of retirement in case it has a 10-times return in the next six months. None of this is optimism. It's stupidity.

The antidote to pride, is, of course, humility. Humility is acknowledging you're not the exception. It's admitting you're not some infallible financial wizard. It's knowing your limits and respecting time-tested strategies for wealth-building.

Remember, the humble investor will always beat the prideful investor in the end. Patience versus haste. Tortoise versus hare. Choose your character wisely.

8

Marketing & Consumerism

We buy things we don't need, with money we don't have, to impress people we don't like.
–DAVE RAMSEY

Do you remember the last time you were "influenced"? I'm not talking about alcohol here. I mean emotionally, socially, financially . . . influenced. Influenced to purchase by some*one* or some*thing*. Maybe it was an Instagram influencer you follow, a targeted ad, a celebrity you admire, your best friend with good taste, or a perfectly crafted marketing email.

For me, it was my friend and coworker Cody. Here's what you need to know about Cody. He's 6'2", lifts weights, and looks like a lumberjack/Patagonia model. I, on the other hand, well . . . let's just say what I lack in height and lumberjack-ness, I make up for with a great personality.

One day, I see Cody walk into work drinking what looks like a tallboy beer can. We get to talking, and it turns out it's just canned water with some rock 'n' roll branding. To set up what happens next, let me tell you a fact about the human brain. My friend Dr. John Delony says that our brains run on ancient technology and are constantly asking these three questions: Am I safe? Do I belong? and Does it feel good? These questions apply to everything in life—including what we buy.

Almost immediately, my brain starts telling me why this purchase is a no-brainer (*ba dum tss*): "Drinking this canned water will help you *belong* to the cool kids' club like Cody! Plus, it will *feel good*, putting out the Happy Hour vibes while keeping you *safely* hydrated."

Cody and I wrap up this conversation, and just minutes later, as I'm scrolling Instagram, what do I see? An ad for this canned water! Turns out my phone was listening the *whole* time. It gave me the creeps, the heebies, *and* the jeebies—all three at once. And yet I'm intrigued, so of course I tap on the ad. At the website, I reluctantly accept the cookies (since they don't even give you the option to reject them anymore), and I casually peruse the site. Later, I'm watching a YouTube video and it cuts to an ad . . . for this canned water. I pull up Facebook to see how my mom is doing, and there's yet *another* ad for this canned water. I'm Googling, and what's at the top? *More* targeted ads for this canned water! I think to myself, *This is the universe telling me I* need *this canned water. This is my destiny.*

Next, I did what any tech-loving, convenience-addicted millennial does—I used the Amazon app to get two-hour delivery from Whole Foods to experience this magic water for myself. Turns out, these bad boys cost $1.50 per can! For *water*! I know, I know. You're probably saying, "George, come on man! You're above the influence. What were you thinking? How could you fall for a $1.50 can of water?"

Fair point. But here's what you need to know about millennials: Tap water is basically poison to us. And if it ain't carbonated, we're irritated. So I bought it. I tried it. I enjoyed it. Was it worth the hype? *Meh.* Did I fall prey to some old-fashioned consumerism and new-fashioned influencing? *Mmhmm.*

QUIT PLAYING GAMES (WITH MY BRAIN)

We often buy things based on referrals from friends, online reviews, or ads. This looks different depending on your age and personality. Some people love going through flyers in the Sunday paper to see what's on sale. Some people enjoy physically going to stores and shopping 'til they drop . . . some coin. Some people still watch TV commercials and insist on finding out for themselves if Arby's truly has the meats. For others, scrolling social media is their kryptonite, and they'll stumble upon micro-influencers promoting viral products like pillow slides and USB electric lighters using affiliate links. This purchasing phenomenon even has its own phrase: "TikTok Made Me Buy It."

Neuroscience and technology have gotten so frighteningly advanced that marketers and algorithms know more about you than *you* know about you. And hear me say loud and clear that marketing is not a bad thing. Selling stuff is not evil. Both marketing and selling can be done tastefully and effectively to help people improve their lives. They're a huge part of what makes our economy grow. Heck, we do plenty of marketing and selling here at Ramsey Solutions. It's probably part of the reason this book ended up in your hands—and for that I'm grateful.

But here's a problem with marketing and selling. When we're not intentional and hyper-aware, we buy, buy, buy. Ain't no lie. (NSYNC had a way with words.)

We live in the most marketed-to culture in the history of the universe. Over $522 billion was spent on advertising, worldwide, in 2021—and experts predict it will be over $835 billion in 2026.[99] And companies are not in the business of losing money. That means they're going to make *way* more than that $500–$800 billion they spent. How? By getting our attention. I mean, Google Ads alone garners almost 30 billion impressions per *day*.[100] The hope is that those impressions turn into clicks, which turn into consumer spending.

No one can say for sure, but the average person sees somewhere between 5,000 and 10,000 ads every single day. That's wild. And not all that far-fetched. Think about it. You're likely desensitized to it, but those ads add up quickly thanks to social media, TV, streaming services, radio, podcasts, movies, logos, websites, apps, articles, emails, billboards, magazines, stores, and recipe blogs. Goodness, those recipe blogs are exhausting. Listen, I just want to learn how to make a kale salad—not learn about your cherished childhood memories in Memaw's garden while you sneak-attack me with 27 ads.

Regardless of the medium or platform, you interact with marketing every day. I want you to think about this in sports terms. Companies are on the *offense* trying to connect their stuff (the ball) to your bank account (the goal). That means you need to be

[99] "Digital advertising spending worldwide from 2021 to 2026," Statista, 2023, https://www.statista.com/statistics/237974/online-advertising-spending-worldwide/.

[100] Jay Leonard, "How Many Ads Does Google Serve In a Day?" Business 2 Community, April 7, 2023, https://www.business2community.com/online-marketing/how-many-ads-does-google-serve-in-a-day-0322253.

on *defense*. And if your defensive game is anything like mine back in Little League soccer, it leaves *a lot* to be desired.

WELCOME TO THE (MARKETING) MACHINE

"Welcome to the Machine" is the second song on Pink Floyd's 1975 album *Wish You Were Here*. The lyrics sum up how society, or "the machine," tells us what we need and dictates our dreams and desires. Decades later, that message is more poignant than ever. If you don't make a plan for your money, companies will. And they use every angle to aggressively compete for your dollars.

Therefore, you and I must rage against the marketing machine. It starts with understanding the many ways companies go after your money. Once you have that awareness, you can be more intentional about spotting and stopping their tactics before they get in your head and persuade you to dip into your piggy bank. To that I yell, "DE-FENSE! DE-FENSE!"

Okay, let's have a look at their tactics.

Personal Selling

Personal selling is all about one-to-one human interaction. This is alive and well today, whether it's in-person, a phone call, a video call, an email, a text, or a social media message. It's one of the most dangerous tactics, especially if you're a recovering people pleaser like me. Why? Salespeople are *trained* to convince you to buy.

The most ruthless salespeople of all go by the name . . . Girl Scouts. Seriously! Highly trained. High closing ratio. Nearly impossible to ignore. It's a feat unto itself to get past them without opening your wallet. I've learned to just close my eyes and say a quick prayer, "Lead me not into temptation but deliver me from Thin Mints." I mean, you want to talk about accepting cookies? It might be easy to decline those online, but good luck declining real-life cookies from a Girl Scout stationed in front of your grocery store.

Multilevel marketing and network marketing rely on personal selling. We've all received that message on social media from that girl from high school we vaguely remember: *Hey, how you been! Long time no talk. I saw you got a dog! So cute. Oh, and that vacation looked amazing. Cabo is so gorge. Anyways, I'm working with this amazing company, and I thought you'd be perfect for it. Would you be at all open to creating an additional income if it wouldn't interfere with what you've already got going on?*

No, thank you, Susan. I have plenty of Tupperware already, and the only oil that's essential in this house is my organic, cold-pressed, extra virgin olive oil. And I will not hesitate to block you.

But for real, personal selling is one of the hardest things to resist because you're interacting with a real person, who's playing into your real emotions and weaknesses, who's been trained to convince you to buy.

The next time this happens, remember these two letters that form one word: *No*. Practice it to the point that you sound like a toddler who's just discovered they can refuse bedtime. If you want to soften the blow, you can add "thank you" to the end of that. "No, thank you." But stand your ground. Don't let anyone pressure you into buying something you don't need or can't afford.

Product Placement

Companies *pay* to have their products placed strategically. When you walk into the big-box stores, do you think they're putting their *least* expensive TV out front? No! They put out the 85-inch Samsung Q90T Series QLED 4K Crystal HDR UHD Smart TV. (By the way, what the heck is going on with TV product names? These companies are one letter shy of shoving the whole alphabet in there.) On this TV, you can see the individual pores on the athletes' faces. As their sweat drips down, you start dreaming about buffalo chicken dip and cracking open some canned water with the boys this weekend.

When you walk into a bookstore (for those of you who remember that they exist), do you think they've displayed the objectively *best* books on that front table? (Not unless they're Ramsey books. *Hehe.*) Publishers *pay* for that primo space, to the tune of thousands of dollars. Why? Because it sells more books.

Grocery stores are the OG masters of product placement. They study how you work the aisles better than any other retailer. I love to shop at wholesale clubs because, who doesn't love being part of an exclusive club that only millions of people can join?

A hot-ticket item at this club is a whole rotisserie chicken for just $4.99. And guess where they place them? At the very back of the store. This means I must pass every single sample station, which for some reason is always run by a cartel of 78-year-old women, *and* pass every endcap spilling over with new and exciting products that I had no idea existed 10 seconds ago . . .

All of it is on purpose.

The crazy part about that rotisserie chicken is—it's a loss leader. That means they lose lots of money *intentionally* in order to draw customers into the store. And it works, because it expertly takes advantage of basic human behavior. You walk in to buy a $5 chicken and you somehow leave with seven items for a total of $185. They don't check that receipt to make sure you didn't steal anything; they check it to make sure you spent $100 minimum!

Next time you're in a store, don't follow your eyes (or your nose). Follow a plan and follow a budget. Because companies position their products in such a way that we see them, we feel them, and we touch them. So stay hyper-aware and keep your eye on the prize—and by "prize," I mean the stuff you really came to buy.

Brand Association

Fun fact: 85 percent of cellphones in America are smartphones.[101] (I guess 15 percent of folks are still clinging to the simpler times of the Nokia brick phone?) And the majority of smartphone users have an Apple iPhone.[102] Those people—iPhone people—are my people. All of you Android people, Samsung people, Motorola people . . . I love you. I just don't want to get a text from you. And it's not your fault. You did nothing to deserve this. You're probably a good person. But Apple has turned us against you. And all it took was one simple color: green.

You see, when I get a text from my iPhone people, who I *belong* to (and it *feels good* to belong), I see a beautiful blue text bubble. When I get a text from a non-Apple device, it's *vomit green*. It's jarring. I can't even look at it. I've started deleting those contacts and just telling myself I'll find new friends. JK. Mostly.

If our brains are asking the question, "Do I belong?" then brand association is the way companies are looking to answer that. The products you buy tell a story about you. If you buy Patagonia, you're not just a millennial who takes pretentious walks in the forest called hikes. No. You, my friend, are an *advocate for the planet*. You exist to reduce your carbon footprint. You have become one with nature and you befriend wildlife.

---

[101] "Mobile Fact Sheet," Pew Research Center, April 7, 2021, https://www.pewresearch.org/internet/fact-sheet/mobile/.

[102] Federica Laricchia, "Share of smartphone shipments in North America 2015-2022, by vendor," May 2, 2023, https://www.statista.com/statistics/632574/smartphone-market-share-by-vendor-in-north-america/.

If you drive a Harley motorcycle, you're *not* just a middle-aged guy named Ronald who's going through a midlife crisis. You're a freedom fighter who lives in black leather and goes by "Ronnie Roadkill" on the weekends.

And when my friend Dr. John Delony buys a Gibson guitar, he's no longer a mediocre guitar player with a wife and two kids in the suburbs. No. He transforms into Slash from Guns N' Roses, shredding solos for millions of adoring fans . . . in his basement.

Branding is about perception. Companies are trying to find shared values to create good perceptions. They want you to feel like your best self. They want you to feel like you're living out your values and your passions through the products they sell you. What does that do? It creates *brand loyalty*. It makes you a part of their *tribe* and keeps you coming back. For life (they hope). And maybe you pass that brand loyalty down to your kids, and maybe they pass it to their kids, and so on.

Again, there's nothing wrong with buying stuff. But your best defense when it comes to brand marketing is to make sure that what you buy aligns with the person you really are.

Sales & Promotions

I love a good deal. Nothing gives me tiny joy like typing in a promo code that actually works. It's a simple marketing tactic that gets you to buy more. So are Presidents' Day sales, Labor Day sales, Fourth of July sales, Black Friday, Green Monday, Taco Tuesday, clearance aisles, buy-one-get-one (BOGO), 20 percent off coupons, and free shipping with purchases of $50 or more. Good golly, it's exhilarating and exhausting.

We can justify spending as long as it involves saving. Remember how your brain is constantly asking, "Does this feel good?"

Your noggin floods with feel-good dopamine whenever you not only get to buy something, but something you also got a *deal* on. Basically, you feel like you won double. As it turns out, though, you can go broke while "saving" money. Isn't that ironic? Sometimes "saving" costs us more than we ever bargained for.

To play good defense against this tactic, *never spend just to save.* Always think about how much you're *spending*, not just how much you're saving. Do you want the best deal of all time? Everything is 100 percent off when you don't buy it! Sale of the century right there.

Now, if you're a sucker for sales via email, let me give you a pro tip. There's a *tiny* link at the very bottom of that email in three-point font with near-invisible ink labeled "Unsubscribe." What happens when you click that link? It takes you to a page that says, "We're sad to see you go!"

No! They're sad because they want your money. They can pretend all they want that they're bummed I won't belong to this tribe of canned-water lovers anymore. They'll be alright without me.

There's nothing wrong with sales and discounts and promo codes. I'm a huge fan of researching and strategizing to figure out how to lower my total. But only take advantage of these offers if you're saving on something you *already* planned to buy.

For my coupon clippers and promo fiends out there, here's your new mantra: Don't let discounts drive decisions. *Don't let discounts drive decisions.* Namaste . . . on a budget.

Convenient Payment Methods

Making a purchase has become so easy that spending money is *painless*. Thanks to our handy dandy smartphones, we hardly need wallets or physical cards anymore. We just Apple Pay, Google Pay,

Venmo, PayPal, or Cash App it all—so easy and breezy. Even your favorite stores, restaurants, and coffee shops have their own app you can load up and pay with. We love that convenience. The problem is, there's almost no awareness that we spent money when we use these payment methods. Companies know this, and they *love* it. Apple Pay's original tagline was "Cashless made effortless." They know that the easier it is to spend, the *more* we'll spend.

This is the consumerism strategy I struggle with the most. My wife and I will occasionally treat ourselves to a Starbucks run. Sometimes we'll even take our French bulldogs and get them a "puppuccino." (Don't worry, it's not coffee—just whipped cream. Don't call PETA on me.) Here's how frictionless this experience has become.

I pull up to the drive-thru window and I don't even hand over a card or my phone. Instead, I do the *most millennial* thing and pay with the Starbucks app on my Apple Watch. Extending my wrist to the barista, I feel like a tiny king who's waiting for them to kiss the ring. I can only imagine the restrained disdain the barista has toward me as I'm handed that Grande Nitro Cold Brew.

Truthfully, it's hard to emotionally or mentally process the $5.76 that just left my bank account. Partially because the money had *already left* my bank account when it was loaded onto the app long ago. (Another genius strategy on their part.) Mostly because of how pain-free the whole process was. Now, of course, I planned for this purchase with a line item in our budget. But the principle remains: These convenient payment methods cause us to spend more often and just spend more in general.

I love convenience as much as the next guy. Amazon One-Click, Instacart, Auto Ship, Same-Day Delivery—these are modern marvels that I'm thankful for. The danger is that you can now tap one button and 17 boxes show up at your front door like it's

Christmas morning. And you open them with only a vague recollection of what you ordered at 11 PM last night while in bed on your phone.

Here's a daring idea to combat these all-too-convenient payment options: Make paying *less* convenient. Take away the debit card information saved on your frequently used apps and sites. Turn off auto-reload for the apps you're most likely to spend on. Switch to physical cash envelopes for a while instead of using your plastic or your smartphone. The key here is to slow yourself down enough to curb the impulse spending and intentionally feel some pain when you spend.

Financing

Financing is the most convenient of all ways to pay because you don't *actually* pay for it . . . right now. You just kick it down the road into payments and borrow the money. A few of the most widely used financing options include buy now, pay later; 90 days same-as-cash; and store credit cards. Let's take a look.

One of the slickest financing tactics companies use is *buy now, pay later*. These short-term payment plans have exploded in popularity lately. They're a modern take on the old-school concept of layaway. Here's the difference. With buy now, pay later, you make payments over time, but instead of having to *wait* to get the item until you make all your payments, you get it *now*. Because this is America. We have the patience of a preschooler. The problem is, instant gratification is a real wealth killer.

Right below that Add to Cart button for a $40 product, you'll see an option that says, "Or pay 4 interest-free payments of $10." And that old pay-later trick creates a whole lot of profit. The market size of buy now, pay later was valued at $112 billion in 2022 and is predicted to reach $725 billion by 2030.[103] That's insane! For comparison, the credit card market is anticipated to hit $294 billion by 2030. These buy now, pay later companies are wildly successful in part thanks to their slick marketing to younger generations. Check out some of their taglines.

Afterpay: "Shop now. Pay better"
Affirm: "Pay at your own pace."
Klarna: "Get financial breathing room."

Klarna even claims they want to create "financial freedom" for their customers . . . by chaining them to payments for months. How does that give you financial breathing room? *Make it make sense.*

What's the catch with these short-term loans? A study from Consumer Reports found that these buy now, pay later companies don't always clearly disclose late fees and interest. Meanwhile, they confuse borrowers about which options *have* fees and interest and which ones don't.

Anyone using these services tells themselves they'll make the payments and pay off the item with no problem. Yet a third of US consumers who use a buy now, pay later option fall behind on one or more payments, which can trigger crazy interest of up to 30 percent along with late fees.[104] The worst thing about these

---

[103] "Buy Now Pay Later Market by Channel, by Application, by End User—Global Opportunity Analysis and Industry Forecast, 2023-2030," Research and Markets, May 2023, https://www.researchandmarkets.com/reports/5792483/buy-now-pay-later-market-channel-application#tag-pos-3.

[104] Anna Irrera, "As 'buy now, pay later' surges, a third of U.S. users fall behind on payments," September 9, 2021, https://www.reuters.com/technology/buy-now-pay-later-surges-third-us-users-fall-behind-payments-2021-09-09/.

services, though, isn't even the interest and fee traps—it's how they're so sneaky at getting you to *overspend.*

They're not shy about this fact. Klarna brags to potential retailers that they'll see a 45 percent increase in the average order value when a customer uses Klarna's interest-free installments.[105] Finally! A company that's brutally honest about how they're screwing consumers!

Don't fall into the buy now, pay later trap—it's a short-term convenience with a long-term cost.

Switching from new school to old school, another financing trap is 90 days same-as-cash. You see this when you buy big-ticket items such as appliances, electronics, or furniture. The promise is, you won't pay interest for the first 90 days. The problem is, *most* people *don't* pay it off perfectly in 90 days, which means it not only converts to payments, but they get back-charged insane interest through the *entire* 90 days. Yikes.

Do you know what's the same as cash? *Cash!* Pay for it in full, or don't buy it. It's that simple.

One last financing trap is the store credit card. I'm a TJ Maxx fan. Who doesn't love browsing a quarter-mile-long checkout where you can smell a Coconut Sunset candle and grab a bag of dark chocolate-covered almonds to add to your purchase? Once you're at the register, the 17-year-old cashier says, without even making eye contact, "Would you like to open a TJX rewards credit card to save 10 percent today?" And you think to yourself, *This is my chance to become a Maxxinista! I'll get 10 percent off this throw*

---

[105] "Installment payments that delight and attract customers," Klarna, accessed September 5, 2023, https://www.klarna.com/us/business/products/installments/.

pillow that says, 'Bless This Mess' and this plush blanket that says 'Live, Laugh, Love.' I already have it in navy, but I'd love one in gray!

You sign up and promise yourself you'll cut up and cancel that store card as soon as it comes in the mail. But by then, they've already emailed you more bait—another sale, another incentive, another reward—and you're hooked.

Don't kid yourself that you're being a smart shopper by playing their games. The bottom line is that companies don't give out discounts if they're not coming out ahead. They. Are. Winning. But there's a no-brainer way to stop getting roped into this financial tug-of-war: *Never finance a purchase.*

No store credit cards.
No buy now, pay later.
No 90 days same-as-cash.

It's never worth the payments—or your peace.

BORN TO RUN (FROM BAD SPENDING HABITS)

Always pay for purchases in full, with money you have right now, for stuff you already budgeted for. That's how you secure more peace, more wealth, and a lot less regret.

Forget about "affording the payment." I want you to think about whether you can comfortably afford the *whole* purchase. This way, your mind, your heart, and your bank account are all in sync when you buy, buy, buy. (And yes, that was the *second* NSYNC reference in this chapter. I make no apologies.)

I may come off like a real fuddy-duddy when it comes to consumerism, but it's because I want to see *you* get rich instead of making other people rich while you stay broke. I'm not mad at spending, but you've got to do it smart—in a way that adds value to your life without detracting from your goals. In a later chapter,

I'll show you how to spend with self-control, and I'll give you a foolproof method to avoid impulse, regret, and debt.

For now, remember that *you* call the shots when it comes to your money. You can stiff-arm the marketing tactics, unsubscribe from the spam, go in with a plan, and say no to the cookies (the online ones and the edible ones). You have the power to turn away temptation and take away the noise. You have agency and autonomy over your spending decisions.

Believe me, your future self will thank you for building these healthy spending habits now. I love picturing future George being proud of current George for abandoning his cart. The power is in your hands. Tap, click, and swipe with caution.

9

Breaking Free from the System

The truth will set you free, but first it will piss you off.
—JOE KLAAS

There's an iconic scene in the 1999 sci-fi action movie *The Matrix.* (Spoiler alert ahead. But honestly, if you haven't seen it by now, were you *really* ever going to watch it?) Let me set the scene. Morpheus, rocking his signature shades-and-trench-coat look, has just blown everyone's minds by revealing that what we *thought* was real life is *actually* a simulation cooked up by some power-hungry robots.

Morpheus offers Neo, played by the uber-cool Keanu Reeves, a choice between a red pill (which will reveal the truth about the Matrix) and a blue pill (which will let him continue his life in simulated ignorance). Neo chooses the red pill and is awakened to the real world, which in this case is a post-apocalyptic dumpster fire where the few remaining free humans fight against the machines.

While entertaining and thought-provoking, the plot of *The Matrix* was made up by talented writers. The stuff in *this* book, however, is 1,000 percent real life. No simulations here (although I'm sure some of you have your conspiracy theories).

The brutal truth is that you've been lied to. Social media feeds, slick marketing, sketchy companies, well-meaning family members, misguided guidance counselors, and of course, your impulsive inner child who actually made the decisions—they've all lied to you. Some with more malice than others. Just as terrible, they've robbed you, stealing your paycheck and your joy.

One of the worst feelings in the world is realizing you got duped. Like that time I got scammed on Craigslist after shipping a pair of Nikes to a guy's "cousin" in Nigeria (can't make this stuff up). I still remember the pit in my stomach when I realized the payment was fake. There was anger, regret, confusion, shame, guilt . . . and initially, panic. While I don't wish those feelings on anyone, I know firsthand that there's power in using them to fuel some serious life change. Once you get got, you're on high alert for good.

If you're disgusted at your situation, riled up and ready to fight back over being robbed and deceived . . . good. That means you're sick and tired of being sick and tired. This is your "I've had it!" moment where you draw a line in the dirt, quit complaining, and start doing something about it.

Remember, it's not (all) your fault, but it is your responsibility. And that's the best news—because it means *you* get to decide what happens next. You get to choose to unplug from this simulation. You get the empowering opportunity to rise above a system that has been gamed against you and live life on *your* terms—not theirs.

THE TRUTH SETS YOU FREE

Now, I'll be the first to admit I'm not nearly as cool as Morpheus, but I've tried my best to unveil the money matrix to you over the past several chapters. Too many of us are willfully choosing to live in our own simulated ignorance—chasing status, credit scores, airline miles, cash back, crypto, shiny cars on payments, and huge mortgages. And what's the next level to keep the simulation going? We work jobs we don't like, to continue buying stuff we can't afford, with money we don't have, to keep up our lifestyle and credit scores, which continues a cycle of discontentment, debt, and anxiety—all the while somehow believing that this is "freedom."

What an awful, exhausting existence we've created for ourselves. America has become the land of the free, home of the broke.

So here I am, standing on my proverbial street corner with my little megaphone and cardboard sign, trying to tell you the *truth* about money. That's all I can really do. The rest is up to you. I can lead the horse to common sense, but I can't make him drink. *You* have to be the one to wake up and recognize the money game for what it is: a simulation that's not even remotely serving your best life.

If you've felt the gnawing sense that there's more to life than this never-ending Peloton ride of earning and spending and anxiety, then you're ready to take the red pill. Take control of your money and create a life that doesn't drain you—financially, emotionally, or otherwise.

It's time to break free from the money matrix. Reclaim what you've been robbed of: options, margin, peace, and joy. You're worth that. *I* know you are, but you need to know it too.

Freedom is worth working toward. The rest of this book will unpack the proven plan that has helped more than 10 million people live it.

I'm one of those 10 million. And you will be too. So load up that sling, because we're about to take Goliath down and prove that the little man *can* get ahead. Just like David did. Heck, he literally got . . . a head—Goliath's. (Gross. But also, pretty freakin' rock 'n' roll.)

Alright, let's do the dang thing.

10

Budgeting Is Freedom

A budget is telling your money where to go
instead of wondering where it went.
—JOHN MAXWELL

There are few things I love more than old-timey slang. *Happy cabbage. Gigglemug. Nincompoop.* The list is wonderfully endless. One of my recent favorites is *ditty bopper*. As legend has it, the phrase originated during the Vietnam War. It's thought to be derived from the Vietnamese term *di di mau*, meaning "to go quickly." American troops started using "ditty bopper" to refer to someone walking with an over-the-top swagger. Specifically, the patrolman walking in enemy territory without paying attention to his surroundings. That careless confidence put him and other members of the patrol at risk.

Back in 2013, I was the quintessential ditty bopper when it came to money. My spending was so out of control, you could have mistaken me for a member of Congress. My subconscious motto was: *As long as I don't overdraft, I'm good.* I'd buy stuff on credit and go out to eat whenever I felt like it. If I had money to cover rent, utilities, and minimum payments on my debts by the end of the month, I thought I was winning the game of Monopoly® Broke Millennial Edition. (Not a real edition . . . but man, that would crush in sales.) But ditty bopping doesn't get you far in life. I wasn't making any progress with my money.

What exactly is required to put a stop to the ditty bop? Well, for most people it takes an *"Oh, crap!"* moment. That moment looks different for everyone. Your card getting declined at the grocery store. A job layoff. A busted HVAC in the middle of a heatwave. A medical bill you can't even cover the small monthly payments on. Maybe it's less dire—you really want to be a homeowner, pursue that business idea, or just add guac without thinking twice about the upcharge.

It's a fact of life that humans aren't willing to change their ways until the problem is big enough or the frustration is strong enough. I never thought I'd say this, but we need to take a page out of Taylor Swift's songbook and admit, "It's me. Hi. I'm the problem. It's me." The good news is, if you're the problem, you're also the solution.

It can be a life-altering moment when unaware broke people become aware that they're . . . broke. And let me clarify that *broke* has nothing to do with income, considering that 51 percent of people who earn more than $100,000 report living paycheck to paycheck.[106] So where do we go when we're ready to make a

---

106 "New Reality Check: The Paycheck-to-Paycheck Report," PYMNTS, January 2023, https://www.pymnts.com/wp-content/uploads/2023/01/PYMNTS-New-Reality-Check-January-2023.pdf.

change with our money? If recklessness and carelessness are what got us here, then discipline and intentionality will get us out. The first and best step is to pay attention to your money by creating a budget. (Reminder: You have access to the world's best budgeting app for three months as my gift to you. You'll do yourself a huge favor by following along this chapter with your unique Every-Dollar budget. Redeem your offer and get started at georgekamel .com/resources.)

THE POWER OF LOVE (AND LANE-KEEP ASSIST)

The way I see it, budgets are the minivans of the financial world. They get a bad rap for being uncool, unhip, and boring. Not in my book. I think they're wildly underrated, understated, and under-appreciated. On a Venn diagram, these common traits would end up in the inner circle:

1. **They're powerful.** A budget gives you plenty of power to take control of your money and puts you in the driver's seat. The Honda Odyssey comes standard with a 3.5-liter V6, generating 280 horsepower. Come at me, bro.
2. **They give you breathing room.** Sticking to your budget will help you live on less than you make, creating plenty of margin for your money goals. The Chrysler Pacifica has more than 40 cubic feet of space behind the second row. So much room for activities!
3. **They offer peace of mind.** A budget gives you confidence for your financial future and curbs the anxiety that comes with not paying attention to your money. The Toyota Sienna earned a five-star safety rating thanks in part to features like a blind spot monitor with rear cross-traffic alert. You love to see that.

4. **They help you arrive at new destinations.** You never just wing it when you're trying to get somewhere you've never been—whether that's wealth or West Virginia. Instead, you use your handy dandy maps app and follow the directions. (Or if you want to party like it's 1999, you print it out from MapQuest.) And if you're rollin' deep in the Kia Carnival, you'll get some help on that long drive with features like lane-keep assist and lane-departure warning. A budget also rolls like that, giving you clear guardrails for where each dollar should go.

A METHOD TO THE (MONEY) MADNESS

Now that you're sold on budgets and minivans, we've got to choose our make and model. Even in the budgeting world, there are a lot of options. Like the 50/30/20 method, which says you should spend 50 percent on needs, 30 percent on wants, and 20 percent on savings. Or the reverse-budgeting method, where you start with a savings goal, don't track any expenses, and then hope you have enough to get you through the month. Then there's the 80/20 method, where you allocate 80 percent of your income to expenses and savings, and the other 20 percent to spending and YOLO.

The problem with these options is that they're either super rigid, they ignore your current financial state, or they reduce your control, awareness, or accountability with your money. Allow me, then, to save you from hours of wasted research and fill you in on the *only* budgeting method you'll ever need: zero-based budgeting. With this method, your income minus all expenses equals zero, meaning you've pre-planned what every dollar is going to do. For you visual types, that's

Income – Expenses = $0

Let me be clear here. You're not shooting for zero dollars in your checking account (you want a buffer of $100–$300 in there). The idea is that you need to give every dollar a *job*—you don't want your dollars unemployed! I use and highly recommend the EveryDollar app, which was built around this idea of zero-based budgeting.

Many people think a budget is just an annoying set of rules that will limit their freedom to spend. (And in this here country, *no one* limits our freedom!) This is why it's no shock that 6 out of 10 people in America don't do a monthly budget.[107]

When I finally started budgeting, that myth got busted. Instead, here's what I found: A budget doesn't *limit* your freedom—a budget *gives* you freedom! It's an intentional spending plan that grants you *permission* to spend.

This isn't about getting a gold star for being a nerd. It's about mastering the art of mindfulness toward your money. You're creating the margin to accomplish your financial goals like paying off debt, covering emergencies, saving up for that new minivan (you know you want one now!), and investing for the future.

If you've never used a budget, it might seem overwhelming at first. Or maybe you tried it in the past and gave it up after a month. Don't judge the budget just yet. I'll show you how to create a simple one that you can stick to. Who knows? Once you experience how it boosts your financial confidence, you might even be inspired to go after some of your next-level dreams that always felt out of reach because . . . you never had the money.

I'm telling you, that can change. Keep reading.

---

[107] "The State of Personal Finance 2021 Q1," Ramsey Solutions, August 29, 2022, https://www.ramseysolutions.com/debt/state-of-personal-finance-2021-q1-research.

HOW TO CREATE A BUDGET

PRO TIP | Before you do anything else, log in to your bank account or pull out your latest bank statements. This info will be extra helpful as you create your budget.

Step 1: Add Your Income

- This is your total take-home pay (after taxes) and, if you're married, your spouse's too. Anything that shows up in the bank or your wallet needs to show up in your budget. *Any* source of income. This includes full-time jobs, second jobs, freelance pay, Social Security checks, and the cash the sweet neighbor lady gives you for pulling her weeds.
- List each source of income on a separate line: your first paycheck of the month, your second paycheck, your spouse's paychecks, and any other income by category.
- If your income fluctuates, give it a conservative estimate based on the lowest amount earned in the past few months. You can always adjust this later.

INCOME	Planned
Paycheck 1	$
Paycheck 2	$
Side Hustle	$
TOTAL	$

Step 2: List Your Expenses

- List *all* the expenses you anticipate having this month by category: housing, food, utilities, transportation, insurance, entertainment, and so on.
- I like to start by setting aside a chunk of my income toward giving and savings goals.

GIVING	Planned
Church	$
Charity	$
TOTAL	$

FOOD	Planned
Groceries	$
Restaurants	$
TOTAL	$

HOUSING	Planned
Mortgage/Rent	$
Utilities	$
TOTAL	$

- Think about your regular bills (mortgage, electricity, etc.) and your irregular bills (quarterly or biannual payments like insurance) that are due for the upcoming month. After that, include other costs like groceries, gas, subscriptions, and clothing.
- Use your bank account or monthly statements to help estimate the amounts for each expense.

Step 3: Budget to Zero

- This is where you make sure your income minus expenses equals zero.
  - If there's money left over, you're not quite done. Get those dollars to work by putting any "extra" money toward your current money goal.
  - If there's a shortfall, don't freak out. Look for categories where you can cut back and find ways to increase your income ASAP.

Step 4: Track Your Expenses

- Do not skip this step! Tracking is how you avoid overspending, keep yourself accountable, and understand your spending habits.
- If money comes out of your wallet, bank account, Venmo, or whatever is hip by the time you read this—it needs a home in your budget.
- Track your expenses regularly. Get in the habit of doing this once every day or two. That way, it never gets overwhelming. Do it while you're waiting in line, waiting

on your coffee, or waiting on the world to change. All it takes is a quick tap, type, drag or swipe.
- As the month goes on, make tweaks as needed to keep that budget happy.

Step 5: Make a New Budget Before the Month Begins

- You need a special, unique budget every single month because your life is one-of-a-kind.
- Carry over the previous month's budget as a template and adjust for any different expenses or costs. (PS: EveryDollar makes this a one-click breeze.)
- Consider month-specific expenses like holidays, birthdays, weddings, seasonal purchases, or quarterly and annual bills.
- Create a special category for these expenses and adjust your budget accordingly. You can always delete them next month.

And *boom*! Just like that, you're a bona fide budgeter!

Although this may seem like a lot of steps at first, I promise you, with some practice, you'll be a pro. For most people, it takes about three months of budgeting to get it dialed in. If at first you don't succeed, try, try . . . for 90 days.

FIRST HESITATIONS (AND SECOND OPINIONS)

We humans are wired for growth yet resistant to change. What's funny is that you can't have one without the other (such fickle creatures we are). With any habit that's new and different, our brains will come up with all kinds of excuses as to why this one is *not* for us. Let's breeze through the biggest hesitations people have when it comes to budgeting and give your brain some food for thought.

I don't know how to budget! You do now. *Income minus expenses equals zero.* Track it like it's hot. Adjust as needed. Rinse. Repeat. Rejoice.

A budget is too restrictive! False. We've already covered how a budget doesn't limit your freedom—it gives you freedom. It's *present* you giving *future* you permission to spend—with the guardrails up that you decided on.

Budgeting takes too much time! It's funny how we can somehow make time to binge-watch an entire Netflix series, but five minutes of budgeting feels like a daunting time suck. While your very first budget may take an hour or so, beyond that, you should be able to whip up a new monthly money plan in just a few minutes. If you're using EveryDollar, it's super easy to track spending with a few swipes and copy over last month's budget to make it snappy.

I'm afraid of what I'll find! Looking in the financial mirror might give you a jump-scare at first. But living in la la land and ignoring your spending hasn't been working for you. Turns out, reality is a lot less scary than the unknown. Once you see it and face it, you can change it and control it. That's empowering.

My income differs every month, so I can't do a budget! For anyone with an irregular income, you *definitely* need a budget. This includes self-employed folk such as contractors and freelancers, commission-based jobs (like real estate agents or certain sales positions), gig-economy workers, and seasonal workers.

If that's you, budget based on the lowest estimate of what you normally make. (You can adjust later in the month if you make more!) Then create a *prioritized spending plan* of what gets paid first (like the "Four Walls"). Make your way down the list of priority expenses until the income runs out that month.

When times are good, put money aside in a separate savings account for leaner months. This way you're covered if you have a no-income month for some reason (like a temporary layoff, an injury, a short gap between gigs, or your invoice for this month's project won't be paid until next month). Do *not* dip into the emergency fund just because you have a low-income month! Get creative, aim to have no interruption of income, focus on needs and priorities, and stick to the plan.

I don't know what percentage I should use for each category! Don't let that stop you from doing a budget. Budget percentages are different for everyone, depending on a whole bunch of factors like income, location, family size, and lifestyle. The three percentages I *do* recommend regardless of those factors is 10 percent toward giving, no more than 25 percent toward rent or mortgage, and 15 percent toward investing during Baby Steps 4 through 6. Outside of that, be reasonable and live on less than you make!

My spouse isn't on the same page! This is a tough one. It's hard to make progress when you're not budgeting together. In this situation, be transparent about your feelings, and encourage your spouse to do the same. Ask questions to understand their perspective, and no matter what, avoid raising your voice (turning it up to 11 never helps). Lastly, show some grace. This stuff is hard. If you can't get traction, it's worth reaching out to a financial coach or marriage counselor to help work through the root issues.

MY BEST BUDGETING TIPS

Now that I've been budgeting for over a decade, I've learned a whole lot about the bumps in the road and how to smooth them out. Since I don't gatekeep, I'll happily share those tips, tricks, and hacks.

Surround yourself with the right people. You become who you hang around with. If you hang with broke people and impulsive spenders, you'll eventually be "twinning" with them. Find friends who respect your goals and won't pressure you to derail your momentum with unplanned spending.

Make budgeting easy with an app. As a millennial, I'm not even sure where to find a pen and paper in my house. And if I open Excel, my day is ruined. I prefer the EveryDollar app to budget on-the-go. My phone is always with me—therefore my budget is too.

Define your *why*. You're budgeting with a purpose. Maybe it's to get control of spending, pay off debt, stack up savings, upgrade the car, invest for the future, or be more generous. When things get tough, boring, frustrating, or downright annoying, remember your *why*.

Find better ways to deal with stress than spending. If you respond to stress with "Add to Cart," replace that habit with a better one. There are much healthier and less expensive ways to cope. Here are a few ideas to jog your noggin: a relaxing bath, a captivating book, a hilarious stand-up special, a cup of tea, a walk or run outside, or a board game with friends. Think low-cost, high-endorphin activities.

Find an accountability partner. You don't have to do this budgeting thing alone! Get yourself an accountability partner to help you stay the course. I guarantee you have some friends who would love some companionship on this journey to money maturity.

Create a "miscellaneous" line item. It's the little stuff that can throw us off track. A miscellaneous budget line is a great bucket for those expenses that catch you off guard. But don't let this become a crutch to get sloppy or overspend. If you see a pattern, plan for it next time!

Ditch the credit cards. A budget and credit cards don't mix. Using credit to pay for expenses and then making a big payment at the end of the month is a terrible management system. Just because you can pay the lump sum doesn't mean you're making progress. Stick to a debit card so the expenses can't hide from you.

Learn to say no (or not now). Budgeting is offense *and* defense. To win with money, you've got to add "no" and "not now" to your vocabulary. Setting boundaries, building discipline, and delaying gratification are strategies that will get you across the goal line.

Give yourself grace. Remember, it usually takes three months to get a handle on this budgeting thing. You're bound to "fudge the budge" the first or second time. But you'll get the hang of it! Offer yourself grace as you go. No shame in the budget game.

I GOT A PEACEFUL, EASY FEELING (THANKS TO BUDGETING)

Playing "Where's Waldo?" with your paycheck gets really frustrating after a while—much like a three-hour game of Monopoly when you don't own Park Place or Boardwalk. The ditty bopping was fun while it lasted, but it's time to look in the financial mirror and make a change.

When I finally got serious about reversing my financial situation, the biggest and best change I made was making a budget every month. There is no more peaceful, easy feeling than taking control of your money. When you make those bucks behave, they work harder for you. It will feel like you got a raise. It will help you rein in your spending, reach your savings goals, and be more generous. And when you start to mind your money, it takes money off your mind. That's straight-up brain freedom!

No matter what your past with money has looked like, the future is bright when you create and stick to a budget. So own it. Go strap into that financial minivan and drive it with pride. The destination? Wherever you want your money to take you. You've got this.

MAKE THE HABIT STICK (WITH AN OFFER YOU CAN'T REFUSE)

It takes three months to get used to budgeting. The first month you do a budget, you're going to be off. The second month will get a little better. By the third month, your budget will be your BFF. Lucky for you, I've gifted you exactly three months of Every-Dollar (with all its premium features)—because I believe in it that much. And I believe in *you*. That means for the next 90 days, you can supercharge your financial progress through awesome features like bank connectivity, a financial roadmap, pay-check planning, goal setting, group financial coaching, custom budget reports, and one-click tracking. If you haven't already, redeem the offer code in this book and start your budgeting journey at georgekamel.com/resources.

11

Spending Is Self-Control

The wise man saves for the future, but the foolish man spends whatever he gets.
–PROVERBS 21:20 TLB

The alarm goes off, jolting you from your sleep. As you hit snooze, your thumb glides across the crack in your phone screen—a sharp reminder (literally) that it's time to upgrade to the new iPhone. An avalanche of notifications awaits, and your brain is already craving a hit from that dopamine screen. Before you've gotten out of bed, you've seen an Instagram ad for that shake powder your friend talked about at Happy Hour last night. But you *already* ordered some shake powder from that high school acquaintance who sells for an oddly named multi-level marketing company.

Bzzz. Amazon alerts you about those leggings you left in your cart—*and* that time is running out to get the Lightning Deal! You get free two-day shipping and an extra 5 percent off by using your Amazon credit card. Why not?

You go to make your coffee, only to realize that your Keurig from college ain't spitting out that burnt bean water like it used to. This is a national emergency. In a foggy daze, you add a fancy Nespresso machine to that Amazon cart, because you've heard it's like Keurig did a semester abroad in Italy and came back with much better taste.

But for now, if you're not caffeinated, you're irritated. Nothing Starbucks can't fix. The app just notified you it's Double Star Day, and you thank your lucky stars for those sweet bonus rewards. You place a pickup order for your standard grande no-whip half-caff white chocolate mocha with a single pump, made with soy. You know what? Scratch that. Coconut milk. You're doing full keto. It's $7.08 after tax, but hey, Momma needs her fix.

On the way to work, you're applying mascara at the stoplight because *of course* you're running late. You hate how this brand clumps, and you harken back to that TikTok influencer who said Maybelline Lash Sensational Sky High is having its moment right now. You add that to the cart too.

At work, your headphones are on the fritz, and you desperately need something to drown out the dissonant symphony of Slack notifications, email dings, and Rick loudly talking about Lord knows what. You really want a pair of AirPods Pro with noise cancellation, but *dang* they're pricey. No worries, you'll put it on four "easy" payments with Apple Pay Later. That's a problem for future you.

Around noon, you realize you forgot to pack a lunch and decide to DoorDash a taco bowl for $12. Well, technically, after tax, delivery fee, service fee, and tip, it's $25. But who's counting at this point? While you're waiting, you open Instacart to get some real food for the week since you feel guilty about all that expensive DoorDash-ing. You add some bags of kale and spinach—although you subconsciously know that one week from today, you'll be throwing away unopened bags of kale and spinach. It's the thought that counts.

You make it home to find Amazon boxes forming a miniature fortress by the front door. The Instacart groceries have been delivered. You forgot what you even ordered two days ago—it feels like a spending eternity.

After all that unboxing and unbagging, you're wiped. Time to unwind. You turn on your Smart TV and see your eight streaming subscriptions glaring back at you. So many limited series . . . so much limited time. Choice paralysis kicks in. After what feels like an hour, you settle for a murder documentary series, only to be pummeled by a sense of restlessness, unrelated to, you know . . . the murders.

You look around at the room full of cardboard boxes and impulsive purchases, and it's a sobering reminder of why your bank account is always running on low. And truthfully, you're running on low too. You're feeling tired, overwhelmed, worried, and broke.

As you lay in bed that night, with the faint glow of your phone hypnotizing you, you wonder if there's more beyond the screen, the cart, and the constant chime of consumerism demanding your attention—and your money.

CURB YOUR CONSUMERISM

America has a love affair with stuff. We can't get enough of it. I feel that. I mean, some of my favorite stuff is stuff! But we've reached a breaking point here. Drive down your street and you'll find that garages aren't for parking cars anymore. They've become a pack-rat palace, brimming with boxes and crap we *might* use one day, or *used* to use back in the day. And even with the square footage of homes increasing over the past few decades, we're *still* running out of space. We rent tiny houses called storage units just to hold *extra* stuff we can no longer shove in our attics, garages, and basements, to the tune of—get this—about $58 billion in 2023. And the self-storage industry is estimated to hit $72 billion by 2028.[108]

We've created a monster through the endless acquisition of stuff. And it's not just the physical items in our life that take up space and eat up our paychecks. It's fancy cocktails, eating out, subscription boxes, memberships, video games, in-app purchases, vacations, concerts, sporting events, and expensive hobbies. Heck, if you piled up all the receipts from your purse, wallet, and inbox, they would make a tiny book about why you're broke.

In moderation, none of these things are inherently bad. But when they're mishandled, it leaves us $1 trillion in credit card debt—somehow unhappier than we were before. That's the reality we're living in today. It feels like we have less time and money than ever, yet *more* screen time, debt, and anxiety than ever. That's no coincidence.

I may sound like an ultra-minimalist by the way I'm talking here. But I'm talking to myself too. Even living debt-free and on a budget, I'm still prone to unchecked consumerism. I'm not mad at the idea of spending money, but we've got to do it with intentionality. If we're going to free ourselves from the clutter, impulse, and financial stress that is burying us, we need to develop

---

[108] "Self Storage Market Size & Share Analysis—Growth Trends & Forecasts (2023–2028)," Mordor Intelligence 2023, accessed September 6, 2023, https://www.mordorintelligence.com/industry-reports/self-storage-market.

something called *self-control*. Keyword *self*. Remember, it's not (all) your fault, but it is *your* responsibility.

HOW TO BECOME A S.M.A.R.T. SPENDER

In the "Marketing & Consumerism" chapter, I shared six ways companies (and people) come after your money. I unpacked their offensive game plan (pun intended), and now it's time to unpack *your* defensive game plan. It's a plan I came up with to help you (and me) spend smartly, once and for all. The best part? It's an acrostic that spells out the word *smart*. We love a good acrostic.

Self-Awareness
Motive
Affordability
Research
Timing

The process here is simple. If you can answer five questions with a resounding *yes*, then you can purchase with confidence and intentionality instead of impulse and regret.

1. Will this add value to my life? (Self-Awareness)

Self-awareness is a fun buzzword these days, but it's sort of lost its meaning. In the context of money, self-awareness is how clearly we see our values, passions, emotions, and behavior. A huge part of this is understanding your money tendencies and how you're naturally wired. My friend and fellow Ramsey Personality Rachel Cruze talks about this at length in her book *Know Yourself, Know Your Money*.

She says that money is just a magnifying glass: It makes us more of whoever we are. That's all it does. It's a tool. Value is about identity as much as utility. Ask yourself: "Will I actually use this thing?" Not just *once*, but often enough to get your money's worth? If you won't consistently use it, rent or borrow instead. *Every purchase must serve a purpose.* If this purchase will help you live out your values and add long-term utility to your life, then check this one off with a big ol' "Yes!"

2. Am I buying this for the right reason? (Motive)

Be aware of what's happening psychologically as you're making the spending decision. What's driving your thinking? There's often an outside force involved. Maybe it's a sense of urgency from slick marketing (hey, mattress companies, it's not a limited-time flash sale if there's *always* a limited-time flash sale). Maybe it's pressure from friends or family. Maybe it's retail therapy because you're sad or tired, or you had a long day at work and you "deserve it." Maybe it's driven by insecurity or the need to impress someone. Whatever the case may be, here's a great question from Rachel to gut-check your motive: "If nobody sees this purchase, do I still want it?" *Oof.* That'll preach.

When we buy things with the wrong motive, it always ends in guilt, shame, or resentment. We don't need any of that. If we're being real, most purchases can and should be stopped in this step.

3. Is this in my budget? (Affordability)

It should come as no surprise that there's a financial question in this quiz. Here's a wild thought: If we all answered this correctly, America wouldn't be in debt. If you can't pay for it in cash today, then you *don't buy it today*. Period. No monthly payments. No debt. Pay for it in full—or wait until you have the money to cover it.

There's an old Arabic saying: "الجمل بقرش وما معي قرش." I'll save you the Google Translate. According to Mama Kamel, this roughly translates to "The camel costs one cent and I don't have one cent." Meaning, even if something is on sale for *one penny*, if you don't have that penny—you don't buy it! Ya gotta love that classic Kamel camel wisdom!

4. Is this the best option, retailer, and price? (Research)

Most people overpay because they're simply not doing the research. Don't skip this step. Compare prices online. Search for promo codes. Ask for discounts. Use that coupon. Look up price-matching policies. Check the clearance section or tab first, just in case. Buy used when it makes sense. Get all the information you can before making a purchase.

That's what this comes down to—less impulse, more information. Simply slowing down and doing your homework can help you save money and avoid knee-jerk spending.

5. Is now the right time to buy it? (Timing)

This question is about opportunity cost. What opportunities might you be giving up by making this purchase? For example, could the money be better spent on an experience, an investment, or paying off consumer debt? (PS: The answer is *always* paying off consumer debt if you have any.) Look at your priorities, your budget, and your financial goals, and figure out if that money would be better spent elsewhere right now.

When there's urgency around a purchase, and it feels like it can't wait, ask yourself *why*. Generally, it's due to impatience, a hot sale, FOMO, a scarcity mentality, an aggressive salesperson, or really good marketing. A great way to curb that urgency is by applying the 48-hour rule. Before you make a big purchase, wait 48 hours. At least. (The bigger the purchase, the longer you should wait.) After a couple good nights of sleep and recovery from the dopamine rush of *almost shopping*, you'll probably decide against it. Maybe you talked it over with your spouse, figured out it would be stretching your budget, or realized it was more of a want than a need. If you *do* end up still wanting the item, at least you know you've thought it through.

There you go. Five simple questions. If you can answer *yes* to all five, you can confidently make that purchase. If you answer *no* to any of these questions, it's a "not now." Work on adjusting your motive, your lifestyle, your budget, your savings, and/or your patience until you can confidently and unanimously say *yes* or decide you don't need it.

That might mean saving up $100 a month for six months to afford a $600 purchase. That might mean finding new friends you don't need to impress or keep up with. That might mean setting boundaries with your mother-in-law. (Hey, nobody said it was easy.) To rein in your spending starts with slowing down to factor in self-awareness, motivation, affordability, research, and timing.

Whether it's a $20 purchase or a $20,000 purchase, the person with the most patience, the most information, and the most options always wins. Always.

THE SIMPLE PATH TO PEACE

We're drowning in a sea of stuff. And stress. And debt. And to-do lists that are longer than a CVS receipt. We're running at an unsustainable pace and spending like we're in Congress. And just like in Congress, it's *your* hard-earned money being spent. But you have the power to fight back and take control of one of the only things in life you *can* control: your spending.

I know it's tempting to think the next purchase is going to be the gamechanger. That it'll make you *feel* better or *look* better or *be* better, at least temporarily. Whether it's the trip, the car, the gear, the purse, the app, or the grande no whip half-caff white chocolate mocha with a single pump, made with coconut milk. Sure, money can buy you some fun for a little while, but my friends The Minimalists put it this way: "More stuff won't make you more complete." In fact, the more you own, the more you have to worry about.

Having financial peace is so much more than just getting your money act together. It's realizing that you can't spend your way into a meaningful life. It's realizing that the most fun you'll have with money isn't through spending—it's through giving (which we'll get to later). All this to say, if you're craving more peace, contentment, and simplicity in your life, stop searching for it in your shopping cart. It's trapped beneath the avalanche of clutter and chaos we've brought into our lives. The answer is simple. Literally. We've got to *simplify*.

The only way to move forward is by cutting back. It's time to Marie Kondo this bad boy—starting with closets and junk drawers and garages, and continuing through to our calendars and brain clutter. It's time to find contentment in the things that truly matter—relationships, experiences, and growth.

Spending can be a wonderful thing, but without self-control, it will control you. It will stifle your freedom, your peace, your margin, and your joy. Money doesn't make decisions; *you do*. Never forget that. Once you know it—and your actions follow—you'll be on your way to becoming a SMART spender.

12

Margin Is Breathing Room

Money isn't the most important thing in life, but it's reasonably close to oxygen on the "gotta have it" scale.
—ZIG ZIGLAR

On the count of three, take a deep breath. One, two, *three.* Hold, hold, hold . . . *and* exhale. Didn't that feel nice? Here's what just happened. That deep breath told your body to chill out by sending more oxygen to your brain, which made you relax, feel less stressed, and even feel a bit happier. Man, if only there was a way to do that same thing for our finances! (JK, there is.)

One of the recurring themes from callers on *The Ramsey Show* is that there's just too much month at the end of their money. Lots of money outgoing and not enough incoming. Maybe you've been there. Maybe you *are* there.

If you're feeling the pinch (which feels more like a punch), you're not alone. Most Americans are running a million miles an hour, trying to stretch every dollar they can, but it's stretched thin thanks to debt payments, cost of living, inflation, expenses, emergencies—and feeling stretched thin themselves too. It doesn't have to be like this. I'm confident that when it comes to your money, you can go from stressed to #blessed.

DON'T STOP 'TIL YOU GET ENOUGH (MARGIN)

How do you go from stressed to #blessed? One magical word: *margin*. Margin is breathing room in your bank account—and in your life. It's space. Cushion. Buffer. Margin is knowing your card's not going to get declined at the grocery store. It's knowing you can cover the car repair without going into debt for it. It's seeing a financial need among your friends and family, and instead of *just* offering thoughts and prayers, you're also able to drop an envelope of cash at their door. It's moving beyond living paycheck to paycheck. You're not just getting *by* anymore—you're getting *ahead*. That's #blessed right there.

How do we get this margin? Well, it involves some math. Don't worry. No imaginary numbers or Pythagorean theorems involved. It's a simple formula:

Spend Less + Make More = Margin

Thanks for coming to my TEDTalk.

Alright, probably not as mind-blowing or lifehacky as you were hoping for. But this equation *works*. Let's dive in and cover my favorite foolproof ways to create financial breathing room once and for all.

THE FOUNDATION OF MARGIN

Before we get to work building this margin, we need to lay the groundwork. It's not the most glamorous part of building a house or building wealth, but it's necessary if you want to create something that lasts. Here are three foundational boxes to check before you do anything else:

1. Make a monthly budget

Sneak attack! We've covered this in the "Budgeting Is Freedom" chapter, but it truly is the key to creating margin. A monthly, zero-based budget is *the* number-one way to find margin. Paying attention to your money is the only way to keep it and have some left over. No leapfrogging this step.

2. Get out of debt

Yep. Debt is the margin killer. If you still have consumer debt hanging around your neck, it doesn't take a genius to figure out that eliminating those monthly payments could give you some breathing room. I cover the best and fastest way to do this in the "Debt Is a Thief" chapter.

3. Audit your budget

Auditing isn't just for the IRS. Go through your budget, bank account, and every single transaction. Ask,

Do I really need this right now?

How can I shave this expense?

Am I getting the best bang for my buck here? Can I negotiate this down with a quick customer-service chat?

Can I do better? What if I canceled that subscription or membership for a while?

You'll be shocked at where all that money's going, and you'll be amazed at how much of a raise you'll give yourself with this simple audit.

Those three things are the foundation for what we're about to cover. They're a great start, but you can do even more to gain extra traction. Let's start with some financial trimming and cover my favorite ways to cut down those pesky expenses.

SPEND LESS MONEY

To have more margin, the first thing you need to do is *spend less*. (Hey, I told you this isn't a life hack.) Deep down in your heart, you *know* you can do better in your spending, but your head is *really* good at justifying every purchase in the moment. This one is hard, but here are 10 ways to make it easier.

1. Try a no-spend month

This is a 30-day challenge where you don't spend a dime on *anything* except the essentials. That means covering basic bills, gas, groceries—and *nothing else*. No eating out, no new clothes, no entertainment, no "just for fun" purchases. You know what's fun? Not being broke.

It sounds rough, but it's only 30 days. Here are some pro tips to survive this:

- Set a clear savings goal.
- Pick a good month for you.
- Plan your meals.
- Avoid browsing (both in-store and online).

- Make a wish list instead of buying.
- Use old gift cards.
- Find free entertainment.
- Limit social media.
- Track your savings (for encouragement along the way).
- Get an old-school calendar and write a big red *X* through every day you make it without spending. The goal? Don't break the chain!
- Stay focused on *why* you're doing this crazy challenge: to gain major money traction.

2. Shop smarter for groceries

Try these ideas for starters:

- Switch to a more affordable grocery store (like Aldi).
- Eat rice-and-bean tacos instead of the pricier carne asada tacos.
- Buy generic brands since they're often made in the same factories as name brands. Put the generic cereal in the name-brand box. Your kids won't even notice—crunchy sugar is crunchy sugar.
- Calculate the price per ounce or unit to know when it's worth buying in bulk.
- Beware of "shrinkflation," where companies reduce the product size while keeping prices the same. They hope you won't notice your favorite snack going from 1.8 ounces down to 1.5 ounces. Sneaky.
- Before you shop, research what's on sale, create a meal plan, and stick to a list.
- Try pickup options if you're prone to in-store temptations.

3. Eat out less

Eating out is a luxury and entertainment—not a priority or necessity. If you're working on paying off debt, cut this one out entirely. Even if you're out of debt, cutting back on this will save you bigtime. Because . . . not-so-fun fact: Restaurants need to mark up ingredients 300 percent on average to cover overhead, labor, and make a profit.[109] That means you spend $16 for a meal that *would* have cost you $4 per serving at home. You'd save about $190 a month just by cooking those meals yourself. Learn to love leftovers and you'll suddenly have some money left over.

4. Evaluate subscriptions

Streaming services, in-app purchases, digital storage fees, grocery delivery apps, gym memberships, delivery kits—it's out of control. I dare you to go tally up all your recurring monthly or annual subscriptions. You'll quickly see that you're spending hundreds or more every year on these money leaks. The average person has 12 subscriptions and pays $219 a month.[110] How? Why? That's more than $2,600 a year out the window. Most of these expenses (if not all of them) are wants, not needs.

Stop it with the subs, would you? If it's not food, utilities, housing, transportation, or insurance, it can go for now.

---

[109] "Guide To Average Markup Of Food Costs For Restaurants," BNG Payments, September 7, 2021, https://bngpayments.net/blog/average-markup-food-restaurants/.

[110] "Subscription Service Statistics and Costs," C+R Research, May 18, 2022, https://www.crresearch.com/blog/subscription-service-statistics-and-costs/.

5. Flex on travel

Disclaimer: I love to travel. I'm all about experiences over things. But if you're feeling the strain right now, this is a great place to get creative. The cost of flights, transportation, lodging, and attractions have all gone up in recent years, making travel crazy expensive. If you're in debt, trips are on the backburner anyways. If you're out of debt and want to travel affordably, be sure to research for deals, keep it closer to home, choose something more outdoorsy and less pricey, and be flexible with your booking dates and destination. Sometimes arriving or returning on another day, on a different week, or in a different city can mean the difference between a vacation and a staycation.

6. Do an insurance checkup

People often forget that insurance is one of their biggest recurring expenses. There are 10 different types you *might* need, depending on your situation. Even with the right coverage, you could be overpaying. I recommend working with an independent insurance agent who can shop for quotes and find you the best deal. I love hearing from people who tell me they saved $500–$1,500 per year just by re-shopping their home and auto insurance. Gamechanger.

> PS: We created a Coverage Checkup tool to help you figure out what insurances to add, tweak, or drop in five minutes flat. It's free and can help you save big. Try it for yourself at georgekamel.com/resources.

7. Get creative with entertainment and date nights

Who says you've got to go big for a good time? Have a picnic in the park, enjoy a game night at home, search for free local events or museums, cook a steak dinner on the old cast iron, throw an at-home movie night without getting price-gouged on snacks, go for a bike ride, be a tourist in your own city, or mix up a cocktail or mocktail at home. The options are endless—unlike your budget.

8. Use apps to save

The best apps help you *save* money, not spend it. Scrap the budget line item for books and use an app that allows you to rent ebooks and audiobooks for free with a linked library card. Save on fuel with apps that help you find the cheapest gas near you. Reduce food costs with in-app grocery store coupons and cashback apps. Remember, it's *smart* savings we're after, so use these apps wisely. Don't drive 30 minutes to save a dollar on gas. And *never* spend just to save.

9. Hunt for discounts, coupons, and promo codes

Save time and money using websites and browser plugins that search for promo codes and automatically apply them at checkout. Don't forget about traditional coupons either, whether it's through email sign-up offers, birthday freebies, or physical paper coupons. Your budget loves a BOGO.

10. Borrow, rent, or buy secondhand

Paying retail prices is for the birds. You don't need to buy *everything* brand new. Ask your neighbors, friends, or family to borrow that chainsaw you may never need again. Borrow that fancy dress for the black-tie wedding from a friend instead of dropping $300 on one. Should you need a special tool or equipment that they don't have, many auto-parts stores, home-improvement centers, and even some libraries, offer either free or low-cost rental options. It's way cheaper than buying something you'll use once. If I *am* needing to buy, I like to search Facebook Marketplace and other reselling apps for gently used stuff that will get the job done.

MAKE MORE MONEY

Now that you have all these ideas to help you spend less money, here are 10 ways you can make more money. Just so you're not shocked, I'll warn you: Many of these require this little thing called *effort*. More effort equals more income. That's how the world works—I don't make the rules.

1. Sell stuff you already have

Collect all those dusty doodads taking up space in your spaces and turn them into dust-free dollars. Electronics, appliances, furniture, décor, clothes, sports gear, baby gear, collectibles—you name it, someone will buy it. (I mean, *you* did at one point.) List it on Facebook Marketplace, Nextdoor, eBay, a forum at work, or one of the many apps for reselling. You can always go old-school with the classic yard sale too. There's no greater feeling than decluttering *while* making money. It's capitalism meets minimalism, baby.

2. Flip stuff

Consider flipping items like furniture, appliances, collectibles, or art. Look for deals at yard sales, thrift stores, or online. Spotting a $5 item at a yard sale that goes for $50 on eBay? That's called profit! Be strategic here, though. Research the item beforehand to see if you're able to make some decent money on it. Then smartly buy low, refurbish it, spruce it up, and resell for profit. Don't forget to factor in shipping costs, platform fees, and your time.

Pro tip: You can search for things on eBay and filter by "Completed" and "Sold" to gauge a potential selling price. Some people do so well with this, it's their full-time job!

3. Delivery apps

We live in the convenience age, and people will pay good money for you to take them places and bring them stuff. With just a driver's license and a reliable car, you can deliver people, food, groceries, and packages in exchange for money. Check out delivery apps like Amazon Flex, Uber, Lyft, Uber Eats, DoorDash, Grubhub, Shipt, Instacart, or whatever ones are hip by the time you read this. These are generally super flexible, so you get to choose when you work and how much. You can make anywhere from $15–$30 per hour depending on your location and peak hours.

4. Change your tax withholdings

In 2023, the average IRS tax refund was $2,753. That was *not* a gift from the government. That means people *overpaid* all year long and gave Uncle Sam an interest-free loan. If you're expecting to continue to get tax refunds above $500, look into decreasing your withholdings. (PS: There's a helpful article that walks you through this at georgekamel.com/resources.) A $2,400 tax refund means you could've taken home an extra $200 per month instead. Instant margin!

5. Pause investing (if you have consumer debt or no savings)

This one may sound crazy—but hear me out. Let's say you make $60,000 and you invest 4 percent into retirement. That's $200 per month. If you hit pause, you'd instead have that $200 at your disposal to pay down debt or save up an emergency fund. To be clear, you're not withdrawing any money that's already invested. You're simply not *adding* any more temporarily. Considering that it takes people about two to two-and-a-half years on average to complete Baby Steps 1 through 3 in our plan, you'll be back to investing in no time. And when you're back, you'll be investing *15 percent*, not a measly 4 percent. Plus, hitting pause will light a fire under you to pay off debt and save faster—because you'll be jonesin' to get back to investing.

6. Babysit/pet sit/dog walk

Do you love babies, or even fur babies? Human parents and dog dads alike need trustworthy people to care for their two-legged kids and four-legged creatures. These days, you can make $15–$30 per hour through childcare, pet sitting, or walking dogs. Platforms like Care.com, Rover.com, Wag!, Nextdoor, and even Facebook groups make it easy to find opportunities. Plus, these gigs can sometimes flex around your schedule. Bonus: You may not even have to leave your neighborhood! And by completing a babysitting certification course (like one from the Red Cross), you'll have an advantage over your childcare competition.

7. Clean houses

If you're a clean freak and don't mind a little manual labor, house cleaning is the side hustle for you. You'll be surprised how many people value a sparkling clean home but lack the time or energy to maintain it. Rates typically run $25–$50 an hour or $100–$200 per visit, depending on the size and condition of the house. You can set your own schedule while making someone's day so much brighter (literally, that shower tile just got three shades brighter thanks to you).

8. Indoor/outdoor home maintenance & repair

You may not know this, but rich people are scared of leaves. You brave souls who enjoy working with your hands can make great money doing landscaping, lawn mowing, leaf blowing, weed pulling, pressure washing, and handyman work. Lots of homeowners (like me) are *happy* to outsource this stuff due to a lack of time, equipment, or know-how. If you have a neighborhood Facebook group or local social-networking app, post about your services, do an amazing job, and watch as word spreads. Realistically, you can pull in $40–$80 per hour doing this stuff.

9. Freelancing/consulting/tutoring

You may have skills that can pay the bills (and more). Skills like graphic design, writing and editing, web development and IT, marketing and SEO, photography, virtual assisting, bookkeeping, and consulting are very marketable. Even tutoring in subjects like math, science, music, foreign languages, or test prep can earn you $20–$75 per hour. Turn that brainpower into profit!

10. Car detailing

If you love cars, cleaning, and the great outdoors, this one's for you. You can make $100–$250 per car by washing, waxing, wiping, and vacuuming the crumbs and dog hair out of someone's car. This can be done on your schedule, and in a customer's own driveway.

MO' MONEY, LESS PROBLEMS

Now that you're loaded up with a whole lot of ideas, I have a challenge for you: Commit to trying at least four ideas from each of these categories over the next thirty days. To get excited, do the math on what kind of margin that would give you per month.

Let's say you currently have $0 at month's end to throw at debt or savings or other goals. Here's what it could look like to apply some of the tips for spending less:

No-spend month: +$200
Shop smarter for groceries: +$100
Eat out less: +$100
Evaluate your subscriptions: +$50
Do an insurance checkup: +$50
Spend Less Monthly Total: $500

And that's just half of the equation! What if you *also* applied some of the tips for making more?

Sell stuff or flip stuff: +$100
Change tax withholdings: +$200
Pause investing: +$200
Side hustles and freelancing (4 nights per week): +$500
Make More Monthly Total: $1,000

Total Margin Created: $1,500

WHAT MARGIN IS REALLY ABOUT

Did you catch the transformation that just happened? We went from having $0 in margin to having a *surplus* of $1,500 a month! Of course, these are all rough estimates, and your numbers could be lower or higher depending on your location, skills, effort, and time.

Think about what that newfound margin does for you. You can *breathe* again. You can pay off debt faster. You can save up that emergency fund and cut up that false safety net of a credit card. You can increase investing to 15 percent and retire with dignity. You can begin investing more in your kids' college fund so they're not plagued by student loan debt. You can pay cash for your vacations and not still be making payments on them six months later. You can pay off the house early and cut out your largest fixed expense. You can give more generously, because when you're not worried about your own money, you're more likely to give it away and bless others. That's legacy and impact. That's what we should be aiming for.

And with more margin in the bank, you'll have more margin in your life. When your mind isn't occupied by money stress, you can focus on things that really matter to you. You've got more time and money than you've had in years—maybe your entire life. You're more present with your family. You're more focused at work. You're a more giving (and therefore happy) person. That's what it's all about. Having more money at your disposal is just a tool to get you there. Do whatever it takes to create that margin because it unlocks so much more for your life.

Margin leads to *options.*
Options lead to *freedom.*
Freedom leads to *peace.*
Peace leads to *joy.*

And *all* that, my friends, leads to a more meaningful life. A life *well spent.*

13

Debt Is a Thief

The rich rule over the poor, and the borrower is slave to the lender.
–PROVERBS 22:7 NIV

I love a good oxymoron. *Act naturally. Working vacation. Genuine imitation. Devout atheist. Social distancing. Honest politician. Fashionable Crocs.*

But the one that really grinds my gears, boils my blood, and salts my apples? *Good debt.* By now, I hope you're convinced *all* debt is *bad* debt. (And yes, while mortgages are the exception to the "no debt" rule, your life is *better* without a mortgage, and you should pay it off as early as you can once you're in Baby Step 6.)

My controversial hot take is that there is *no debt* worth keeping alive like a pet Tamagotchi. Debt makes banks and lenders rich and keeps you broke. Debt is not a tool to be "leveraged," despite what you hear from social media and your broke friends. Debt steals from your paycheck. Debt robs from your future by demanding that you pay for the past. Debt is a trap. Debt is a *thief.* As ruthless as the Wild West bandit Jesse James and as relentless as Swiper the Fox from *Dora the Explorer*. And America has gleefully accepted this thievery for far too long. I say it's high time we took a stand and yelled, "Swiper, no swiping!"

Total household debt in the US is at an all-time high of $17 trillion. Truthfully, our mere mortal brains can't fathom a number that big. To put it in perspective, that's *twice* as much household debt as Americans had back in 2004. Simpler times.

Here's how the US numbers break down as of this writing:

- Total credit card debt: $1 trillion
- Total auto loan debt: $1.58 trillion
- Total student loan debt: $1.57 trillion
- Total HELOC debt: $340 billion
- Total mortgage debt: $12 trillion[111]

Those are ginormous numbers, I know. Applied more personally, the average household debt in America is now more than $100,000[112]—*apart from* a mortgage.

Let's zoom in and break this down by types of debt:

---

[111] The five breakdown figures are from "Total Household Debt Reaches $17.06 Trillion in Q2 2023; Credit Card Debt Hits One Trillion," Federal Reserve Bank of New York Center for Microeconomic Data, August 2023, https://www.newyorkfed.org/microeconomics/hhdc.

[112] Chris Horymski, "Credit Scores Steady as Consumer Debt Balance Rise in 2022," Experian, February 24, 2023, https://www.experian.com/blogs/ask-experian/consumer-credit-review/.

- Average credit card debt: $5,010[113]
- Average auto loan debt: $22,612[114]
- Average student loan debt: $38,290[115]
- Average HELOC debt: $41,045[116]
- Average mortgage debt: $236,443[117]

Y'all—this is *madness*! And we haven't even touched on personal loans, payday loans, medical debt, or IRS debt. It's no wonder that more than half of Americans surveyed feel stuck in a cycle and say they can't get ahead with their finances.[118]

The harsh reality is that you will *never* win with money as long as you struggle with debt. As long as you continue justifying, rationalizing, and normalizing your use of debt, you will *always* be normal. And normal sucks. Normal is broke.

---

[113] "Record Levels as Consumers Navigate Challenging Economic Climate," TransUnion, May 11, 2023, https://newsroom.transunion.com/q1-2023-ciir/.

[114] Chris Horymski, "Average Auto Loan Balances Grew 7.7% in 2022," Experian, April 26, 2023, https://www.experian.com/blogs/ask-experian/research/auto-loan-debt-study/.

[115] Chris Horymski, "Americans Shed More Than 10% of Total Student Loan Debt Since March 2020," Experian, August 25, 2023, https://www.experian.com/blogs/ask-experian/state-of-student-loan-debt/.

[116] Chris Horymski, "HELOC Balances Rise 3.5% Reversing 10-Year Decline," Experian, June 16, 2023, https://www.experian.com/blogs/ask-experian/research/home-equity-line-of-credit-study/.

[117] Chris Horymski, "Total Mortgage Debt Increases to $11.2 Trillion in 2022," Experian, March 27, 2023, https://www.experian.com/blogs/ask-experian/how-much-americans-owe-on-their-mortgages-in-every-state/.

[118] "State of Personal Finance in America Q1 2023," Ramsey Solutions.

If you're not angry yet, go tally up all your monthly debt payments. Then calculate how much *interest* you're paying on all that debt. It's so much freaking money! Imagine that money working *for* you. Putting it into investments instead of toward payments would make you a whole lot *more* money.

Yet our society is so brainwashed that living *without* debt is considered weird. Hey, after seeing those stats, I'll take abnormal over normal any day. Normal is living paycheck to paycheck, working your whole life like a hamster in a wheel with nothing to show for it. Just like Sisyphus had nothing to show for his perpetual rock-pushing (except for amazing calves probably). In order to stop spinning that wheel and trudging up that hill, you'll need a different way of doing things. Because what you've *been* doing probably hasn't been working. As you know, I was $36,000 in student loan debt and $4,000 in credit card debt at one point, thinking I could somehow spend and borrow my way out of this hole. I was a financial genius who was broke.

THE ONLY (GOOD) WAY TO GET OUT OF DEBT

Since the goal is to create wealth and be outrageously generous, you need to stop letting debt take the wind out of your paycheck's sails. Not to muddy the waters with more boat analogies, but debt payments are like a leak in the bottom of your boat, constantly draining that income you work so hard for. How do you stop the leak and get out of debt once and for all? You need a leakproof method that works. Let's get to plugging and patching.

Stop borrowing money

It sounds obvious, but it had to be said. No more debt. It's useless trying to bail water out of the boat while letting *more* water in. When you decide to pay off debt, that means you're *breaking up* with debt. For good. Cut up that credit card so you can't swipe it for another airline mile. No more financing a car you can't afford. No more debt consolidation or other debt-settlement tricks. Enough with the credit card balance transfers. You need to get *rid* of the debt, not just move it around. You need to take debt completely off the table and decide to live without it.

Figure out exactly how much debt you have

To pay off your debt, you have to face the reality of your total debt amount. I know it's hard to stomach, but burying your head only gets you a crick in your neck and sand in your mouth. You *can* face your debt demons. But before you perform a financial exorcism, you've got to know exactly what you're up against. (Sorry, that analogy got real dark, real quick.) Look up *all* your debt balances and write them down. If you need help finding out what you owe, you can get a free copy of your credit report (every 12 months) from each credit reporting company at annualcreditreport.com.

Get on a budget

Surprise, surprise . . . George talking about budgets—again. But for real, if you've ever heard someone do their Debt-Free Scream on *The Ramsey Show*, you know that as they share about their journey, we ask, "What was the key to getting out of debt?" Most of the time, their answer is "The budget." Makes sense. A budget corrals every single dollar into the right place. A budget helps you figure out exactly how much you can throw at debt and shows you how making more and spending less could speed up your debt payoff. Read the "Budgeting Is Freedom" chapter if you need a refresher on this.

Pay off all debt using the Debt Snowball

With the Debt Snowball method, you pay off your debts in order of smallest to largest balance, *regardless* of their interest rates. Here's how the method works:

> **Step 1:** List your debts from smallest balance to largest.
>
> **Step 2:** Make minimum payments on all debts *except* the smallest, throwing as much extra money as you can at that smallest debt. (The ideas in the "Margin Is Breathing Room" chapter will come in handy here.) Once that one's paid off, take the entire amount you were putting toward that debt and apply it to the *next* smallest debt on your list, while continuing to make minimum payments on the rest.
>
> **Step 3:** Repeat the process with the next smallest debt until they're all paid off. The more you pay off, the more money you can throw at your next payment—like a snowball rolling downhill, getting bigger and faster as it goes! It's the positive momentum Sisyphus always dreamed of.

THE DEBT SNOWBALL METHOD WORKS

More than 10 million people have followed this exact method to pay off their debt. It works every time you work it. Why? Psychology. As you pay off the smallest debt, you get a pep in your step. An early win that motivates you to keep going. You start to believe in this process because you're getting this cool feedback called *success*.

As humans, that feedback is critical for changing our behavior, our habits, and to stay on the horse. When you're doing something difficult or new, you *need* to see progress or else you'll quit.

The Debt Snowball works because it's all about *hope*. Hope has more to do with this equation than math ever will. The Debt Snowball method exponentially amps up the momentum to get out of debt. Winning with money is 80 percent behavior and only 20 percent head knowledge. If you can get that person in the mirror to behave and change their habits, there ain't no stopping you.

NOW WALK IT OUT, NOW WALK IT OUT (A DEBT-FREE EXAMPLE)

To help you wrap your brain around this, let's walk this out with a real-life example. Let's say you have a total of $30,000 in debt across four different types with combined minimum monthly payments of $520. Here's the breakdown:

Debt #1: $500 medical bill—$50 monthly payment
Debt #2: $2,500 credit card debt—$75 monthly payment
Debt #3: $12,000 car loan—$250 monthly payment
Debt #4: $15,000 student loan—$145 monthly payment

Using the Debt Snowball method, you make minimum payments on everything *except* that $500 medical bill—since it's the smallest debt. And because you're intense about this, you've followed the advice to spend less and make more, and created an extra $950 in margin to put toward your debt.

The medical debt is obliterated immediately with $500 left to throw at the credit card debt. Next month, you take the $1,000 (the $950 margin plus the $50 monthly payment from the medical bill) and attack your credit card debt, throwing $1,075 at it ($1,000 plus the $75 minimum payment). In two months, you give Capital One the ol' "Bye, Felicia!"

Next, you punch that car loan in the grill to the tune of $1,325 a month (the $250 minimum payment plus the $1,075 you freed up). Nine months later, that $12,000 car loan is now a $0 car loan.

By the time you reach that student loan, you've got $1,470 a month to throw at it (the $145 minimum payment plus the $1,325 you freed up). Ten months later, Sallie Mae goes away and you're *done.*

Bada bing bada boom—you're debt-free! With all your hard work and sacrifice, throwing extra money into the snowball and staying focused on the goal, you'll have paid off $30,000 in less than 22 months. *Booyah!*

PS: Wondering what your debt-free date will be? Our Debt Snowball calculator can show you just how fast you can get there. Give it a whirl at georgekamel.com/resources.

YOUR BURNING DEBT-PAYOFF QUESTIONS ANSWERED

Wouldn't it make more sense mathematically to pay off high-interest debt first?

Well, yeah, *technically*. But counterpoint: If we were doing math, we wouldn't have credit card debt, would we? (That was rhetorical. The only right answer is *no*.) That pay-the-high-interest-debt-first approach is called the Debt *Avalanche* method. The math might look good on paper, but that's where the buck stops. Debt is only *partially* a math problem. It's *way* more of a behavior problem.

With the Debt Avalanche, you may not see progress on your first debt for a *long* time, which motivates *nobody*. With the Debt Snowball, you crush the first debt fast and build momentum, which motivates *everybody*.

Fun fact: Back in 2012, *TIME* magazine published an article on the Debt Snowball and said, "Turns out Ramsey is right. People who pay off the smallest debt first are more likely to be successful at eliminating all of their outstanding balances."[119] A more recent study from *Harvard Business Review* found that "people are more motivated to get out of debt not only by concentrating on one account but also by beginning with the smallest."[120] Looks like *TIME*, *Harvard Business Review*, Dave Ramsey, and 10 million people who have successfully done this stuff are all in agreement. The Debt Snowball is the best debt-payoff method out there.

That settles it for me.

When should I start my Debt Snowball?

You're ready to begin your Debt Snowball once you're in Baby Step 2. That means you've already completed Baby Step 1 by saving up a $1,000 starter emergency fund. I know $1,000 won't cover *every* emergency (that's why it's a *starter* emergency fund). But it's enough to take care of those ankle-biters (like an aching tooth or a flat tire) while you focus on working your Debt Snowball.

---

[119] Martha C. White, "The Verdict Is In: Tackle Smaller Debts First," *Time*, August 16, 2012, https://business.time.com/2012/08/16/the-verdict-is-in-tackle-smaller-debts-first/.

[120] Remi Trudel, "Research: The Best Strategy for Paying Off Credit Card Debt," Harvard Business Review, December 27, 2016, https://hbr.org/2016/12/research-the-best-strategy-for-paying-off-credit-card-debt.

Is there ever a time when I would pause the Debt Snowball?

Yes. There are certain life situations that make this a wise move. Some examples would be having a baby on the way, losing your job, experiencing a health crisis, going through a divorce, or dealing with an outstanding IRS bill. I call these pauses "Storm" or "Stork" mode. If you're in one of those scenarios, focus on minimum debt payments and prioritize other financial needs. Once you're out of the storm (or Mom and baby are home safe), restart your Debt Snowball and regain that momentum.

What debts should I include in my Debt Snowball?

Your Debt Snowball should include any *non-mortgage* debt. (And just so we're clear, debt is owing *anything* to *anyone* for *any* reason.) Some examples of non-mortgage debt are student loans, medical bills, car loans, credit card balances, personal loans, and payday loans. (PS: IRS debt is special in that it trumps all other debts and gets a fast pass to the front of the line. The IRS can seriously screw up your life, so you want to attack this debt *first.*)

What should you do about the mortgage? You'll tackle that big kahuna later in Baby Step 6—*after* you've paid off all your consumer debts and saved up an emergency fund of three to six months of expenses. Don't worry, you're going to knock out the mortgage too.

How long should the debt-payoff process take?

On average, it takes people 18–24 months to pay off all consumer debt using the Debt Snowball method. Depending on your shovel-to-hole ratio, you might need more or less time. For people with hundreds of thousands of dollars in consumer debt, it could be three, five, or even seven years (that would be a big hole). For some folks, they can clear their debt in six months (that's a small hole and probably a big shovel). All that to say, don't get wrapped up in how long it takes *other* people. Set an aggressive goal for *yourself* and then do your best to hit that goal, or even better, beat your goal.

What's the best way to pay off my mortgage early?

If you're in Baby Step 6 and paying off the mortgage early, don't overcomplicate it. The best way is to simply apply extra money toward the principal balance along with your normal monthly payment. Once you're in Baby Step 4 and beyond, it's okay to move from *intense* to *intentional.* You're investing 15 percent into retirement, investing some for college (if you have kids), and throwing whatever is left at the mortgage.

Check with your mortgage company on this, though. Some only accept extra payments at specific times or may charge prepayment penalties. Be sure to select or add a note that you want that extra payment applied to the *principal* balance—*not* to the following month's payment. Oh, and never pay extra fees for some sort of "mortgage accelerator" program. You can accelerate it just fine on your own with the strategy I mentioned. What *will* accelerate things is looking at your amortization schedule and seeing how much interest you'll save by paying it off early.

When my wife and I paid off our mortgage back in 2021, I did the math on what we had saved in interest. If we'd made normal payments on our 15-year fixed-rate loan, we would've shelled out around $49,000 in interest. Had we opted for the 30-year loan, that number would have been $106,000! Instead, we paid just over $9,000 in interest by paying it off crazy early. Being "normal" and paying on a mortgage for 30 years would have cost us almost $100,000 *extra* in interest!

PS: Our free mortgage payoff calculator will show you just how much interest you'll save through your discipline and diligence. Get to number-crunching at georgekamel.com/resources.

DON'T STOP ME NOW ('CAUSE IT'S PAYING-OFF-DEBT TIME)

I'm aware that what I'm asking you to do is no small task. Getting into debt is remarkably easy. Getting out is *hard*. I still remember the long days and long nights of side hustling, freelancing, selling stuff, and waiting for Lean Cuisines to go on sale for 5 for $10. All that sacrifice was *not* easy. But I would do it again for the financial peace I have today.

Knowing what you know puts you at quite the financial crossroad. You *could* continue down the "easier," familiar path white-knuckling the timing of your paychecks and payments, giving lenders your income, and praying someone or something (Congress? Powerball? A surprise inheritance from a distant relative?) eventually turns your financial situation around. But it turns out that path isn't so easy after all.

Both paths are hard. The major difference is that the debt-free path involves short-term sacrifice for long-term freedom and peace. The path most people take is about instant gratification that will keep them broke now *and* later.

So what's it going to be? Will you let debt continue to rob your freedom and wealth, or will you do the hard work to reclaim what's rightfully yours? If you're still on the fence, here's one last question to tip you in the right direction: *What could you do if you didn't have any payments?*

Answer: *Anything you want.*

Seriously. Imagine no car payments. No student loans. No credit card bills. No mortgage payment. All the money you earn is yours. Freedom is the best feeling ever.

Every weekday, visitors from all over the world and from all walks of life stop by the Ramsey Solutions headquarters in Franklin, Tennessee. I love meeting them and hearing their stories, whether they paid off a whole bunch of debt, paid off their house, got their kids through college debt-free, or became Baby Steps Millionaires. They share a common thread that never fails to inspire me: All of them one day recognized *they* had the deciding vote in what their future would look like. They realized debt was an obstacle to their wealth and freedom—and it was an obstacle they could overcome.

You're reading this book because what you've been doing probably hasn't been working (or hasn't been working well enough). Right now, your debt may feel to you like Jesse James has targeted your bank account or Swiper the Fox is sneakily swiping your paycheck. But every villain eventually faces a hero. That's you. *You're* the hero in this story. It's time to confidently step into that main-character energy and freakin' show those robbers who's boss. It's time to take a stand and get debt out of your life once and for all. When you do (and I know you will), I can't wait to hear you scream, at the very top of your lungs, "I'M DEBT-FREE!"

KEEP ON SAILING

What got me fired up on my debt-free journey back in 2013 was a course called *Financial Peace University* (or FPU if you're hip with it). It takes the principles in this book to a whole new level. It includes nine video lessons taught by Dave Ramsey, yours truly, and some of our other stellar Ramsey Personalities. What makes it so powerful is that it combines the knowledge, tools, motivation, structure, accountability, coaching, and community you need to truly change your habits and behavior. In the first 90 days of the plan, the average person pays off $5,300 of debt and saves up $2,700. There's a reason it's the number-one personal finance course in America: *It works.* Try it before you buy it with a free sample at georgekamel.com/resources.

14

Savings Is Peace

An emergency fund turns a crisis into an inconvenience.
–DAVE RAMSEY

There I was, driving my little Chevy Cobalt down the interstate, minding my own business, when I heard that dreaded rattling sound. I'm no Tim "The Toolman" Taylor, but I do know anything that rattles comes from the devil (mainly snakes and engine problems).

I get the car to a mechanic, who, bless his heart, tried to explain the diagnosis: "The timing chain jumped teeth and the pistons hit valves." Y'all. That was a brand-new sentence for me. The only word I truly understood in there was "and." A whopping $802 later, I swiped my credit card to cover the repair and was on my merry way, feeling less than merry.

That was a long time ago, but isn't it funny that when you're broke, you remember exactly how much an emergency costs? These days, I couldn't tell you what my last emergency amounted to. I must've just grumbled, paid for it, and moved on with my life.

As much as I'd like to avoid having another emergency during my lifetime, I realize there's more where that came from, just by nature of the world we live in. I hate to be the Danny Downer here, but as sure as the sun will rise, we're all going to see some rain in the seven-day forecast of life. That's why you need a rainy-day fund, aka emergency savings.

WHY DO I NEED A RAINY-DAY FUND?

Imagine a *giant* umbrella that keeps you dry from the storms of life. More of an awning, really. These savings will help protect you from ever going back into debt for emergencies. No more turning to credit cards, 401(k) loans, or a GoFundMe to cover the bills. You just . . . go fund yourself. *You* have the money to pay for it. What a concept! And it's a concept that, sadly, many people haven't grasped.

Only about one-half of Americans have $1,000 or more in savings. One-third of Americans have no savings at all.[121] As in, *zero* dollars. That's frightening. Think about this. Even with no debt, when you don't have money for the unexpected, you'll eventually end up *back in debt*, in a paycheck-to-paycheck cycle. We're aiming for financial peace here, not financial drama. We've had enough of that.

Dream with me for a second. What if you had $20,000 in savings and no debt payments to anybody? Every dollar of your

---

[121] "The State of Personal Finance: Trends for 2023," Ramsey Solutions, accessed September 6, 2023, https://cdn.ramseysolutions.net/daveramsey.com/media/pdf/SPF2023%20Trends/2023-SoPF-report.pdf.

income works for you instead of lenders. You have an army of Benjamin Franklins ready to go to war for you. Breathe that in. Relax your shoulders. Close your eyes. Wait, bad idea—you're reading a book. But seriously, how much easier would it be to face your next ER visit, fender bender, or job layoff, knowing you had $20,000 saved up and no debt?

Now nightmare with me for a second. You have *no* savings, a bunch of debt payments, and you're living paycheck to paycheck. One emergency hits. Maybe your HVAC system leaked all of its refrigerant and needs a new condenser coil, costing you $1,500. Or maybe your dog ate a sock, requiring a $2,000 surgery. You now have to charge that emergency to your credit card at 22 percent APR, turning an already-stressful situation into months of payments.

That nightmare is many people's unfortunate reality. If that's you, we're going to get you out of this mess if it's the last thing we do. Having that fully funded emergency fund in place will turn your next crisis into an inconvenience.

How full is "fully funded"? Great question. Let's talk emergency fund . . . amentals.

THE FULLY FUNDED EMERGENCY FUND

Remember those 7 Baby Steps we talked about? Well, the very first step is to save up a starter emergency fund of $1,000. The reason the plan begins there is that you need a small buffer between you and life as you begin to pay off debt. The other step involving savings comes *after* you pay off all your consumer debt in Baby Step 2. We call that Baby Step 3. Genius.

In Baby Step 3, you save three to six months of expenses in a fully funded emergency fund. That means you're adding on to that initial $1,000 and building a *forcefield* between you and life.

How do you know how much to save? Well, it starts with knowing your expenses. And you know this already because you've been doing a budget, right? *Right!?* That monthly budget gives you a pretty good idea of how much it takes to operate your household each month.

Now, those numbers are based on *everything* in the budget—including subscriptions, eating out, haircuts, etc. But . . . if (worst-case scenario) you lose your job and need to dip into your emergency fund, you'll want to get on a bare-bones budget that *just* covers the essentials, like food, utilities, housing, and transportation. It's not the time to pay for extras. Some people decide to include expenses like a gym membership if they're that guy or gal who never skips leg day. (I, on the other hand, *always* skip leg day. It's the reason I can still fit into skinny jeans.)

Once you figure out that Goldilocks monthly expense number, multiply it by three, six, or somewhere in-between to set your savings goal. To help you make this decision, here are some pointers.

Save three months of expenses if:

- You're single, with no kids and a stable income.
- You're married and each of you has a stable income.

Save six months of expenses if:

- You're married with a single income.
- You're a single parent.
- Your job is seasonal.
- Someone in your home has chronic health issues.
- You or your spouse is self-employed, works on commission, or has a highly irregular income.

The reason you want to save six months in those scenarios is that if something goes down, you've got a bigger, meaner storm to weather due to your riskier financial position. The less stable your income, the more you want to save. You decide what the number is, but make sure that number gives you and your family security. If you're married, you *both* need to agree on this number. If one spouse wants to lean closer to six months for more security and cushion—do it. You'll sleep better at night knowing your spouse is sleeping better at night.

Pro tip as you begin to build this thing: Automate your savings! Set a monthly amount to transfer into your savings *automatically* from your paycheck. That way, you can avoid temptation and create a forced savings plan that will help you get there faster.

Where should these savings be saved? I was saving that for this next section.

STASH YOUR CASH

You've got to be careful where you store your emergency fund. Do *not* put it in the sock drawer or a piggy bank. Here's why. According to a very strange study by Samsung, 15 socks go missing every year for the average Brit. (We could hypothesize that the sock/loss ratio might be similar between Americans and Brits, but without concrete data, it's merely speculation on my part.) Skip the sock drawer. It's like a Bermuda Triangle made of cotton.

Your emergency fund should be liquid and secure. *Liquid*, meaning you can get to it easily and quickly—like water from a faucet. *Secure*, meaning it's in a federally insured bank or credit union account (look for the letters FDIC or NCUA to be sure). You don't want your money unsecured, or even worse, *insecure*, like that coworker who constantly attempts to one-up everybody's stories.

Here are a few secure and liquid parking spots for your emergency fund:

- A simple savings account connected to your checking account
- A money market account that comes with a debit card or check-writing privileges
- A high-yield savings account through an online bank that pays a higher interest rate

The key is security and accessibility. You want to be able to pay for that vet bill or car repair quickly, with zero hassle and headaches. Do *not* put this money into an investment account or Certificate of Deposit where you could lose money or be penalized for accessing it.

One little heads up here . . . Once this thing is fully funded, you might have $10,000, $15,000, or $30,000—just sitting there. How boring. Good! It should be boring. And soothing. Like watching golf on TV. This is not meant to be an exhilirating, money-making scheme.

An emergency fund is *insurance*, not an investment. It's not there to make you rich; it's there to keep you safe. While investments aim to grow your money, insurance is for guarding what you've got: your home, car, health, even your paycheck. Your emergency fund is meant to protect you. So do not touch it unless you have a *true* emergency.

How do you define a true emergency? I'm so glad I asked for you.

WHEN SHOULD I BREAK INTO THIS PIGGY BANK?

When a sudden expense pops up, and it *feels* like an emergency—how do you *know,* deep down in the bottom of your heart? Ask yourself these three questions before using your emergency fund:

1. Is it *unexpected*?
2. Is it *necessary*?
3. Is it *urgent*?

If you can answer *yes* to all three, you have a real emergency on your hands—and a real need to tap into it.

Before you touch the emergency fund, however, I want to challenge you to first see whether you can adjust your budget this month to cover the expense. It's worth it to skip some extras to avoid dipping into your savings. If moving things around in this month's budget won't cut it, it's *okay* to use it. Don't feel guilty! That's what it's there for.

Remember, an emergency fund is not for emergency *fun*. This is not the "Bass Pro Shops has a killer sale" fund. This is not the "I want a new leather couch" fund. This is not the "I forgot Christmas is in December" fund. This is for *true* emergencies. Let's practice.

- A pipe burst in a winter freeze. *Emergency!*
- The new iPhone just released, and you want to upgrade. Yeah, no. *Not an emergency.*
- Your kid broke their arm. *Absolutely an emergency.* (Get well soon, Ashton.)
- The dishwasher won't run. *A-ha.* Not so fast. This one's complicated.

In the olden days, people used to wash dishes *by hand.* So pretend you live in a little house on the prairie and get a family assembly line going to get those dishes spic and span. But for real, can you watch a YouTube video and fix it yourself? Can you call a handyman and cashflow the repair? Worst case, get a used one or start saving up a sinking fund to get a new one when you can. Sorry, though. Not a true emergency.

By the way, when you *do* have to use your emergency fund, don't forget to *build it back up*. Fast. Buckle down on your budget for as long as it takes to patch up the hole in your safety net. If you need some ideas to speed this up, check out my tips on how to spend less and make more in the "Margin Is Breathing Room" chapter.

MAINTAINING MOMENTUM IN THE MONEY MARATHON

The quick win of $1,000 in Baby Step 1 was awesome. The Debt Snowball journey in Baby Step 2 was an absolute adrenaline rush. But saving up that fully funded emergency fund in Baby Step 3? Kind of a slog, to be honest. So allow me to be your Little League coach and give you some orange slices of hope in the form of a timeline for this journey. It's based on how long it takes the average person following the Ramsey plan with some pep in their step.

- $1,000 starter emergency fund in Baby Step 1: 30 days
- The Debt Snowball in Baby Step 2: 18 to 24 months
- Fully funded emergency fund in Baby Step 3: 6 to 12 months

Adding that up, it's about two or three years in total.

Before you start dwelling on the word *years*, listen to how far you've come: You have *zero* debt (except maybe a mortgage) *and* you have potentially $15,000–$30,000 just sitting there in the bank to protect you from the chaos of life. What an amazing place to be!

That last six months, though, can feel like six *years*. You're discouraged because there's no immediate reward of paying off the debt and seeing that progress. You're in the middle of the marathon, and you may not see the drink station, balloon arch, live band, or spectators cheering you on up ahead. I'm *told* these things happen at marathons. I have no clue. I'm not a runner. Proverbs 28:1 says, "The wicked flee when no one is chasing them" (TLB), and I've really taken that wisdom to heart.

Whatever you're not seeing yet that you'd hoped to see by now, give it a little longer. Do *not* give up! If you stop now, you'll soon revert to your old life. The one where you were stressed out all the time, with no financial or emotional margin, wondering if you'd always struggle with money problems. Remember that?

Don't give up and *don't go back!* Push through. It's so worth it.

Think about it this way. When you're paying off debt, you're making progress to *zero*. You're climbing out of the hole, out of the negative, and back to solid ground. Once you make it to this step, you're in the black instead of the red! Heck, you might have a *positive* net worth for the first time in your *life*. Celebrate that! It's an amazing accomplishment.

GOOD LUCK AND GODSPEED

Having a fully funded emergency fund ready to protect you changes *everything*. Not an exaggeration. This is a huge emotional step for your future.

And the funny thing is, when you get that emergency fund, you sort of . . . stop having emergencies. I mean they still technically happen, but they hardly *feel* like emergencies. When you're broke, it seems like it's hard to have good luck. It's like the adult version of *Alexander and the Terrible, Horrible, No Good, Very Bad Day* (hopefully minus waking up with gum in your hair). When you're not broke anymore, you seem to have more good luck. But it's not really luck. You've just set yourself up in a better position.

You can afford higher-quality stuff.

You can keep up with the maintenance on that stuff to make sure it stays in good shape.

You have margin in your budget to cashflow most of the emergencies that come your way without even dipping into savings.

And on it goes . . .

The emergency fund takes the drama out of life. So make savings a *priority*. It *has* to matter to you. That padding between you and life is like a financial basecamp, offering a safe and convenient location to rest and recoup from whatever adventure life throws at you. It'll give you newfound confidence and peace for the rest of the journey. Maybe for the first time ever, you'll be *excited* about what the future holds for you and your money. The dread will be gone. Those no-good, very-bad days will be a distant memory. And happier days will be ahead, at least when it comes to money.

This is a race worth running, and as a non-runner, that's saying something. I can't wait to see you at the fully funded finish line. (I'll be the guy in the hot dog suit cheering you on.)

15

Wealth Is Patience

Wealth gained hastily will dwindle, but whoever gathers little by little will increase it.
–PROVERBS 13:11

When I was a kid, my understanding of wealth was colorful—mostly because it was measured in crayons. If you had a 64-color box of Crayola's with a built-in sharpener, your parents were for sure millionaires. No questions asked. If your pantry had Pop-Tarts instead of generic toaster pastries, you lived in gourmet opulence. If you peeled open a Lunchable in the cafeteria, that wasn't a meal—it was an *event.*

If you lived on a cul-de-sac, that was French for "we got money." In-ground pool? *Swimming* in money. If you had more than one bathroom, you lived a life of lavatorial luxury. Extra fridge in the garage just for drinks? Welcome to the 1 percent. Second phone line *just* for the internet? Pure extravagance. *Two*-car garage? Palatial parking paradise. And if you had a finished basement with a big-screen TV and a pool table? Borderline billionaire. At least in my middle-class eyes.

Don't get me wrong. I didn't grow up poor, but we for sure weren't *rich*. I grew up in a modest home in the suburbs of Boston. It was 996 square feet, and all four of us shared one tiny bathroom. As immigrants, my parents worked their tails off to give me and my brother a great life. And they did. We never went without, and I loved every second of my childhood.

But there was a clear separation between the rich folks and the rest of us. I always thought wealth was predestined and predetermined. Like genetics. Or the outcome of a WWE wrestling match. I assumed you were either born into wealth or you'd never have it. That's why, when I pictured a millionaire in my mind, I never pictured *myself*. Maybe you can relate.

When I started following this Ramsey plan, I was broke with $40,000 in debt. After a decade of living these principles, I went from a negative net worth to debt-free millionaire. It still blows my mind. And I want you to hit that milestone (if you're not already there). Not because it will solve your life problems, but because it will give you something that's been stripped from you for too long—belief, hope, peace, and confidence in your financial future.

The current wealth landscape is far from that. Research from the Fed reveals that 26 percent of non-retired Americans have $0 in any kind of retirement account.[122] Not great. In research done by Ramsey Solutions, 48 percent of Americans have less than $10,000 saved for retirement. That'll get you about three months into retirement if you're lucky. You might be thinking, *But you're*

---

[122] "Economic Well-Being of U.S. Households in 2021," Federal Reserve, May 2022, https://www.federalreserve.gov/publications/files/2021-report-economic-well-being-us-households-202205.pdf.

not factoring in Social Security! I've paid into it my whole life and it'll be enough to get by!

Good luck with that. According to the Social Security website, the average monthly benefit in 2023 was around $1,700 a month. Try living on that, and you'll see why I call it social *in*security. I mean, that's approaching the *poverty line*. And by the way, that's the average—some people get less than $900 a month.[123]

Here's a final gut punch: At least 52 percent of workers have never stopped to calculate how much money they'll even need in retirement.[124]

While those stats are heartbreaking, I want to assure you—you can opt out of them. The fact that you're reading this book tells me you refuse to be part of the broke folk club. How do we rise above this suck bar and build wealth without needing a degree in finance? I got you. Here's your CLEP course on the quickest (right) way to build wealth.

WHEN TO BEGIN INVESTING

If you've been following along, you know that the right *time* to begin investing is after you've paid off your debt and saved up a fully funded emergency fund. Once you get there, you can shift your focus off debts and what-ifs and start looking up the road. That puts you at Baby Step 4 and beyond. Let's do a refresher on what those next steps look like.

---

[123] "Monthly Statistical Snapshot, July 2023," Social Security Administration, August 2023, https://www.ssa.gov/policy/docs/quickfacts/stat_snapshot/2023-07.html/.

[124] "2020 RCS Fact Sheet #3: Preparing for Retirement in America," EBRI, accessed September 6, 2023, https://www.ebri.org/docs/default-source/rcs/2020-rcs/rcs_20-fs-3_prep.pdf?sfvrsn=f0bc3d2f_6.

Baby Step 4: Invest 15 percent of your household income in retirement.
Baby Step 5: Save for your children's college fund.
Baby Step 6: Pay off your home early.
Baby Step 7: Build wealth and give.

While the first three Baby Steps are done one at a time, with focused intensity, Baby Steps 4, 5, and 6 are done *simultaneously* and in order. The reason we recommend investing no *more* than 15 percent in Baby Step 4 is that you need some money left to save for college and to knock out the mortgage. Once that mortgage is paid off, you'll have a *ton* of extra money to increase investing, spending, and giving.

You start with Baby Step 4 because investing for retirement comes *first*—it's the priority. To figure out what that number is for you, just multiply your gross household income by 0.15. That will give you the yearly amount you should be investing. Math is a whole lot more fun when it's helping you build wealth.

While there's the right *time* to invest and the right *amount* to invest, there's also the right *way* to invest.

THE ONLY INVESTING STRATEGY YOU NEED

I'm all about investing made simple. Are you ready for a five-word investing strategy to make the most of that 15 percent?

Match beats Roth beats Traditional

(Or if you're a Lion King fan, Mufasa beats Rafiki beats Timon.) Let's break this down.

Match: First, take all the company match you can get through your employer's retirement plan (if you have one). For many of you, that's a 401(k) plan. If you're a federal employee or a member of the military, it'll be a Thrift Savings Plan (TSP for short). If you're a teacher or non-profit employee—probably a 403(b) plan. Any match they offer is a 100 percent return on your investment, so it trumps everything else.

Then Roth: Second, do all the Roth you can at work or as an individual (through a Roth IRA). The Roth option means you're using *after*-tax dollars to invest, which then grow tax-free! You're paying taxes on the money *now* so you don't have to pay taxes when you use it in retirement.

Then Traditional: If you've exhausted the options above and *still* haven't hit 15 percent of your income, go back to the traditional tax-deferred plan through your employer until you hit 15 percent. Side note: If your employer doesn't offer a retirement plan, you may still be able to invest through an IRA or non-retirement investment accounts. If you're self-employed, look into options like a Solo 401(k) or SEP IRA.

Frequently Asked Question: **Does my match count toward the 15 percent contribution?** Nope. Don't count it. Invest 15 percent of *your* income regardless of what your employer matches. Think of it more like icing on the cake. (You can write me hate mail later if you end up with too much money in retirement.)

THE ONLY INVESTMENT VEHICLES YOU NEED

All you need to build wealth are retirement accounts like 401(k)s and IRAs. You heard me right. In 2019, Ramsey Solutions conducted the largest study of millionaires ever done in North America: more than 10,000 people who had a net worth of at least a million dollars. How's this for a shocker? The number-one investment vehicle to become a millionaire was a company 401(k) plan, with 80 percent of them saying it was the key to their wealth.[125] No magic. No beans. No stalk. It's so . . . unmagical. Our study found that 79 percent of millionaires attribute regular, consistent investing in retirement plans over a long period as a reason for their success. Really. It's that unexciting. And that hopeful. Because it means they're not special, and you can do this too.

THE ONLY INVESTMENT TYPES YOU NEED

Now that we've chosen our investment vehicles, we need some gas in the tank.

A retirement account is just an empty, tax-advantaged shell. You've got to choose investments to purchase *inside* of it to turn that cold, sterile house into a warm, wealth-building *home*. People tend to get overwhelmed and confused at this point due to all the options. Allow me to free you from paralysis by analysis and choice overload: The only type of investment you need to build wealth is *mutual funds*.

Remember, a mutual fund pools together money from a bunch of investors to buy a diverse range of stocks in different companies. Kind of like a potluck where everybody brings a dish, and you get to enjoy a little bit of everything instead of hoping the one dish turned out great. If one potluck dish disappoints (like Karla's vegan meatloaf), no biggie—you've got plenty of other options to balance it out. And to avoid Karla's vegan meatloaf ever making it to the party, a team of experienced, nerdy, investing professionals

---

[125] "The National Study of Millionaires," Ramsey Solutions, April 12, 2023, https://www.ramseysolutions.com/retirement/the-national-study-of-millionaires-research.

manage these funds, with specialized experts focusing on specific industries. These people have *one job*: to make sure only the best investments are included in the fund, therefore giving the investors better results than they could get on their own. What the fund *does* depends on the goal, aka *fund objective*. If it's a bond fund, the manager will buy bonds. If it's an international stock fund, the manager will buy—you guessed it—international stocks.

For decades now, Dave Ramsey has recommended investing in *growth stock* mutual funds with long track records. These funds focus on companies expected to experience above-average growth compared to others in the market. While they may be more volatile in the short term, they also have the potential for higher returns over the long haul, making them a great option for retirement investing.

To add one more layer of risk reduction to this wealth tiramisu, it's wise to diversify evenly across *four different types* of mutual funds. That means allocating 25 percent of your investment to each type of fund. Here's the breakdown using boat analogies (just because):

Growth and Income funds: The Cruise Ship
These are funds invested in big, established companies like Procter & Gamble, Johnson & Johnson, and Coca-Cola. You might see them listed as "large cap," which is short for large market capitalization. That's a fancy way of saying "huge corporations valued at $10 billion or more." These companies might not grow as fast as others, but they're stable and steady, and are a solid backbone to your portfolio.

Growth funds: The Racing Yacht
These investments focus on companies with the potential for rapid growth, even if the companies may not be as large or established as the ones your mom and dad grew up with.

Amazon, Netflix, and Tesla are just a few examples of the companies you'll find in a growth fund.

Aggressive Growth funds: The Jet Ski
This is the wild child, roller-coaster ride of your investments. (We all have that one, unpredictable friend.) There could be some high highs and probably some low lows. Think companies like Zoom, Square, and Shopify. Good to have in the mix.

International funds: The Globe-Trotting Sailboat
It's smart to keep some of your eggs in the international basket, investing in large non-US companies like Alibaba (China), Samsung (South Korea), and Nestlé (Switzerland). This geographic diversification gives you a good buffer in case the US economy takes a hit.

Mutual funds are great *long-term* investments. (Did you notice there aren't any short-term investments mentioned in this chapter?) If you've scrolled social media lately, though, you've probably seen videos of people aggressively pitching some short-term investment that sounds too good to be true. (Trust me, *it is.*) The frustrating reality is that the internet is a magnet for fraudsters, grifters, shysters, and swindlers peddling this crap to get your views, your clicks, and your money. You've been warned.

What I've shared with you here is a simple, proven method to build wealth without stress. It's the same portfolio I have in *my* retirement accounts, that Dave Ramsey has in his retirement accounts, and that plenty of other Baby Steps Millionaires have in their accounts. None of us are geniuses—in fact, our study of millionaires found that most of them are average investors at best. Yet once again, that gives me hope that even an average George like me or you can do this stuff.

THE EXPONENTIAL POWER OF COMPOUND GROWTH

We've talked about when to invest, how much, and in what—but we haven't talked about *how* your wealth gets built. There's an undocumented quote credited to Albert Einstein, and it goes like this: "Compound interest is the eighth wonder of the world. He who understands it, earns it . . . he who doesn't, pays it." I wouldn't put it past him if he *did* say it, but even if he didn't, it's a great financial principle.

Here's what I'm talking about. In most retirement accounts, around 80 to 90 percent of the balance is *growth* when you get to retirement age. Only 10 percent is your contribution (the money you put in). That's the power of compound growth. Your money makes money, and that money makes *more* money. As you see returns on your investment, you'll keep earning based on its *current* value, not just the original investment.

To illustrate this, let's say you invested $10,000 at age 22 and never put in another dime. Over 40 years, with a 10 percent average annual return, look at what happens:

Years Invested	Account Balance
1	$10,000
10	$25,937
20	$67,257
30	$174,494
40	$452,592
Total Contributions: $10,000	**Total Growth:** $442,592

Now *that* is some math worth nerding out over! Your $10,000 investment turned into nearly half a million thanks to *capital appreciation* (the growth in value of the stocks inside these funds) and *compound growth* (the exponential growth created when your contributions *and* earnings get automatically reinvested).

PS: We could get extra nerdy and go through the equation that creates this effect, but to spare you, there's a slick investing calculator that will do the math for you. Go check it out and start dreaming with zeroes on the end at georgekamel.com/resources.

THE WONDERFUL REALITY OF WEALTH-BUILDING

To get pumped about this process, let's look at a hypothetical yet real-life scenario. Imagine a 32-year-old couple—I'll call them Austin and Sydney. They just finished going through *Financial Peace University*, they're rocking their EveryDollar budget, and they're *all-in* on the Baby Steps. It takes them three years to knock out Baby Steps 1 through 3, getting out of consumer debt and building their full emergency fund.

Three years into this plan, they're now 35 years old and on Baby Step 4, where they begin investing 15 percent of their income into retirement across the four types of mutual funds inside of their employer-sponsored Roth 401(k). Their combined household income is $71,000 (the median household income in America).[126] So that 15 percent comes out to just under $890 per month, or $10,650 per year. (Side note: That nearly $890 of

---

[126] Jessica Semega and Melissa Kollar, "Income in the United States: 2021," United States Census Bureau, September 13, 2022, https://www.census.gov/library/publications/2022/demo/p60-276.html.

margin only exists because Austin and Sydney do a monthly budget, got out of debt, and live on less than they make.)

Now let's pretend they don't have an employer match (which is unlikely), and they work their *whole* lives making that median income and *never* get a raise (even more unlikely). Here's what that money could turn into over 30 more years of their working life, with average returns of 10–12 percent (which, historically, is the average annual return of the S&P 500).[127]

$887 per month invested in a Roth 401(k) from age 35 to 65:

- 10 percent rate of return = $2 million tax-free at retirement
- 11 percent rate of return = $2.5 million tax-free at retirement
- 12 percent rate of return = $3.1 million tax-free at retirement

Even with a more conservative forecast, an 8 percent average annual return would *still* give them $1.3 million tax-free in retirement. Ultimately, Austin and Sydney would have anywhere from $1 million to $3 million in retirement. Guess how much of that was money *they* put in? Less than $320,000. Absolutely incredible. And it only happened because they invested consistently over a long period. Their income was *not* the secret sauce. That tracks: One-third of millionaires we surveyed never made six figures in a single working year of their career.[128]

But what's even more likely to happen to our friends Austin and Sydney is that their income will go up over time, which

---

[127] "Historical Returns on Stocks, Bonds and Bills: 1928-2022," Stern/New York University, January 2023, https://pages.stern.nyu.edu/~adamodar/New_Home_Page/datafile/histretSP.html.

[128] "National Study of Millionaires," Ramsey Solutions.

means they'll increase the amount they're investing. They'll likely have an employer match, which means more free money added to their compound snowball. Following the Baby Steps, they'll pay off their house in under 15 years (probably closer to seven years, per the average Baby Stepper)—and that house will appreciate in value! Once the house is paid off, they'll increase their investing even more in Baby Step 7. All of this means that Austin and Sydney are going to have *way more* money than what I just calculated.

They are also likely to experience a healthier, happier marriage because they're on the same financial page with fewer money problems, less stress, and more money in the bank. They'll be more fulfilled in their careers because they're free to make choices without *needing* that next paycheck. They'll also become more generous because they have the *margin* to be.

Don't you want that kind of life? Of course you do. That's what it looks like when you decide to buck the status quo and follow a proven plan. In order to change your future and build wealth, you've got to turn off the noise, turn off the news, and focus on the right money habits.

My financial turnaround took 10 years—going from broke to millionaire. The two main components of Whitney's and my net worth won't shock you: our Roth 401(k)s and a paid-for house, following the exact strategy in this book. Now, 10 years may sound like a long way away. And it may take you 15–20 years to become a Baby Steps Millionaire, which feels like an eternity. But that time will pass whether you like it or not. So what are you going to decide to do *today*, that you'll look back on 10, 15, or 20 years from now and be grateful for? Don't underestimate the power of time, consistent habits, and compound growth. And more importantly, don't underestimate yourself.

BE A CROCKPOT IN A MICROWAVE WORLD

You need a *long-term* mindset to build wealth and keep it, not the mind of a financial genius. Discipline, simplicity, consistency, and time are the not-so-secret ingredients to crockpot happiness. Don't mess with it. Don't get caught up with investment theories and too-good-to-be-true strategies. Just start investing and don't stop. Time *in* the market beats timing the market. Just let compound growth do its thing.

I know it's tempting to give in to the pressure of our culture that moves at a breakneck pace. Instagram. Instacart. Instapot. We want instant results and instant gratification. Patience? Ain't nobody got time for that! But here's something to chew on from Hebrews 12:11: "No discipline seems pleasant at the time, but painful. Later on, however, it produces a harvest of righteousness and peace for those who have been trained by it" (NIV). The antidote to a lack of patience is *delayed gratification*. If you can master that, you will have the prescription for long-term wealth.

Henry Ford said, "Whether you think you can, or you think you can't—you're right." Building wealth starts with the *belief* that it's possible for you, regardless of where you're at today or the mistakes you've made in the past. Belief is half the battle. The other half is consistent habits, delayed gratification, and giving that crockpot some compound cooking time. Turns out, the quickest (right) way to get rich is to get rich *slow*. I think you can. I hope you think so too.

BUILD WEALTH WITH MORE CONFIDENCE

You don't have to know everything about investing to do it well. And you don't have to do it alone. There are pros who can educate and guide you when it comes to retirement, college savings, and other investing goals. I've got one in my corner, and Dave Ramsey does too. Learn more about getting investing guidance at georgekamel.com/resources.

16

Generosity Is Joy

We make a living by what we get. We make a life by what we give.
—WINSTON CHURCHILL

For Amir and Connie, the journey to becoming millionaires didn't begin until later in life. They didn't get "enlightened" about money until their early forties. They knew they needed to make a change, but they were lacking the right plan to do it. Driving through Atlanta one day, Connie saw Dave Ramsey on a billboard and took it as a sign. (Nothing like a *literal* sign to be your sign.) She immediately signed them up for a local *Financial Peace University* class. That class set Amir and Connie on a 10-year journey to pay off $986,000 in debt—the majority of which was their mortgage.

Fast-forward a decade. *They did it.* On December 12, 2018, they showed up at the Ramsey Solutions headquarters to do their

Debt-Free Scream live on *The Ramsey Show*. I'll never forget that day. I met their whole family in the lobby and instantly connected with their story. Amir was an immigrant from the Middle East—just like my parents. Their kids, Naseem and Naveed, were first-generation Americans—just like me and my brother. They were even the same age as me! Pretty wild.

Amir and Connie, being the incredible parents they are, had put their kids through *Financial Peace University* (which, by the way, was one of 13 classes they ended up coordinating over that 10-year journey). Because of that basis of knowledge and wisdom, their kids were debt-free except for their mortgages. But what happened next shocked us all.

They had an ace up their sleeve. Amir and Connie shared their story on-air of paying off $986,000, which was already awe-inspiring. Then, right before it was time to scream, Amir told Dave Ramsey, "We don't have any secrets; our kids have been right there with us. But there's *one* thing we kept from them. And the secret is . . . just because they're here, and they're going to scream 'Debt-free' with us, we would like them to know that *their mortgages are paid off.*"

Yeah, that's right. They sneak-attacked *two* extra mortgage payoffs on top of their own.

My eyes started sweating profusely. Every bystander caught a case of the feels, and there wasn't a dry eye in the building. I was overwhelmed with emotion just *imagining* the joy and awe their kids were feeling, and the even greater joy Mom and Dad must have been feeling. I had just witnessed something magical called *outrageous generosity*. It was the coolest thing ever. As I dried the transparent tears from my translucent face, I remember thinking, *That's the kind of legacy I want to leave. I want to be them when I grow up.*

THE SURPRISING ANTIDOTE TO A WORLD OF PROBLEMS

There are only three things you can do with money: You can save it, you can spend it, and you can give it. Now, which do you think is the most fun? At first blush, you might say spending. No doubt, spending can be an absolute blast. But the truth is, *giving* is the most fun you'll ever have with money. And that's not just one man's opinion. There's plenty of social proof to back it up.

We've all seen viral videos of random acts of kindness and generosity on social media. If you have even half a heart, the videos tend to make your eyes leak a little liquid joy. And if you have the other half of a heart, you dream of being that kind of person one day. The kind who would be in a financial position to give that much of your money away without flinching so that someone else could have something they want, or even more likely, need.

I'm not the first to tell you that we live in a world full of greed, selfishness, envy, materialism, negativity, hostility, and suffering. I have this wild theory, though, that the solution could pretty much be described in one word: *generosity*.

Money can be a great tool for achieving the goal of generosity. But for too many people, money isn't a tool—it's an obstacle. It's often a place of stress, anxiety, guilt, shame, embarrassment, pain, or addiction. I told you that nearly 4 out of 5 Americans are living paycheck to paycheck and have no margin. If you don't have the margin to cover your bills and emergencies, it's a whole lot harder to get to that mountaintop of Baby Step 7, where you continue to build wealth and be outrageously generous.

You see, generosity becomes a whole lot easier, in the financial sense, when you create the margin for it. I can already hear you muttering under your breath, "There he goes with the budget stuff again." Yeah. Can't stop, won't stop. That's what *Breaking Free from Broke* has secretly been about—creating financial margin *so that* you can live your best life. And your best life always includes plenty of generosity.

Of course, generosity isn't always monetary. You can be generous with your time, talent, and other resources too. Either way, one of the incredible things that financial margin allows you to do is to be more generous with your money *and* your time.

THE SCIENTIFIC BENEFITS OF GIVING

Whether you like it or not, generosity has some undeniable benefits. (I have no idea why you wouldn't like that.) Of course, you should give with pure motives, not expecting anything in return. But weirdly, there are a plethora of perks that boomerang back when you're generous. I'll name a few, straight from the laboratory.

Generosity is good for your brain.

Have you ever caught someone in the act of giving? If you pay attention to the giver, you'll notice they light up like a Christmas tree. That reaction is nicknamed the "giver's glow." Stephen G. Post, the director of the Center for Medical Humanities at Stony Brook University, found that when we're generous, our brains release happiness chemicals, like dopamine and oxytocin.[129] So the verdict is in—it is scientifically better to give than to receive.

---

[129] Elizabeth Renter, "What Generosity Does to Your Brain and Life Expectancy," *U.S. News & World Report*, May 1, 2015, http://health.usnews.com/health-news/health-wellness/articles/2015/05/01/what-generosity-does-to-your-brain-and-life-expectancy.

Generosity makes you—and those around you—happier.

Generous people are fun to be around, aren't they? I mean, who wants to get drinks with the Grinch, Mr. Krabs, Mr. Burns, and Scrooge (Ebenezer *or* McDuck)? You know, now that I say that out loud, it'd be quite entertaining. Just be ready to cover the bill.

Generous people aren't only open-handed with their money—but with their time, talents, and words. Their attitude is inspiring and contagious. Whether you're the giver or receiver, generosity makes you want to spread that warm, fuzzy feeling.

Generosity can help you live longer.

Do givers outlive the greedy? One could make the case. Research shows that generosity lowers stress levels, which is a big deal since stress is a huge risk factor for chronic diseases and heart attacks. A study from Carnegie Mellon University found that people who volunteer around four hours per week are 40 percent less likely to develop high blood pressure than those who don't volunteer.[130] Ask your doctor if volunteering is right for you. (Said in my most calming pharmaceutical ad voice.)

Generosity counters depression.

Researchers with Project MATCH found that people in Alcoholics Anonymous *double* their chances of success when they

---

[130] Shilo Rea, "Volunteering Reduces Risk of Hypertension in Older Adults," Carnegie Mellon University, June 13, 2013, https://www.cmu.edu/news/stories/archives/2013/june/june13_volunteeringhypertension.html.

help others.[131] It makes sense. Sometimes the key to *self*-help is being *others*-focused. Who knew generosity wasn't just an act of kindness, but also a path toward your own healing and personal growth? Beautiful.

THE SPIRITUAL TRUTHS OF GIVING

It's no secret that I grew up with a faith background (shout-out to my Arabic Baptists). Whether you also have a faith background, or you're "ye of little faith," hear me out—because there are some timeless nuggets of wisdom in this ancient text.

Generosity helps you prosper.

That's right. Proverbs 11:25 says, "A generous person will prosper; whoever refreshes others will be refreshed" (NIV). Now, don't get it twisted: This is *not* advocating a "prosperity gospel" where being a good person and sending checks to television preachers (or even a church or charity, for that matter) guarantees you a jackpot from God. I rebuke that absurdity. Generosity should never be a transactional relationship where you're expecting material gain. This proverb is pointing to the deeper, more meaningful rewards of giving—like recharging emotionally, refreshing spiritually, and living more peacefully. That's priceless.

---

[131] Maria E. Pagano, Karen B. Friend, J. Scott Tonigan, and Robert L. Stout, "Helping Other Alcoholics in Alcoholics Anonymous and Drinking Outcomes: Findings from Project MATCH," December 21, 2010, https://www.ncbi.nlm.nih.gov/pmc/articles/PMC3008319/.

Generosity helps you become who you were made to be.

God is the OG—Original Giver. The G-GOAT—the Greatest Giver of All Time. Why? He gave His one and only Son! And according to Genesis 1:27, humans were made in His image. Fast-forward to Ephesians 5:1 and we're called to imitate God. Let's do the Bible math: If He's the greatest giver of all time, and we're made in His image, and we're supposed to imitate Him, then no bones about it—we were *made* to be givers. Thus, the more generous you become, the more you're imitating the image of God. Man, that is poetry.

Generosity helps you become a better steward.

If you're a person of faith, you understand a spiritual truth that is confusing to the rest of the world: We're *stewards* of our resources. A steward is not an owner, but more like a manager—someone who takes care of the possessions of someone else. Having that perspective completely changes the way you view money. It's actually freeing. You see, it's not really *my* money at that point. If I build more wealth, it just means I've got more wealth to manage. That causes me to be way more thoughtful in how I spend it, how I invest it, and, because I'm made to be a giver, in how I *give it.*

Generosity helps you leave a legacy.

Reminder: You can't take it with you when you paint your final sunset in the sky. With that in mind, you want to be intentional about transferring your wealth to the next generation—that's a huge part of your legacy. Proverbs 13:22 says, "A good person leaves an inheritance for their children's children" (NIV).

Generational wealth, when done properly, can change your family tree forever. Your thoughtfulness and planning can create a ripple effect for generations to come. That's pretty dope.

A BEGINNER'S GUIDE TO GIVING

We've covered lots of great reasons to give. You may be wondering how to do this when you're not at multimillionaire-philanthropist level quite yet. It can be hard to even *think* about generosity when you're juggling bills and family needs. But here's an idea from my friend Rachel Cruze that I hope will set you free: *Give a little . . . until you can give a lot.* It's more about the *spirit* of giving than the amount.

If you're wanting to be more generous, but currently don't have the margin to do it, it's even more reason to follow the Ramsey Baby Steps and the advice in this book. Make the sacrifices needed to get out of debt, get on a budget, and find ways to spend less and make more—*so that* you can give more.

John D. Rockefeller, the wealthiest guy in US history, started tithing with his $1.50 weekly salary. Start giving what you can now, even if it's just a few bucks. You're building a habit, not reaching a magic dollar amount. With time, giving becomes just another part of life, like paying bills (except fun instead of painful). Plus, you become an example to others, especially your kids. More is caught than taught. Your kids are catching everything you do, including your generosity.

THE THREE TYPES OF GENEROSITY

As you develop the habit of giving, you'll realize there are three buckets to choose from. I highly recommend all three, but I'd start in this order:

1. Planned Generosity

This is giving you do on an ongoing basis every single month. For people of faith, this can be done through tithing to your local church. Tithing is an important aspect of faith, symbolizing giving your "firstfruits" instead of leftovers (see Proverbs 3:9). That's why "giving" is the first category in your EveryDollar budget—it should be a *priority* instead of an afterthought.

Quick clarification: God doesn't need our money. But He does want us opening up our hands to help others. And only an open heart will open its hands. So generosity isn't about what's in your wallet—it's about what's in your *heart.* Like sharing toys as a kid, the toy itself doesn't matter all that much, but the kindness behind the act reflects your character.

Regardless of how much you give or what you give to, committing to consistent giving is an awesome way to create a rhythm of open-handedness. Let me offer some other ideas for planned giving:

- Sign up for monthly donations to your favorite charities and non-profits
- Give ongoing to global missions work
- Contribute regularly to a local shelter or food bank
- Support creators on Patreon
- Give extra offerings to your church beyond your tithe

2. Spontaneous Generosity

This is giving on a whim—from the heart—when the spirit leads. My wife and I have a special line item in our budget, and it's the most fun we have with money. We call it the "Bless Up" fund. We set some money aside every month and wait to see who God puts in our path to give to. When you're not preoccupied with *your* bills, you have the bandwidth to think about *other* people's bills. Maybe it's the server who's always serving with excellence. Or a coworker going through some hard times or health problems. Maybe it's a family member who doesn't have the money for that car repair.

Imagine just writing a check, leaving an envelope of cash, or sending a digital payment—all with a note that says, "Hey, I know life is hard right now. I hope this makes it a little easier." That's the good stuff right there. Depending on the situation, you might even do this anonymously. That can be even more fun. While the *target* of your giving may be unplanned, the money itself needs to be planned. Incorporate a plan for the unplanned in your monthly budget. It's a blast. Here are some more fun ways to give spontaneously:

- Try #TipTheBill with a 100 percent tip on your meal
- Contribute to a GoFundMe campaign that you connect with
- Send a surprise delivery (groceries, food, or flowers) to someone in need
- Contribute toward someone's medical bill or vet bill
- Give gift cards to postal and sanitation workers, bus drivers, and teachers
- Cover a pet adoption fee at a shelter

3. Outrageous Generosity

What financial impact do you want to be remembered for? That's the kind of question you can ask when you get to Baby Step 7—with no mortgage, no payments, and plenty of money in the bank. This is the stuff of legends and legacy, where we can impact entire families and change communities. Here's an example.

Back in the day, my church merged with an older church. And with that merger, they inherited $7 million of debt on the building. That amounted to sending a *million dollars* every year to a lender, and it got leadership thinking, *Hey, what could we accomplish with an extra million dollars a year?* As a result, the church got the congregation involved, and the gazelle intensity moved that mountain of debt quickly. In just 12 months, they paid off all $7 million! They even had Dave Ramsey show up to celebrate with a churchwide Debt-Free Scream. It was epic.

Y'all, the stuff our church *gets* to do now and *can* do now—because we're not sending a million dollars a year to a lender—is mind-blowing! We're currently building a new ministry center that includes a community-care facility for mental health and suicide prevention, a cars facility to provide single moms with reliable transportation, a safehouse for kids awaiting foster placement, and a wrap-around center to support the tangible needs of foster families.

What if *those* were the things that all churches were known for? What if every household and church in America became debt-free and managed their money *so well* that they had the margin to be outrageously generous? We could make the government totally irrelevant! To be able to take care of the needs of our communities? That's the kind of life worth chasing after.

I'll wrap this up with some ideas for outrageous generosity:

- Pay the adoption fees for a family
- Clear a school district's lunch debt
- Cover a year of utility bills for widows or single parents
- Give a $1,000 tip to a server
- Start a scholarship fund to help students graduate debt-free
- Buy a car for a single mom—or have hers repaired and detailed

LIVING FREE

Before you build wealth and give, you have to reframe the way you look at money. Money is just a means to an end, like a brick that can either build a home or break a window. In the wrong hands, money can become an idol that controls your life. That kind of greed and obsession is what the Bible is talking about when it says the *love* of money is the root of all kinds of evil. When managed well, however, money can change your life—and other people's lives—in the best way possible.

Another misnomer that needs to be corrected is this: Not all rich people are greedy. In fact, there's a fancy $10 word for generous rich people: *philanthropists.* What *is* true is that money is a magnifying glass—it amplifies what you already are. If you're stingy and broke, you'll be a stingier rich person when you build wealth. If you're a giver when you don't have much to give, you'll be outrageously generous when you have a lot.

I've known people who have wanted to stop being stingy, but because they've never had money before, they hesitate now. Keep this in mind: While *money* won't change who you are, generosity *will.* Generosity is the quickest route from being self*ish* to being self*less*. So take a deep breath and just do it. In no time, I bet you'll be *looking* to give. Generosity feels that good.

I'll be the first to admit that giving hasn't always come naturally to me. I'm a natural saver and a shrewd spender, but tend to be a cautious giver. Giving thoughtfully, spontaneously, and outrageously—that takes a little more effort. That's why making it the first line item in our household budget is so helpful. When you make it a priority, and do it consistently, it becomes a natural habit.

Maybe you relate to my story. Or maybe you're already a poster child of generosity, and you're reading this while volunteering at a soup kitchen after just having donated to your local animal shelter this morning. Either way, this habit of giving will help you move from a scarcity mentality to one of abundance, where you'll discover a newfound sense of joy and fulfillment.

Start by prioritizing giving in your budget. Give a little . . . until you can give a lot. And remember what this money plan is all about—*living free*. Free from stress, free from debt, and free to use your wealth for what truly matters.

And just so we're clear, what *truly* matters when we're gone won't be the stuff we accumulated; it will be the lives we impacted. If that sounded sappy to you, then great. Sometimes we need a little sap. Dave Ramsey says it less sappily: If you live like no one else, later you can live—*and give*—like no one else. Embrace that wisdom and watch as your life becomes more joyful, more purposeful, and *richer*—in every sense of the word.

CONCLUSION

Ignorance Was Bliss

Do not conform to the pattern of this world, but be transformed by the renewing of your mind.
–ROMANS 12:2 NIV

I used to think it was edgy and cool to be cynical. To have a general distrust in humanity and operate as if life wasn't going to work out well. It took me a long time to realize that cynicism isn't wisdom—it's negativity wrapped in fear. It's a lazy way to say that you've been burned and disappointed.

For too long, I chose to drink that poison. I let cynicism steal my joy, and it kept me stuck in a victim mentality, resigned to my "fate" as a mere cog in this money machine.

Nothing changed for me financially until I realized that pity didn't lead to progress. I hated being in debt and barely getting by. I hated being in a financial hole. I hated how it felt. And I worked too hard to feel so broke.

That rock-bottom feeling was when *everything* started to change. Or rather, when *I* started to change. I started learning the truth about money, and I started changing my *mind* about money. I took the first step, planted the seed, and I was ready to try something different.

The fact that you've stayed with me all the way through 16 chapters tells me you're ready too. It tells me you're sick and tired of living in the simulation—chained to a system designed to keep you broke.

We started this book by exposing those chains and forces that keep us tied up: credit scores, credit cards, student loans, car loans, mortgage traps, and investing traps. All of which get amplified by the pressures of marketing and consumerism. When the system seems to be invincible, it's easy to get cynical. And it's easy to stay there. Because negativity and pessimism and victimhood are always the easy route. Turns out, being a huge bummer takes very little effort.

Choosing positivity and optimism even when the deck feels stacked against us? That's a tall order.

That combo of positivity and optimism is called *hope*. You see, cynicism is normal. And normal has no money or margin. Normal gets you nowhere. Hope, on the other hand—is rare. It's weird but awesome. Hope pushes you forward. You can expect that something better is up ahead because you've made up your mind. You're willing to take the next step and do things you've never done. You're not relying on a toxic system, a lender, or the government to solve for your freedom. That's a huge step to transforming your relationship with money.

Romans 12:2 says, "Do not conform to the pattern of this world, but be *transformed* by the renewing of your mind" (NIV). That's powerful. See, I didn't come up with this concept of bucking the system. Dave Ramsey didn't either. God did. He's been dropping these truth bombs for a few thousand years now from the Bible. Transformation requires the renewing of your mind, aka thinking differently. I hope the ideas in this book helped create that kind of paradigm shift for you.

When you're able to *think* differently, you can *act* differently. Once you start *acting* differently, you begin to *believe* that a different future is possible. You start to see some light at the end of the tunnel—and realize it's freedom.

That confidence and belief in your future is what hope is all about. It's the kind of transformation that will create some serious momentum in your life.

CH-CH-CHOICES (TURN AND FACE THE SYSTEM)

You may have noticed that some of the principles involved in breaking free from the system go way beyond money. Virtues like joy, peace, patience, and self-control.

Why talk about these things in a book about money? Well, I've got this wild idea that what we're really after isn't *just* a fix to our money problems.

My intent for this book was to talk about money so we can *stop* talking about money. When money is no longer an obstacle, we can focus on what really matters and become the people we really want to be. Money, then, becomes a tool to help you live a life you're proud of.

After doing this stuff for over a decade now, I've found that this is the only way to truly *live*. People might look at you funny as you challenge the status quo instead of just following trends. They may be confused as to why you're swimming upstream when it's easier to float down the river. Some will take it personally that you're going against the crowd. They'll probably laugh at how optimistic you are. But those people are broke and bound by their chains. Not you. Not anymore.

Ignorance was bliss—until now. You know too much to stay the same. You have autonomy over your life. You have the power to shape your future. You *can* buck the system. The little man *can* get ahead.

The power of choice and hope says that the odds are ever in your favor. Because hope always defeats cynicism. The tortoise always beats the hare. The crockpot always trumps the microwave. And if you think you can, or you think you can't . . . you're right.

You're no longer stuck between a rock and a hard place. I've laid out Option C for you in these pages—a path less taken and yet more likely to lead to the freedom you seek. So if what you've been doing hasn't been working, know that there's another path—a better one. And not only does that path exist, but you are 1,000 percent capable of taking it.

The principles I've shared with you in these pages changed my life, and I know they can do the same for you. It's up to you to decide what happens next. I'm biased, but I *hope* you choose to live more freely. I hope you choose to follow these Baby Steps and build wealth and become outrageously generous. I hope you choose. . . hope. Because a better life is up ahead.

Let *your* transformation begin.

TAKE THE NEXT STEP

If you do *nothing else* after reading this book, you've got to start budgeting. Paying attention to your money is *the* foundation of the plan I've laid out for you. I've made it stupid easy with three months of EveryDollar as my gift to you. Now's the time. Take the next step, tap in that offer code, and start your budget today at georgekamel.com/resources.

A PERSONAL NOTE

I've done all the talking so far—now it's your turn! I'd love to know what you thought of this book. Post about Breaking Free from Broke *along with your favorite quotes or takeaways, and be sure to tag me @georgekamel so that I see it! And if the content was helpful to you in any way, it would mean the world if you'd share it with friends and family and leave a review online. Thank you for reading this book. I meant every word.*

ACKNOWLEDGMENTS

Anytime you see a turtle up on top of a fence post, you know he had some help.
–ALEX HALEY

Writing a book has been a dream of mine since the third grade. But I'll be honest—I had no idea how difficult it would be. While I exerted plenty of effort in the making of this book, it wouldn't exist if not for the unbelievable number of people it takes to make me look good. I'm not a fan of debt, but I owe a debt of gratitude to the extraordinary people who helped turn this dream into a reality:

Whitney Kamel, for your unwavering love and support (while pregnant with our first child). You are the gravity that keeps my world anchored. Words fall short, but know this—my gratitude and love for you run deeper than any acknowledgment can convey.

Dave Ramsey, for your mentorship, leadership, and generosity. Thank you for trusting me with your platform and giving me the opportunity to carry this mission forward.

Tyler Seymour, for being the best brand leader and cheerleader a guy could ask for. You're the real MVP.

Jessi Mestan, for bringing peace and order to my life and calendar (even when it felt like an extreme game of Tetris). Thank you for always serving with the best attitude.

Preston Cannon, for leading this project from inception to birth and for always putting the reader first.

Kris Bearss, for your remarkable editing skills that refined the narrative and polished the words. You helped me find my voice and become a better writer. It was a joy to work with you.

Julia Calvert and *Amy McCollom*, for coordinating no less than a million details to get this project done on time, and with excellence.

Rick Prall, for your sanity-saving help with outlines, stats, and citations. You always came through in the clutch.

Tim Smith, *Kathryn Graeff*, and *Amanda Wiggins*, for your rigorous research and meticulous fact-checking that gave this content even more credibility.

Rachel Miller, *Mike Colling*, *David Porter*, and *David Kakish*, for your feedback that sharpened the content of this book.

Chris Carrico, *Weylon Smith*, *Brad Dennison*, *Carlee Francis*, *Riley Clark*, and *Seth Farmer*, for your artistry that made this book visually appealing, regardless of my face.

Chris Wright, *Alex Chatfield*, *Paul Salveson*, *Bryan Amerine*, *Connor Bowser*, *Steven Russell*, and *Will Rudder*, for bringing my words to life through an incredible audiobook product.

Brian Horvath, *Jeff Miller*, *Tim Scee*, *Jasmine Cannady*, *Candi Williams*, and *Kiah Francis*, for bringing this book to the marketplace—and to its readers.

Sara Small, *Megan McConnell*, and *Curt Harding*, for your expert publicity skills, amplifying the reach of this book further than I could have imagined.

Jeremy Breland, *Suzanne Simms*, *Jen Sievertsen*, *Katie Crenshaw*, and *Daniel Ramsey*, for your leadership and wisdom.

The EveryDollar team, for generously gifting my readers with three months of access to a budgeting tool that will help them live out the principles in this book.

The Ramsey Personalities team, for the friendship and support that makes this wild ride way more fun. It's the honor of a lifetime to work alongside you all.

My parents, *May and Maged Kamel*, for nurturing my passions and encouraging me to explore my talents. Your belief in me has shaped the person I am today.

After writing out that list, it's easy to see why I feel like a turtle on a fence post. I am eternally grateful to these men and women for helping me get there.

Did this book positively impact your life?

If so, it would be a huge help to me if you post about it on social media using #theramseyway. This is how we get the word out to help more people.